J.K. LASSER'S™

PICK
WINNING
MUTUAL FUNDS

Look for these and other titles from J.K. Lasser™—Practical Guides for All
Your Financial Needs.

J.K. Lasser's Pick Winning Stocks by Edward F. Mrkvicka Jr.
J.K. Lasser's Invest Online by LauraMaery Gold and Dan Post
J.K. Lasser's Year-Round Tax Strategies by David S. De Jong and
    Ann Gray Jakabcin
J.K. Lasser's Taxes Made Easy for Your Home-Based Business
    by Gary W. Carter
J.K. Lasser's Finance and Tax for Your Family Business by Barbara Weltman
J.K. Lasser's Pick Winning Mutual Funds by Jerry Tweddell with Jack Pierce

J.K. LASSER'S™

PICK WINNING MUTUAL FUNDS

Jerry Tweddell

with Jack Pierce

John Wiley & Sons, Inc.

New York • Chichester • Weinheim • Brisbane • Singapore • Toronto

Library of Congress Cataloging-in-Publication Data:

Tweddell, Jerry.
   J.K. Lasser's pick winning mutual funds / Jerry Tweddell with Jack Pierce.
     p. cm. — (J.K. Lasser guide series)
   Includes index.
   ISBN 0-471-39771-7 (pbk. : alk. paper)
     1. Mutual funds.   2. Investment analysis.   I. Title: JK Lasser's pick winning mutual funds.   II. Title: Pick winning mutual funds.   III. Pierce, Jack.   IV. Title.   V. Series.

HG4530.T938 2001
332.63'27—dc21

00-053175

Printed in the United States of America.

10 9 8 7 6 5 4 3 2 1

To our wives, Deb Tweddell and Avril Pierce,
for their infinite patience, understanding, and support

Acknowledgments

Any book ever written on finance requires a great deal of outside help, and this one was no exception. Many individuals supplied that assistance and made the task easier.

Three publishing professionals were key in writing this book. Our agent, Laurie Harper, owner of the Sebastian Literary Agency in St. Paul, Minnesota, gave us support and guidance throughout the process with her usual skill and patience, and supplied us with much needed encouragement. Without her, we would not have received a call from Bob Shuman, senior editor at John Wiley & Sons, asking us to write this book. Without Bob's original concept, daily guidance, editorial skill, and extraordinary understanding nature, this book would literally not exist. He was ably assisted by Nancy Gratton, who spent many long hours editing the manuscript making much needed changes, improving the final product. It was a pleasure working with each of them, and we appreciate their efforts.

We want to thank Shelley Tweddell, who actually knows about such things as computer disks and software applications; she expertly prepared most of the charts and graphs in the book. Her technical ability was much appreciated and, in fact, indispensable. Jackie Pierce was very helpful when we were developing the format for the manuscript, and we thank her for the guidance. And Gavin Pierce did something remarkable when one of our computers crashed and had to be replaced with a new machine. He not only diagnosed the original problem, but also saved the entire lost manuscript by transferring it from a broken hard drive to a new computer.

Industry experts were essential to us in preparing ourselves for this book. John Calamos of Calamos Asset Management (who also supplied us with the Japan story—see Appendix C) was especially helpful and kindly granted an interview, enlightening us on the current state of the convertible bond market, a field in which he is a recognized expert. Doug Forcman of TCW Group, and John Rekenthaler of Morningstar both took the time to provide insights about happenings in the mutual fund industry. Ryan Tagal of Cerulli, Inc., supplied us with much needed information on fast-growing managed asset accounts.

Several industry people gave noteworthy interviews for this book. For Chapter 2, on investors' habits, Charles Biderman of Trim Tabs Financial Services provided perspective about investors' buying and selling patterns. We interviewed Rick Imperiale, portfolio manager of Forward Uniplan Real Estate Fund, concerning real estate investment trusts (REITs), and he helped us with that sometimes hard-to-understand market. And our interview with Alan Carr, portfolio manager of two H&Q closed-end funds made the discussion of closed-end funds more complete. We also want to thank John Duggan for his assistance. With his long experience as a bond trader and manager, he was extremely helpful to us when we were working on Chapter 7.

Jerry Tweddell also extends a special word of thanks to Carol Larkin at TD Waterhouse, who has been doing her best the past few years to make new funds available as close to inception as possible. Without her help, the new fund investment strategy could only have been written about as theoretical, rather than actual experience.

Because of the help we received from experts, the complexities of the subjects covered in the book were easier to describe, and we thank them all for their assistance.

Contents

Introduction

Mutual funds are almost ideal investments for most people. They are not complicated, and they provide the opportunity to invest in diversified portfolios that will meet almost any investor's needs.

There are some problems, though. There are too many of them, most don't earn their keep, and many are marketed and distributed irresponsibly. And, most investors misuse them, egged on by an industry waging a fierce battle for investors' dollars. The average investor ends up achieving the seemingly impossible: *lower returns than the very funds he or she invests in.* How can that be? As you'll see, it is remarkably easy.

Technology-driven change is revolutionizing the way Americans invest. Much of a book on mutual fund investing today would have been indecipherable to a reader only 10 years ago. Rapid change provides wonderful opportunity; for example, the vast sea of information available on the Web. The challenge is how to use it. While there have never been so many alternatives, how do you identify the relatively few good opportunities from the ocean of also-rans? While the Internet has simplified and lowered the costs of instant trading, so far, there is no evidence that it improves the average investor's returns. In fact, it may be doing just the opposite.

J.K. Lasser's Pick Winning Mutual Funds is a hands-on guide that leads you through the mutual fund maze: getting the best from both index and managed funds. It shows how the structure of the mutual fund *business* critically affects mutual fund *returns.* In addition, you'll learn about off-the-beaten-path opportunities from new funds, real estate investment trusts, convertible bond, and closed-end funds; how to use them to boost returns without increasing—and in some cases reducing—risk. In addition, you'll learn how to *keep* your fund profits by minimizing taxes and how to avoid the common mistakes made by most investors that so systematically and routinely reduce their returns. Whether you are fascinated by or indifferent to investing, you can find a strategy that suits you—from a disciplined new-fund buying/selling strategy to a "buy it and forget it" indexed portfolio that puts your portfolio on autopilot.

J.K. Lasser's Pick Winning Mutual Funds differs from other mutual fund books in important ways:

- It provides basic well-grounded fundamentals on mutual fund selection and management. Drawing on our combined experience of more than 50 years in the investment business, we will show you how to take control of your mutual funds. You'll learn the critical importance of asset allocation and risk management, how to use both index and managed funds, the importance of minimizing costs and taxes, and how to overcome psychological hurdles that can undo even the soundest plans.

- The book offers new insights: It explains how the structure of open-end funds and the operation of the fund management business have such a profound effect on fund returns—and how most investors make the costly mistake of ignoring (even denying) the laws of probability.

- A step-by-step fund selection process is provided, highlighting critical benchmarks and valuable information sources along the way.

- Two new concepts are introduced and documented: how surprisingly bad the average investor's returns are (the mutual fund industry would rather not talk about this). And how, contrary to prevailing wisdom, new funds outperform those with long track records, and how to profit from the powerful "new-fund effect."

- *J.K. Lasser's Pick Winning Mutual Funds* provides insights and investment strategies that combine new era investing with traditional principles and plain old common sense.

It's relatively easy to be a good investor if you have a sensible plan, stick with quality investments and advisers, control costs, and have the discipline to stay with it. A good plan, the right way to invest, gets good results.

It's also easy to be a "bad" investor—one who doesn't have any plan other than "to make money." A bad investor routinely "takes fliers," relies on "experts" promising unrealistic returns, ignores costs and probability, and invests in whatever is in fashion. The overwhelming majority of bad investors, who invest the wrong way, achieve predictably bad returns.

Once you know the difference between the right and the wrong way to manage your mutual funds, and start using the tools provided in this book, you will begin to enjoy higher returns, a sense of purpose, and peace of mind. You will never go back.

J.K. LASSER'S™

PICK
WINNING
MUTUAL FUNDS

PART 1

Getting Started

CHAPTER 1

Take Control of Your Mutual Funds

> Anyone can turn a
> million bucks into
> two million. The trick
> is to get that first
> million.
>
> —Ric Edelman,
> *Ordinary People,*
> *Extraordinary Wealth*

You should take control of your mutual funds for one reason: No one cares more about your money than you do. While you might think that you lack the experience, time, or interest to invest well, you can do it by learning a few simple principles—the do's and don'ts of fund investing. Our goal is to help you with the process, so we've boiled our research down to the keys to successful fund investing. The chapters that follow are the result; they provide specific guidelines and steps for building a successful mutual fund portfolio. You'll learn how to:

- Find and evaluate the information you need.
- Allocate money between fund types that will be consistent with your needs and risk tolerance.
- Control risk.
- Make the laws of probability work for, not against, you.
- Decrease and control return-reducing costs.
- Invest more in the market and less in the experts.
- Understand what experts can—and cannot do.
- Be as involved or uninvolved as you wish and still achieve good returns.

- Control your own destiny instead of relying on others.
- Minimize taxes.

But first, you need to understand a few basics about mutual fund investing, and what it can mean for your financial future.

First Things First

They say in the medical profession, "First, do no harm." Regrettably, most mutual fund investors fail to heed that simple maxim. Too often, they end up harming themselves by buying unsuitable funds and buying and selling at the wrong time. The sad result is that most mutual funds actually make more money than their own shareholders ever achieve. To avoid this requires that you understand how to make mutual funds work for you by avoiding the most common mistakes of investors.

For most Americans, funds are the investment vehicle of choice. In 1999, according to *Consumer Reports,* investment in funds increased by over $800 billion; 77 percent of which went into stock funds (the various types of funds are discussed in later chapters). Morningstar, the most widely followed fund tracker, reports on over 11,400 funds. This creates a dilemma when you're trying to choose the right fund for your needs. Realistically, you can only follow a tiny fraction of the mutual fund universe.

Nuts and Bolts

Mutual funds are investments made by people with similar goals who pool their money to invest in a portfolio of stocks (also called equities) or bonds, or both. When you buy into a mutual fund, rather than directly purchasing individual stocks or bonds, you invest in a proportionate share of the ownership of the pool's portfolio. Professional portfolio managers invest the money with the objective of meeting their shareholders' goals and expectations, which can range from protecting their principal (the original amount invested) to earning high returns from more aggressive stategies.

Mutual funds are an almost ideal vehicle for the average investor. Here's why:

- *Professional management* While wealthy investors and institutions can afford to hire professionals to manage their portfolios, mutual funds provide the same opportunity for smaller investors.
- *Diversification* Mutual funds are diversified. This means that investments are spread across a broad spectrum of holdings, which reduces risk

---

Heard on the Street

"The rich love their money. They love making it, enjoying it, growing it and keeping it secret. But most of all they love building walls around it.

"Actually, it's stronger than even love. It's compulsion, obsession, you name it . . . The rich would, if they could find a way, take it with them."*

You may not aspire to be among the stereotyped "rich," portrayed here, but it's clear that accumulating—and keeping—wealth doesn't happen by accident.

---

* Excerpted from an American Guaranty & Trust Company advertisement.

---

and volatility (wide swings up and down in the value of the investment). If a few holdings lose value, that loss is offset by others in the portfolio, which may be increasing in value. This reduction in risk and volatility makes the investment easier to "live with," so you're more likely to stay with your investment longer, allowing you to earn good returns over long periods.

- *Liquidity* Liquidity refers to the ease with which you can convert an asset to cash or vice versa. Funds are very liquid—you can buy, sell, or exchange your shares whenever you want to, so you have more control over your investments.
- *Control of risk* Funds allow you to calibrate the amount of risk you want to take with some precision. For example, high-quality, short-term U.S. government bond funds are very low-risk investments; while leveraged (using derivatives such as futures contracts) and specialized sector funds that invest in emerging nations' stocks or specialized technology can be very risky.
- *Variety* In addition to broadly diversified mainstream funds, there are funds that invest in just about any sector, industry, region of the world, or country you desire.
- *Ideal for the small investor* With as little as $50 or $100 per month, you can invest in funds that provide the same diversification and professional management skills used by the wealthy.
- *Regulatory oversight* The Securities and Exchange Commission (SEC) regulates the entire securities industry, including mutual funds, and provides investors a measure of protection against fraud and theft.

- *Convenience* Mutual funds handle your buying and selling transactions and issue regular statements that help keep your record keeping to a minimum. In addition, one-stop shopping fund "supermarkets," such as Fidelity or T.D. Waterhouse, make thousands of funds available from just one source.

Developing an Investment Plan

You've heard it a zillion times: To achieve a successful outcome, you have to plan for it. The first step is to define your goals.

Are you investing for a new or second home? For retirement? For your children's college tuition? People invest for any number of goals, their reasons are as various as the human condition. Whatever your goals, your investments should be tailored to meeting them—you're not investing in a vacuum. Questions you should be asking—and answering—yourself include:

- How much time do you have to meet your goals? Generally, the longer the time horizon, the more risk you can handle.

- How much do you have to invest? If your goal is high, you may have to invest more and/or allow your investments to grow over a longer period.

- What is your risk tolerance? You should construct a plan you can live with, so that volatility doesn't cause you to abandon it. You'll learn in Chapter 4 how to allocate your assets in accordance with your investment objectives and the degree of risk you find comfortable. The older you are, the more you might want to make bonds an important part of your portfolio, because they're less risky than stocks. Some experts feel that when you are age 60 your portfolio balance should be 50 percent stocks and 50 percent bonds; and at age 30, the split should be 70/30. But you have to make the final choice.

- What are your priorities? You probably can't expect to achieve all your life's goals at once. If you prioritize, however, you can achieve them—one goal at a time.

- Do you have the time, energy, and interest to research investments on your own? If not, you'll need to enlist professionals to help.

- Are you looking at your total financial picture? If you are paying high credit card interest and earning low investment returns, you're going backward. If you're bouncing between conflicting advice given by your broker, CPA, banker, and insurance salesperson, it's time to make choices.

- Are you objective about your goals? If emotion seems to drive many of your investment decisions, it would be wise to bring in an objective third party to help define them more rationally.

- Do you keep putting off constructing a plan? In the magic world of compounding, delayed investing takes a terrible toll on ultimate returns. Don't delay any longer.

Keeping Score

"Taking control" of your mutual funds doesn't necessarily mean that you have to be continuously involved. If, for whatever reasons, you don't want to manage your own fund portfolio, you can hire others to help—there's no shortage of people eager to take over for you (see Chapter 6). But no matter whether you decide on a "hands-on" or "hands-off" plan, as long as you are keeping score, *you still are in control.* What does keeping score mean? Comparing your funds' returns with the major indexes and returns of similar funds. This scorekeeping function is critical. If you find that you don't like doing it, aren't good at it, or lack the time and energy, hire someone who can do it for you. Just remember: No matter how much capital you have, there is no time to waste, and every year that goes by with your funds earning subpar returns puts you further behind.

Expected Returns

Scorekeeping starts with the most basic measure of the value of one share of any mutual fund, the net asset value, or NAV. *Investorwords.com* defines the NAV as follows: "The dollar value of a single mutual fund share, based on the value of the underlying assets of the fund minus its liabilities divided by the number of shares outstanding. Calculated at the end of each business day." In evaluating any investment, you should think in terms of *expected returns.* This refers to the amount by which a stock, bond, or mutual fund can realistically be expected to increase in value over time. But how can an investor figure out how much of a return he or she should expect? History gives us guidance, but no guarantees.

Since the Standard & Poor's Index began in 1926, 10 percent has been the approximate total annual rate of return on stocks, and that's probably as good as any other guess, estimate, or bet for the twenty-first century. There were long periods when stocks returned more and others when they returned less. Future returns will be just as variable, but when you're trying to gauge an expected rate of return you have to start somewhere.

But the expected increase in value of your investment is not all you need to determine when calculating your expected return. You must also take into account the costs—including fees and commissions—associated with your investment. Many investment brokers charge fees and commissions totaling as much as 2.0 percent or more per year of your invested capital. It doesn't sound like much, but siphoning off that amount year after year will significantly reduce your overall return.

Question: Which Is Better—Actively or Passively Managed Funds? Answer: Neither/Both

In Chapters 5 and 6, you'll learn about passively managed index funds and the actively managed funds, run by investment professionals. Right now, all you need to know is that there's an ongoing debate as to which is better. That debate won't be settled here, because it can't be. But history seems to show that index funds have won the battle in large, efficient markets such as high-volume liquid large-cap stocks and investment grade bonds. On the other hand, actively managed funds have triumphed in relatively inefficient markets such as small-cap stocks, foreign stocks, and junk bonds. For the foreseeable future, then, your best strategy is to include the best of both in your investment portfolio.

Human Nature versus Returns

There is no question that "everyman" is a pretty poor investor. Most mutual fund investors are underachievers: Without changing their investments, most of them could enjoy greater gains with a simple "fix." All they have to do is learn to hold on and resist the temptation to buy and sell so frequently. This fix, however, goes against human nature. Like skipping dessert, investors have to give up current gratification for distant and probable—but not certain—future rewards. Most people find this difficult. It requires gumption to go against the crowd and stay the course with patience, confidence, and fortitude. But even if you are a little short on fortitude, if you have knowledge, you can beat the crowd and maximize your returns.

"Good" Funds, "Bad" Funds

Most folks invest in "good" funds—funds that have performed well in the past, and you can't fault that. Nevertheless, most folks who have invested in good funds garner "bad" returns. You *can* fault that.

How can good funds give bad returns? Because an investment strategy based on buying good funds has the logic backward. Almost all good funds—as the public perceives them—have the wind at their backs. They look good because they've done well in the recent past. But while good past performance can hint at superior future returns, it doesn't guarantee it. Nonetheless, what does the average investor do when trying to predict a winner in the mutual fund performance race? He looks in the newspaper at past winners and assumes they are going to continue to outperform their peers in the future. He fails to recognize that funds' returns, like the weather, can't be foretold that way. Storms pass, seasons change, . . . and markets go through cycles. In the chapters to come, you'll learn that there's a much better way to select funds.

"Taking Things Personally"

If you were building a house, you wouldn't frame, plumb, wire, and sheetrock before you laid the foundation. A house with a poor foundation will never function well. The same is true for investing: Before anything else, you have to build a strong foundation that is designed to achieve your specific goals.

Picking a fund (or funds) is not a one-size-fits-all decision. Your investment decisions must make sense in the context of your personal situation. When it comes to mutual funds, your foundation is built through asset allocation: determining the best mix of stock funds and bond funds, and which types of each are most appropriate for meeting your goals.

Asset allocation is the foundation of a well-put-together investment portfolio. Many experts may claim they can determine the right foundation for you, based on their predictions of what the future holds. But that's nonsense. The best asset allocation plan is not based on somebody's crystal-balling the future, but is chosen to support you and your loved ones' goals, dreams, and fears. In Chapter 4, you'll learn the fundamentals of asset allocation, so that you can make better investment decisions.

So Many Funds—So Few Dollars to Invest

But how can anybody possibly choose the right funds when there are thousands to pick from—more mutual funds, in fact, than there are stocks on the New York Stock Exchange? If you do your asset allocation homework well, you will be shopping for only one or two funds at any one time, and you'll be looking for funds in specific categories. This simplifies your choices by immediately eliminating about 90 percent of all possibilities. Of the 10 percent remaining, you can exclude half by cutting out funds that charge sales commissions (called "load funds"). Next, examining the remaining 5 percent will eliminate the ones that consistently underperform similar funds. In very short order, you can thus eliminate 97 to 98 percent of all funds, and that's before you begin any serious analysis.

Once you've narrowed your fund choices this much, the next step can be easy. Since you've done your asset allocation homework, you've already identified the categories of funds you need. If you are looking for a fund in efficient markets, say a large-cap stock or high-quality bond fund (discussed in detail in later chapters), you can end your search at this point by simply selecting an index fund that closely tracks the S&P 500 or Wilshire 5000 Index. If your asset allocation plan points to a sector where a managed fund makes more sense, we provide guidelines for selection. But all this assumes that you've taken basic, preliminary steps—to determine how much you need to put into which categories of investment, otherwise, your search for the right funds will be long and painful because you will have no idea what you are looking for or where to begin or end your search.

Less-than-Respectable New Funds—Nobody Likes Them (but You Should)

The most often repeated dictum heard in the mutual fund universe is: "Past performance is no guarantee of future returns." Coming in at a close second is: "Only invest in funds with solid, long-term track records." But if funds with long-term records are the only funds you invest in, you are missing some great opportunities to be found among new funds. Why? Because there is no time in the life of a mutual fund when the interests of management and the shareholders interests are more closely linked than when a fund is new.

When a new fund debuts, the fund's management has to invest heavily in start-up costs and often in seed capital. These investments can run in the many hundreds of thousands or even millions of dollars. From the fund management's perspective, the only way to make the fund really pay off is to attract bushels of investors' dollars to the fund and capturing the coveted Morningstar four- or five-star ratings. How do they attract these investors? By offering superior fund performance. If they're successful, the money gushes in *after* early investors have made superior returns. By then, savvy new-fund investors have cashed in and moved on to other, newer funds.

FUNDAMENTAL FACTS

Caution. You can't be a sloppy new-fund investor, following the crowd into the sector du jour because Wall Street has that nasty habit of shoveling out new funds in overheated sectors that are about to turn tepid, cold, or even rancid. So you have to be discriminating and know what characteristics to look for. But if you do, returns are rewarding—and occasionally—spectacular.

So Many Experts—Which Do I Choose?

Experts come with all kinds of advice: The only commonality they all share is that every single one wants some of your money. There's nothing wrong with that—they have to make a living; giving financial advice is not their hobby. The issues are, how much are they worth and what added value do they provide? Here are a few rules of thumb to keep in mind when shopping for investment expertise:

Rule 1. You can't afford most experts. Most of the time, however, if you are willing to forgo some personal service, you can turn to the Internet, books, and periodicals to get quality services and information in areas like asset allocation guidance and fund selection. You can also get basic advice from companies that sponsor no-load funds and, of course, you can go to experts who charge a fee for their advice.

Rule 2. You want service providers whose self-interests are most closely linked to yours or whose fees are very low. Examples:

- *New funds* During their first three years, new funds are in a race for the stars—their Morningstar ratings. As already mentioned, there is no other time when your objectives are more closely linked to the interests of a fund's management.

- *Institutional investment managers who have recently entered the mutual fund business* These powerful managers, who have earned their stripes with large private accounts, need to make themselves known. The only way they can muscle into the already-crowded market is to post stellar returns, and they often have the resources to achieve them.

- *Fee-based advisers* These are professionals whose ongoing compensation is based directly on your returns. It's in their best interest to maximize your returns, so they're a better bet than commission-based brokers who get paid up front regardless of how well your investments perform.

Rule 3. Keep it simple. Avoid funds with tangled fee structures—up-front charges, sales commissions when you sell your sales, trading costs, and so on. Such complexity can be bewildering to shareholders, making them more dependent on the experts than they need to be. Complexity seldom enhances returns; usually, it does just the opposite.

What's the Market Going to Do?
What If It Crashes?

The future for any investment can take only one of three directions: up, down, or sideways. Legions of experts are eager to take your money for predicting which direction it will take, but they don't really know any more than you do. One thing we do know: Two-thirds of their possible choices will be the *wrong* ones. That being the case, the best investment strategy is to prepare for all three possibilities. And the best preparation, the best defense against uncertainty, is to develop a good offense: Work out a sound asset allocation for yourself.

If your time frame is long (20 years or more), you can afford more volatile funds in your portfolio because even if stocks drop in the near future, there is plenty of time for them to make a comeback. Therefore tilt your portfolio toward more stock funds and less toward bonds; held over the long term, stocks are likely to earn a higher return.

If time grows short (5 years or less), you're best advised to do the opposite. You might not have the time to wait for a dip in the market to turn itself around, so you want your portfolio to favor more bonds and bond funds, which have a lower likely rate of return but are far more secure than stocks. If you find yourself staring at the ceiling at 2 A.M. after a bad day for stocks, you've got your allocation wrong; adjust your portfolio to favor less risky bond investments.

A terrific way to capture fine returns without having to try to predict the market's direction is to choose convertible bond funds. They hold portfolios of bonds, each of which can be converted into common stocks (see Chapter 11). Most retail investors consider them complicated, and few understand them— let alone have enthusiasm for them—but this only makes these funds an even better bet. The relatively painless experience of investors in Japanese convertible bonds versus stocks and more recently in Asia makes them even more desirable if you worry about a similar future crash in U.S. stocks.

"Things Are Too Uncertain—I'm Going to Wait (or Watch 'It') for a While"

Many people postpone investing because they want to wait until the market seems safer. So they simply sit back, claiming they're going to watch it for a while before jumping in. But what is "it," they're going to watch? More importantly, what is it they're going to do after they've watched it? Watching is a poor substitute for doing. If you're watching and the stock market goes up, you've "missed it." If it goes down, you "knew it was too high." If it goes sideways, you "knew it wouldn't do anything."

But where does all this watching get you? Nowhere. Indeed, things are uncertain in the stock market right now—so were they 10 days ago, 10 weeks ago, 10 months ago, and 10 years ago. And so will they be 10 days, weeks, months, and years from now. That's no reason not to do something. In fact, this uncertainty is precisely why you should do something: You want to plan for an uncertain future. And among the wide range of available mutual funds, there are strong candidates to suit the goals and affinities of any investor.

"I Don't Invest in Stocks, I Only Buy Real Estate"

Unlike the commentary from the 1970s, you almost never hear, "I only buy real estate" anymore, at least from mutual fund investors. Today everybody's betting on the technology sector. But that means that real estate investment trusts (REITs) are overlooked. REITs—and REIT mutual funds—have been laggards for the past decade, even though the industry has gone through some major, and positive, changes. But if REITs are such a good deal, why isn't everybody snapping them up? Most investors don't care about REITs because they're too busy chasing the tech-stock of the day, and today many investors don't even understand what REITs are. They confuse them with real estate limited partnerships (where individuals invest their money with a general partner who runs the operation—buying, selling, and managing the properties) that caused so much grief during the late 1970s and early 1980s. Today's investors hear "real estate" and envision partially occupied buildings mismanaged by incompetent and often unscrupulous managers.

What today's investors don't understand is that the landscape of real-estate investment has changed. Today, REIT managers have to put their own money into their projects, and lenders won't give developers construction loans unless their projects are half leased up. Institutions, which customarily keep between 10 percent and 20 percent of their assets invested in commercial real estate, understand this; and so does Warren Buffett who has invested in REITs the last few years. REITs, yielding 6 to 10 percent returns, from dividends are a compelling alternative to many popular stocks that are yielding only 1 to 1.5 percent. At some point, the public's perception of REITs is likely to improve, and in the meantime REIT fund buyers are amply rewarded for their foresight.

Funds at a Discount—Closed-End Funds

Closed-end mutual funds, which can be bought at 10, 20, and even 30 percent discounts to their underlying portfolios may seem like real bargains, and sometimes they are, as discussed in Chapter 6. More often, however, you get what you pay for—most closed-end funds have unfortunate track records. And since they have a captive audience of shareholders, unlike open-end funds where new owners can come aboard or depart daily, it's fair to wonder if many closed-end fund managements have as much dedication as they would have if their investors could pick up their marbles and go home.

Still, there are pockets of opportunity among closed-end funds. Some well managed funds sell at unusually steep discounts; some are being pressured to convert to open-end funds or merge. Others provide access to very small sectors of the market, or participation in venture capital opportunities. While they aren't mainstream, some closed-end funds provide intriguing opportunities if you want to take an opportunistic approach to fund investing.

Beyond Mutual Funds—Individually Managed Accounts

One of the reasons mutual fund asset growth has slowed in recent years is the growth of individually managed accounts (IMAs). IMAs are customized, professionally managed portfolios of individual stocks and/or bonds. They require a fairly large initial investment—$100,000 or more—but they have some real advantages over most mutual funds. They can be managed to be sensitive to your particular tax situation, which is not true of most mutual funds. You can also get a greater sense of participation with them, because instead of owning shares of a fund that owns securities, you own the stocks and bonds themselves.

Like most services, IMA providers are popping up on the Web, vowing to provide increased services at lower costs. But whether they do so remains to be seen. In fact, IMA costs can be higher than the costs associated with some mutual funds, and they often provide less diversification. And don't let anyone tell you that IMA managers as a group are any more talented than fund managers! In fact, they may be the same people—some fund managers also manage IMAs.

Taxes: It's Not How Much You Make— It's How Much You *Keep*

If your investment account is taxable and you are a successful investor, your account can become a tax monster—one you have to feed. The monster exists because you are taxed on income and all realized gains from your funds, whether you receive or reinvest them. And when you sell a fund at a nice profit, it's not all yours to keep; you pay more taxes.

Studies have shown investors lose an average of 2.5 percent of mutual funds' annual returns to taxes. The grand total for U.S. investors in 1997 and 1998: $50 billion in federal taxes. But there are ways to lighten the load. Among the options are tax-efficient funds, tax-managed funds, and tax-free municipal bond funds, all of which are discussed in later chapters. There are also general guidelines for minimizing the IRS's claim on your investments' returns.

Kitchen Table Economics: The Rule of 72

Why children are allowed to complete junior high school without knowing the *Rule of 72* is one of the great mysteries of the educational system. It's very simple: Divide any annual percentage return into 72, and you get the number of years it takes to double any sum of money. So, if you've got a 6 percent return, you double your money in 12 years—72 divided by 6 is 12. Ten percent doubles your money in 7.2 years, and 15 percent gets you there in less than 5 years. And of course, after the first doubling, the rule holds for every subsequent doubling. The Rule of 72 is a wonderful mental shortcut and helps us understand the wonder of compound returns.

Do your kids, grandkids, nephews, and nieces a huge favor: Before the week's out, make sure they know the Rule of 72 and don't let them forget it—it could

TABLE 1.1 Rule of 72: The Magic of
Compounding ($1,000 Invested at Age 30—
Final Returns)

AGES	6%	10%
40 (10 yrs)	$1,790	$ 2,590
45 (15 yrs)	2,400	4,180
50 (20yrs)	3,210	6,730
55 (25 yrs)	4,290	10,830
60 (30 yrs)	4,980	17,450
65 (35 yrs)	6,510	28,100

See Appendix B for complete compound interest table.

make investors out of them. Table 1.1 shows how the Rule of 72 works over time. You can see that if you invest $1,000 in a mutual fund at age 30, and your average annual return is 6 percent per year, you will have approximately 6½ times your money at age 65, or $6,510. If your return averages 10 percent a year in the same period, it will grow to $28,100—over 28 times your money! The longer you can invest, and the higher the return, the more powerful is the compounding.

To repeat: No one cares more about your money than you do. But caring about your money is not enough—you also have to know how to take care of your money. Despite what the experts want you to believe, it's not that difficult, and it's what this book is about. But there is no one right way. To borrow a tired old cliché, you have to plan your work and then work your plan. Chapter 2 will help you take the next step—breaking out of the "average investor" mode, who so often receives below average returns. We point out why this is so and how these unsatisfactory results are self-inflicted through classic mistakes that are repeated with regularity. We list these all-too-common errors and show you how to avoid the pitfalls that cause disappointing returns and losses.

Why You Can't Be an Average Mutual Fund Investor

If at first you don't succeed, try, try again. Then quit. There's no use being a damn fool about it.

—W.C. Fields

The elephant in the living room—everybody knows it's there, but nobody really wants to talk about it. An elephantine problem faces mutual fund investors today: Their returns are generally lower than the gains earned by the mutual funds they invest in.

Studies show that mutual funds outperform most of their own shareholders. They reveal that investors hurt their own returns because they break the fundamental rule of successful investing: They buy when prices are high and sell when prices are low. Most investors have come to understand that cutting costs and eliminating fees improves the returns on their investments. But reducing these drains on your return doesn't help much if you are buying and selling at the wrong times.

Because investing in mutual funds is so "easy," most people should find it is an almost ideal way to invest. Why then, is it so hard for the average investor to achieve even near-average returns? Much of the damage to investors' returns is self-inflicted. Too many people make classic mistakes and then repeat them during every market cycle:

- Investors ignore the most hallowed of all principles, reasonable asset allocation: how to divide up money between stocks, bonds, large and small companies, foreign stocks, and so on. They fail to realize that the fuel driving their returns comes from the powerful forces that move industries and major sectors of the economy, such as interest rates and corporate earnings—not the star mutual fund managers that get so much press.

- Investors are risk-averse when stocks are down and virtually ignore hazards when they are up. When stocks are down, "things" are too "uncertain" or downright "bad" to invest. When stocks are up, they espouse nifty rationales explaining how this time "things are different" and why risk-worries are passé.

- Investors ignore probability. They pile into growth funds sporting torrid performance long after asset bloat has guaranteed that the hypergrowth is unsustainable.

- Investors ignore valuation. They are unconcerned about whether the stocks are historically overpriced or underpriced in relation to earnings, dividends, and other benchmarks. Instead, they tend to buy funds that hold the most expensive stocks, because those funds have the "best track records."

- Investors ignore costs. They allow "experts"—brokers, advisers, fund managers, and the like—to siphon off too much of their money. They invest too much in the experts and not enough in their portfolios. A typical professionally managed mutual fund can cost 1.5 percent to 2 percent annually, whereas excellent index funds are available with a cost of as little as 0.15 percent a year.

- Investors expect too much from experts. The market is going to do whatever it is going to do. While a minority of so-called experts provide added value to market returns, most charge too much for their services and reduce your returns.

- Investors place inordinate faith in "proven track records," in their pursuit of above-average returns, even though history shows that past performance is almost meaningless in predicting superior future performance.

- Investors try to improve returns by trading more often, even though it has been shown that more frequent trading systematically reduces returns.

While returns on stocks, bonds, sectors, and indexes are measured to the third decimal, studies of the mutual fund investor underperformance phenomenon are relatively rare, largely because it's in nobody's self-interest to document how badly investors do. Certainly not the brokers or fund companies that have the most resources and data to do such studies.

Imagine an ad in a finance magazine showing a prosperous middle-aged couple sitting on their private dock, beaming at the camera. The caption reads:

"We're cool. Our Tapioca Fund's annual return for the past five years has been 22.7 percent." Running alongside, however, is a story with a table showing that the *average investor in Tapioca Fund* garnered only a 5-year return of 11.2 percent. Why the difference? First, it's because there aren't many 5-year investors any more—the average mutual fund investor stays put for only around 2.5 years or less. Second, more investors put money in funds during periods when prices are up and take it out when they are down.

Underperformance Studies

All of the studies available agree that the average investor fails to stay even with the returns from their own mutual funds. The only differences in the studies are the time periods measured and the degree of underperformance discovered. One study, reported in *Mutual Funds* magazine (May 2000), showed that from 1984 to 1996 the average fund investor's returns were 7.3 percent, trailing well behind the 10.7 percent earned by the average stock mutual fund. That's a significant shortfall—a $10,000 investment in the average *fund* delivered $45,942 at the end of 12 years, but the average *investor* managed to capture only $28,773. The $17,169 difference is *almost twice* the amount of the original investment.

This was one of the first large studies to chart investors' returns, and it was widely circulated and challenged because reported investors' returns were so miserable. It found that both load and no-load fund investors' returns lagged behind returns of small-cap stocks by more than 57 percent and the Standard & Poor's 500 Index by more than 75 percent! It concluded that the amount of underperformance was a result of the frequency of investors' trading. The study may or may not have been flawed, but subsequent studies by others indicate that while it may have overstated the magnitude of investors' underperformance, it pointed in the right direction:

- *Forbes* compared the "dollar-weighted" returns (*investors'* actual average annual returns) and "time-weighted" returns (the *funds'* average annual returns) of Fidelity Magellan and 20th Century Select Funds for the decade ending December 31, 1987. The shortfall for investors was striking:

	Time-Weighted (Funds') Returns (%)	Dollar-Weighted (Investors') Returns (%)
Fidelity Magellan	31.0	13.4
20th Century Select	24.3	11.5

The reason for investor return shortfalls was poor timing and too much of it. Converting the percentage differences between investors' returns and their own mutual funds' returns into dollars on a $10,000 investment shows that their funds bettered them by almost four times:

	Funds	Investors	Funds' Advantage
Fidelity Magellan	$148,837	$35,166	+$113,671
20th Century Select	88,046	29,699	+ 58,347

The study used two of the top-performing funds of the 1977–1987 period (Peter Lynch was at Magellan's helm), and the message is clear: Even in great funds, *most investors timed themselves out of most of the profits.*

- A *Money* magazine study reported that in 1996, Dreyfus Aggressive Growth Fund earned 20.7 percent, but its average shareholder *lost* 34.9 percent. During the same year, Van Wagoner Growth Fund returned 26.9 percent, yet its average shareholders lost 20.0 percent.

- Frank Russell Company, in collaboration with Morningstar, studied 35 funds over 13 calendar quarters ending September 30, 1997. Compared with the funds' returns, traders reduced their average annual returns by almost 12 percent. A sample: T. Rowe Price Mid-Cap Growth Fund—rapid fund switching reduced traders' returns by 2.99 percent *per quarter.*

- Investors bailed out of stock funds after the October 1987 stock market "crash." As stocks recovered, they continued pulling out more money than they put into funds in 17 of the following 18 months. Only *after* prices exceeded precrash levels, did they resume their previous stock fund buying pace. A classic example of selling low and buying high.

Mistiming is not restricted to mutual fund investors. Terry Odean, a professor at the University of California Business School, Davis, conducted a study of 97,000 stock trades at a large discount broker. Odean found that the most active traders achieved the lowest returns. He tracked the performances of the stocks sold and compared them with those that replaced them. One year after the trades, the most active traders trailed the market by 7 percentage points.

FUNDAMENTAL FACTS

When buyers outnumber sellers, open-end mutual funds *create new shares* and the shareholder population expands. When there are more sellers, shares are effectively canceled; they cease to exist. We can be somewhat certain of the success or failure of fund investors because the open-end mutual fund shareholder population is elastic. Measuring expansion and contraction of the number of shareholders versus fund share prices provides insight into investors' returns.

Bond investors are similarly afflicted. In 1994, a year of falling bond (and bond fund) prices, bond funds experienced net redemptions (more money being taken out than being invested) in all but one month during the following 13 months—February 1994 to March 1995. Bond fund investors didn't resume net buying until *after* bond prices exceeded previous highs.

Divided Loyalty

Fickle fund buyers are not a new phenomenon. During the 1970s, when stocks were suffering from rising interest rates and the OPEC embargo, fund buyers were anything but enthusiastic. In all but one year from 1972 until 1980, investors sold more funds of all types than they bought: In seven out of eight years, *the entire mutual fund industry was in net redemption.* As the 1980s dawned, marking the beginning of history's greatest bull market, there was less money invested in funds than at the beginning of the previous decade; total assets didn't surpass the 1972 peak of $59.8 billion until 1982.

A much more specific example of investors' love/hate relationship with funds can be found in the history of Fidelity Select Technology Fund, launched in 1981. It got off to a terrific start, returning 162 percent for the 12-month period ending June 1983, and investor enthusiasm swelled assets to $670 million—a big fund in those days. But then technology stocks began a long fade, and the fund returned only 0.6 percent annually for the rest of the decade. Meanwhile the S&P 500 Index return averaged 19.7 percent a year. Disillusioned Fidelity Technology investors hit the bricks, and by the end of the decade, the fund's assets shrank by more than 89 percent, bottoming out at $71 million, and the Morningstar rating was down to one star. In 1990, the technology cycle turned up, and the fund's average annual return rebounded to 28.5 percent for the next 10 years. The investor stampede reversed also—by the end of the 1990s, assets had increased more than 70-fold, to $5.1 billion, and topped $7 billion in early 2000, just in time for the beginning of another technology swoon.

Investors have become trigger-happy, switching in and out of funds in search of the highest possible return. Today, fund switching is reaching remarkable dimensions. Table 2.1 shows one sector fund's exploding asset growth when its sector became popular in 1999 (the fund provided these statistics only on the promise of anonymity). Column 3 provides the net asset value (NAV), in dollars per share.

In a 6-month period, assets grew over 50-fold; in just 3 months, by over 30 times.

Index funds, supposedly the investment-of-choice of more patient investors with long-term objectives, are not immune from fickle fund investors. S&P 500 Index fund returns, driven by their large-cap weightings, were immensely

TABLE 2.1 Explosive Fund Asset Growth

DATE	ASSETS ($ML.)	NAV
12/31/97	3.00	10.00
01/31/98	3.08	10.26
02/28/98	3.16	10.49
03/31/98	3.19	10.59
04/30/98	3.17	10.47
05/31/98	3.16	10.35
06/30/98	3.05	10.03
07/31/98	3.10	10.11
08/31/98	2.48	7.93
09/30/98	2.93	9.11
10/31/98	3.19	9.88
11/30/98	3.53	10.56
12/31/98	3.91	11.44
01/31/99	4.48	12.03
02/28/99	4.36	11.44
03/31/99	4.42	11.19
04/30/99	4.36	10.94
05/30/99	4.45	11.11
06/30/99	4.96	12.43
07/31/99	5.19	12.91
08/31/99	6.13	14.62
09/30/99	6.38	14.62
10/31/99	6.89	15.16
11/30/99	9.05	16.92
12/31/99	14.75	20.02
01/31/00	38.97	24.20
02/29/00	302.79	40.74
03/31/00	273.96	27.31
04/30/00	273.06	26.16

Rearview Mirror Investors

"THE NEW CLASS OF MUTUAL FUND INVESTOR:
THE LAST CLASS . . . IN RIGHT AT THE TOP"—

"The way I look at it, there are only two things in the stock market: shares of stock and the money to buy them," said Charles Biderman, a former *Barron's* editor, and president of Trim Tabs Financial Services, Santa Rosa, California (trimtabs.com), in an interview in May 2000. His firm tracks liquidity, the "net action of the corporate investor," and other data for institutional investors ($7,000 minimum annual fee).

Biderman says, "Stock prices have nothing to do with value." If you can track "float" (the supply of stocks) and "net liquidity" (the money to buy them), you can tell the direction of the market. When the net liquidity/float balance tips in favor of stocks as happened in 1994, it drives stocks higher. When net liquidity reverses, as it did in February 2000, Biderman forecasted lower stock prices.

Wonderfully simple as the idea is, rounding up liquidity and float statistics is a huge task that includes collecting data from government agencies, the Federal Reserve, the U.S. Treasury, Wall Street, mutual funds, and the banking system. Further complicating the task is that some of the data is delayed requiring some "massaging and interpreting" based on seasonal patters and Trim Tabs' experience.

Biderman's firm collects data from over 500 equity mutual funds with $750 billion in assets; a Wharton School-sponsored study determined that it was over 99 percent accurate. The study found that "mutual fund flow is strongly related to same-day market returns, and to previous-day market returns."

Biderman's assessment of fund investors' buying and selling patterns: "They invest with their eyes firmly on the rearview mirror and wonder why they crash regularly. The more [mutual funds] have gone up, the more likely they think they are going to continue to go up."

Interviewer: "What about this year (mid-year 2000)? Investors didn't sell on the dip like they usually do."

Biderman: "Anecdotally, this year, we're seeing a new class of investors—the last class. These are the people who have been waiting, waiting, waiting; they think now that there is absolutely no risk in the market. Now they're in—right at the top."

Once more, investors trying to time the market, (an impossible task), probably got it backward.

popular in the late 1990s, garnering 40 percent of investors' new money in 1999 alone. In early 2000, as technology stocks skyrocketed, investors began to switch out of index funds and into technology funds. The industry was anxious to accommodate. In April 2000, Morningstar told the *Wall Street Journal* that there were 30 funds invested exclusively in Internet stocks, "with more in the works."

A flummoxed spokesperson for Vanguard, the largest index fund sponsor, was quoted in the April 2, 2000, issue of *Investment News:* "We are astonished at the speed at which investors are willing to punish a fund. Index investing has turned into a sport. If you didn't get a 100 percent return last year, your country club membership is in jeopardy." Perhaps the problem boils down to one simple human truth: *People want to own winners.* No amount of Wall Street analysis and interpretation about companies' growth rates, managements, market shares, or valuations equals the irresistible appeal of stocks that are going up. The same is true for the mutual funds that own them.

Researchers have found a strong correlation between the market's direction and investors' decisions: When the market drops, people sell their stocks. A study of monthly trading activity draws the same conclusion. In 1997, Bridge-water Associates, a research and consulting firm based in Wilton, Connecticut, published a study of a 6-year period (from 1990 to 1996) of monthly "net exchanges into and out of equity mutual funds by households." Their report reads in part:

> In the history shown, which goes back until 1990, there have not been too many monthly dips in the equity market, but we do see that *every* month in which the S&P declined in price was accompanied by net exchanges *out* of equity mutual funds and into other forms of investment. The size of exchanges has been proportionate with the size of the equity market declines. Conversely, nearly every upward move in equity prices has been accompanied by net exchanges into equity funds out of cash and bonds. Of course, these fund flows could be causing the market moves, but given the relative size of net exchanges, this is not really likely. Rather, it is most likely indicative of the *trend following approach that households take towards equity investing.* (emphasis added)

But this trend-following approach is precisely what we have been warning against—it causes investors to buy high and sell low, a classic recipe for poor returns.

Past versus Future Returns

While a fund that *has risen* may be a good fund, a really good fund is one that *will rise.* Those, of course, are harder to spot ahead of time, as the fund-picking services have consistently demonstrated. You can get your arms around good past performance: It's tangible. Is there anything more beautiful than a Morningstar report on a fund that has left all its peers in the dust? It is so easy to project those results into the future. And that's what most investors do—over 90 percent of all new money flows into funds displaying four- and five-ratings.

Privately, the industry calls this phenomenon "performance chasing," a not-so-flattering term for buying funds on the basis of their good returns in the past. Performance chasing reached epic proportions in 1999. The September 1999 issue of *Mutual Funds* magazine reported, "In the first quarter of 1999, the 25 funds with the highest net sales took in a stunning 96 percent of all net fund inflow, according to Financial Research [Corp., Boston]. (Nearly every one is a large-cap growth fund.) The other 5,702 funds tracked by the firm accounted for just 4% during early 1999."

Nondurability of Above-Average Returns

The problem is, above average performance is usually not sustainable, as the following statistics show:

- A 1994 Lipper Analytical Services study found that Morningstar's five-star rated funds underperformed the average stock fund each year during the 1990–1993 period.
- A Financial Research Corp. study reported that from late 1987 to late 1997, the top-selling funds in the typical 12-month period yielded returns that were below the average fund during the following 12 months.
- *Forbes* columnist and publisher of the *Hulbert Financial Digest*, Mark Hulbert tracked Morningstar's top-ranked, no-load, equity funds for almost 7 years and found that they lagged behind the stock market by "an average of nearly three percentage points per year."
- Financial Research Corp. examined the returns of 365 Morningstar-rated funds for the December 31, 1994–September 30, 1998, period. They found that two- and three-star rated funds outperformed four- and five-star funds for the entire period, and that five-star funds performed worst of all.

The reason so few above-average funds continue to turn in above-average performances is that rising prices expand valuations. The stocks in their portfolios are bid up to unrealistic prices because of investors' expectations. As a fund's portfolio valuations rise, the ratio of risk to reward becomes more and more unfavorable, reducing potential appreciation and exposing shareholders to more risk.

To return to that 1999 *Mutual Funds* study: An examination of the large-cap growth sector that received the "stunning 96% of all new money" shows the inverse relationship between price and value. Table 2.2 shows how the Morningstar fund categories rated at the beginning of that quarter, according to two of the commonest valuation measures—price/earnings and price/book ratios. The price/earnings (or P/E) ratio compares the price of a stock with its earnings per share. Those earnings are calculated by dividing the total earnings of a company during the past four quarters by the number of shares outstanding. So, if a company with 1 million shares reported earnings of $2 million, the earnings per share would equal $2. If its share price was $26, the P/E ratio would be 13. If the share price was $40, the P/E would be 20.

The price/book ratio is calculated similarly. The book value of a company is its theoretical value as it appears on its balance sheet equal to total assets minus liabilities, preferred stock, and intangible assets. This figure, divided by the number of shares outstanding in that company, gives you the book value per share. Dividing the current share price by the book value per share provides the price/book ratio.

Table 2.2 shows how the valuations stood at the beginning of 1999, and where most of investors dollars were flowing.

Buying when prices are high violates the law of supply and demand, to say nothing of common sense. Economic theory holds that consumers will buy less of a product or service as prices rise. When it comes to baskets of blueberries or cans of peas, the theory holds true—consumers snap up bargains, and buy less when prices rise.

Investors, however, don't buy to consume, they buy stocks and funds to own. While consumers want *value*; investors want *valuableness*. Most investors see

TABLE 2.2 Morningstar Fund Sector Valuations—December 31, 1998

MORNINGSTAR SECTOR	PRICE/EARNINGS RATIO	PRICE/BOOK RATIO
Large-cap growth	38.2	9.3
Mid-cap growth	38.8	8.1
Small-cap growth	34.9	6.9
Large-cap blend	30.4	6.9
Mid-cap blend	27.9	5.1
Small-cap blend	23.9	4.6
Large-cap value	23.8	4.0
Mid-cap value	22.0	3.3
Small-cap value	18.7	2.5

rising stock and fund prices and unrealistically extrapolate present trends into the future; they see the rising prices as a confirmation that their investments are becoming ever more valuable. After all, that's the reason for investing in the first place. And it takes only a small leap of faith to convince themselves that today's rising prices will go on indefinitely.

But investors who fall into this kind of thinking are looking at only one part of the equation. They see rising prices, but they don't also take into account the fact that value is being extinguished. Judging from where they put their new money, most fund investors in early 1999 were counting on a continuation of the uninterrupted, and unprecedented, 5-year trend favoring large-cap growth stocks. They weren't in pursuit of "just" average returns, and certainly not below-average returns. But how likely was it that 96 percent of investors' new money, in any sector, would achieve above-average returns in recent years? As one wag remarks, "Universal acclaim is not the birthplace of outstanding investment opportunities."

Heard on the Street

"Have any bubbles survived? Has there ever been a new era? No. My colleagues looked at every big asset class this century: gold, oil, cocoa, dollars, yen, pounds, and stocks. Each one had at least one bubble and each bubble gave back all its gains, reverting to the mean. To make matters worse, I have in the last year asked about a dozen gatherings of investment professionals if they could suggest a single new era or bubble that did not burst. Not a single one has been forthcoming."

Jeremy Granthem, in "Global Markets"—*Forbes Magazine*, November 1, 1999.

Paying the Piper

The undoing of fund performance chasers that "buy high" is the relatively unforgiving mathematical principle called "reversion to the mean." This principle operates much like a pendulum: It calls for prices to retreat (revert) from extremes toward the middle. Buying at the high end of the pendulum's swing is a recipe for disaster. When you start hearing Wall Street's most dangerous phrase, "But this time it's different," you know you're somewhere near the peak of a cycle—the pendulum is near the extreme end of its swing. If your asset allocation plan is in place, unlike most fund investors, you're diversified and you aren't nearly as vulnerable. At this point you're probably well advised to stay put.

The problem is cyclicality; what's "good," doesn't always stay good. While most studies have found that bad performing funds tend to stay bad, *Money* magazine's Jason Zweig notes, "The average five-star fund sustains that rating for only six months." Zweig went on to cite a finding by two professors: "A five-star fund stands about the same chance of remaining superior as a three-star fund has of becoming superior." Morningstar's John Rekenthaler doesn't disagree: "I wouldn't worry about whether the fund has three, four or five stars."

It's not hard to understand how reversion can play havoc with fund switchers; they get caught when the pendulum begins its inevitable swing back to the middle. There are long-term fund investors who avoid this fate, but if the average investor holds for two to three years, there are legions that hold their funds for considerably less. And if those short-termers typically buy near peaks, they inevitably suffer when their funds revert to the mean. If they then sell their "bad" funds to buy new "good" funds that are near *their* peak, these investors systematically degrade their returns. Done often enough, the "strategy" converts returns into losses.

FUNDAMENTAL FACTS

Moving Averages Explained

Moving averages are used to graphically smooth out historical price fluctuations. To construct a 50-day moving average of the S&P 500, you add up the index's closing prices for the past 50 days, divide that sum by 50 and plot the resulting average number. Tomorrow, you add the day's new closing price and subtract the oldest (the 51st day), repeat the division, and add that point to your graph. Plotted over time, moving averages show the main trend—incoming and outgoing tides—not every breaking wave.

A good way to understand reversion to the mean is to look at a graph of two moving averages—one calculated on the basis of 200 days, the other based on 50 days. The graph of the Dow Jones Industrial Average shown in Figure 2.1 is an example of how reversion to the mean works. The 200-day moving average smooths the index's price movement more than the 50-day average. As time passes, the more volatile 50-day average oscillates to greater extremes and then tends to revert back from extremes to the center, or to the opposite extreme. Since reversion occurs more often than not, a methodology that systematically buys when prices are near extreme highs and sells near extreme lows is obviously badly flawed. It's not hard to see why investors who chase

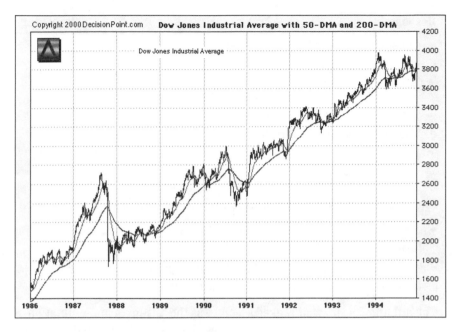

FIGURE 2.1 Dow Jones Industrial Average.
Copyright 2000 DecisionPoint.com.

performance fare badly and why the more they do it, the worse their returns become.

While "roller coaster ride" is a cliché that is often used to describe stock price fluctuations, it may be even truer than we realize. Unlike the relatively slow speed with which prices click their way up, they drop with frightening speed. If you aren't prepared, it may be your last ride.

Ad-ding Fuel to the Fire

Chasing performance without considering your asset allocation needs is investing done in the wrong way, because it makes a fund's performance the first selection criterion when it should be one of the last. Still, most investors don't seem to recognize this basic point. Investors' typical way of thinking is shown in their responses to a major telephone poll in 1996, in which 100 investors were asked the following question:

"When you see a mutual fund advertisement, what is most likely to get your attention?"

Response	Percentage
a. The fund's performance	46
b. The fund's objective	8
c. The investment sector's market strength	4
d. The strength and reputation of the mutual fund company	26
e. The fund's independent rating(s)	9
f. Don't know	6
g. Refused to answer	1

The responses to this poll are instructive:

- "The fund's performance," the factor *least likely* to determine future returns, got the *most* attention.
- The "investment sector's market strength," the factor *most likely* to determine future returns, got the *least* attention.

The attention-getter that ranked second was the "strength and reputation of the mutual fund company," which confirms the wisdom of the industry's billions spent on advertising.

Large fund families advertise and offer bushels of helpful literature offering sound, reasoned investment advice and information on topics ranging from taxes and retirement to asset allocation. But these high-minded educational efforts don't attract a lot of money from investors. Attracting even less are marketing programs promoting out-of-favor sectors or funds, even though these probably offer the best value and long-term prospects for serious investors.

Judged by advertising space, the real war for investors' dollars takes place on the battlefields of past performance. Victors advertise funds with the highest returns—the ones that investors are most predisposed to buy—in big, bold type. There are always some of these funds to promote because random chance systematically provides above-average funds no matter *what* the market is doing. When market conditions have been particularly hostile; however, industry advertising shifts its focus from recent returns to long-term performance.

Advertising that emphasizes performance and funds with ultrahigh recent returns has a couple of undesirable side effects:

1. It implies that stellar recent returns are likely to extend into the future. The reality is, however, that they probably won't, and the ads generally deny this rosy prospect in microprint at the bottom of the page.

2. It implies that past returns are *the* key criteria for picking future outperformers—after all, the performance numbers and/or the star ratings usually appear in the largest type. This implication is also false.

The March 2000 issue of *Mutual Funds* magazine provides a microcosm of
fund advertising practice. Advertisements for 76 funds appeared in this issue.
Omitting generic fund family, foreign, and sector-fund ads, there were 38 diversified U.S. stock funds that ran ads showing one-year returns. Some of these
showed 3- and 5-year returns as well, and a few exhibited their star ratings.
Thirty of the advertisers (79%) were growth funds, the fund style category that
had enjoyed the highest recent gains. On the other hand, blend funds, which lie
between growth and value funds, took up only 16 percent of the advertising
space, and value funds, mired in the worst performing category, claimed only 5
percent. This is hardly surprising, since advertising tends to be biased in favor
of funds that have garnered the highest recent returns.

The average advertised fund's one-year performance for 1999 was *86.7* percent—an astonishingly above-average return compared with 27.1 percent for
the average diversified U.S. stock and the "pathetic" 21 percent achieved by the
S&P 500 Index. The majority of advertised funds looked amazingly good: They
had almost doubled in value during the previous year. But for value-conscious
investors, the underlying figures were unsettling. These advertised funds had
valuations that were high compared to the S&P 500, which was itself carrying
above-average historical valuations:

	Price/Earnings	Price/Cash Flow	Price/Book
Standard & Poor's 500	37.3	25.8	10.6
Average advertised funds	46.3	31.7	14.5

Do Something!

When the market comes gunning for your net worth, you're winged before you
know it. But unlike in the movies, it's not over quickly. Days stretch into weeks,
and then months, as prices sink, lurch, and stumble lower. Short, sharp rallies
kindle hopes of recovery that are doomed and dashed within days. Each week's
bad news is worse than the previous week's; and experts, who used to crow
about rising prices, are glibly explaining why prices are now dropping.

Watching months and years of accumulated gains melting away has a corro-
sive effect on any investor's resolve. "Doing nothing," which is usually the best
approach *after* a sharp drop in prices, can be very difficult, particularly if it's
your first experience with a bear market. Your monthly statement arrives,

showing ghastly shrinkage to your account. You're more likely to feel driven to do something—but there really is only one thing to do: Sell!—to save what's left! The point is, you must be prepared for stocks and funds going up and down. Otherwise, when you and millions of others reach the point where all you can think of is selling, the market will be near a bottom. And if you pull out of your funds or stocks at that point you're faced with several unpleasant consequences:

- You convert your temporary losses into permanent ones.
- You eliminate any opportunity to get even.
- You postpone or eliminate the opportunity to build wealth after prices later rebound and go on to achieve new highs.

But you can "do something" far more productive than bailing out after the market falls. You can prepare for a bear market ahead of time as though it is inevitable—because it is. How? By assuming that *starting tomorrow* stocks can drop 30 to 40 percent. Most of all, you want to avoid being driven to sell *after* a drop. Do *not* assume that you—or your adviser—is prescient enough to get you out ahead of time. Aviators prepare, and train, for crash landings while they're aloft, not after they and their planes are spread out all over a cornfield. If you're totally fearless, an all-stock fund portfolio may be your best choice. On the other hand, if you're likely to need to sell during tough times, your portfolio can be made more "bear-proof" by keeping a hefty stake in REIT, convertible, and bond funds. "Know thyself"—and allocate your assets accordingly.

Taxes—The Final Insult

As if the chronicle of the things that can go wrong and the self-destructive behavior of some investors aren't depressing enough, there remains the final insult—taxes. You can successfully jump over all the pretax hurdles in investing and find yourself streaking over the finish line, only to face a hefty penalty by the IRS and your state tax collector.

The folks who impose taxes apparently feel that you owe them a hefty chunk of your investment returns if you are successful. If you're *not* successful, well, that's your problem. It's important to recognize a few tax facts of life.

For example, if you are a successful investor without some kind of tax deferral such as a 401(k) or an IRA (individual retirement account) taxable investing can become very expensive. Woe to you, should you choose to reinvest and build for the future—you'll have to cannibalize some of your investment returns or fork over some of your earnings to feed the ravenous tax beast.

Left unattended, the fund tax bite can be formidable. Vanguard has calculated that taxes (at the maximum rate) reduced the reported annual returns of the average managed stock fund by 2.5 percent over the past decade. To bring this point home to their investors, they have announced that in addition to their normal reporting, they will began reporting their funds' after-tax returns to shareholders. Predictably, competitors howled that Vanguard's move was self-serving because their stable of tax-efficient index funds gives them a competitive advantage. Well, it does—and good for Vanguard! Reports containing information about after-tax returns provide a valuable service. And this isn't the first time Vanguard faced such competitor-carping. Scoffers claimed that Vanguard's 1994 introduction of tax-managed funds was just a "gimmick." A few years later, however, imitators had launched 45 funds with that same gimmick, and the number is growing.

Vicious Velocity?

For investors, the Internet provides an extraordinary amount of information that used to be the sole domain of brokers. Investing has become fun for everybody, but it has had some unfunny consequences. Among these is the systematic destruction of day traders' accounts and the net worth of others who do not understand how to invest sensibly.

The availability and speed of cyberinformation provides neophyte investors with the illusion of competence. While the Internet allows investors to "stay on top of things," most reports tell us it hasn't helped returns. Cyberspace can't endow investors with good judgment or discipline. For some, in fact, it seems to amplify their worst instincts.

Whether it is online or not, the the majority of investors continue to make the same return-reducing mistakes:

- They confuse activity with accomplishment, trading their stocks and funds too often, thereby systematically reducing their returns.

- They believe past outperformance predicts future outperformance, despite statistical proof that it does not.

- They confuse valuableness with investment value, tending to buy funds with high valuations and sell those with low valuations.

- They ignore, and defy, the mathematical principle of reversion to the mean, which causes prices tend to retreat from extremes.

- They project present trends into the future without regard to economic cycles.

- They follow the advice of experts without regard to costs and without taking into account the possibility that those experts may have interests very different from their own.

If you avoid making these average mistakes, you're on your way to increased returns. In fact, doing "the right thing" (e.g., avoiding the crowd) involves no more effort than doing "the wrong thing." It just requires a bit more self-control. An added bonus is that a buy-and-hold investor obviously spends less time and effort keeping up with the financial markets than does a constant fund switcher.

If you have a sound framework and a sensible investment plan, the Internet provides a fantastic opportunity. Information and data that the experts monopolized only a few years ago, are only a few clicks away. You are far less information-dependent than at any time in history.

That's what Chapter 3 is all about—how you can gather the information you need to make intelligent investing decisions and design an investment strategy that suits your needs. We'll give you background on the leading financial sources—the publications, research organizations, and investment professionals that are available. Whether you develop your investment plan completely on your own or seek some measure of professional assistance, what you learn in the next chapter will give you the foundation to chart your future course.

CHAPTER 3

Financial Sources: What You Need to Know and Where to Get It

Knowledge is power.

—Francis Bacon

Before you take charge of your mutual fund portfolio—even before you sit down to work out your asset allocation plan—you need to establish a road map. The purpose of this chapter is to help you find your way in the financial maze. Many organizations and services offer guidance through that maze; you'll discover that you have many choices. You can find an adviser or can decide to go it alone. Either way, however, you need to establish reliable sources of information.

The Personal Connection

Most people feel that they need a personal connection with a provider of financial advice. In a December 1999 study drawn from a random investor survey of "full- and part-time users of advice, and do-it-yourselfers," Fidelity Institutional Services found that all types of investors agreed to some degree with the statement "the Internet provides a lot of information, but for customized advice, you need an adviser you know and trust." Further, 80 percent of full-timers and 74 percent of part-time users said that the ability to meet face-to-face with an adviser was "very important" to them. If you feel in need of help from an adviser before you get involved with investing, you need to know where to go to find one.

Before choosing an adviser however, take a look at who has historically sold mutual funds. Once upon a time, people hardly ever bought funds, they were *sold* funds by commissioned salespeople who generally fell into one of four categories:

1. Large national brokerage firms (sometimes called wirehouses) and regional stockbrokers.
2. Mutual fund salespeople.
3. Insurance salespeople.
4. Mutual fund and insurance salespeople offering financial planning services.

In addition, a few no-load funds were (those with no commissions) available.

The modern era of mutual funds began in the 1950s and 1960s, when sales loads (up-front commissions) of 8.5 percent were common. Understandably, these funds weren't easy to sell, particularly when the market wasn't doing well, because the entry fee was so huge. Brokers and mutual fund and insurance salespeople shared most of the commissions pie. In recent years, however, this picture has changed. Everybody's getting into the act of selling mutual funds, competition for investors has brought costs down dramatically, and no-load funds are a significant factor.

Commissioned Advice

In the 1970s, commission-based financial planners emerged, sporting professional designations and advice about the whole money spectrum—estate planning, insurance, mutual funds, and limited partnerships. Even though they offered a broad range of advice, they earned their money by charging a commission on every transaction they carried out. For a long time, they ruled the field, but they suffered a setback when the 1986 Tax Reform Act crushed limited partnerships by disallowing many of the tax write-offs that helped sell them. Still, investors' demand for advice didn't die completely, and the field was changing. Some people decided they preferred paying others for *managing* money—making investment decisions about the funds carried in fund portfolios—rather than simply *moving* it through buy and sell transactions.

Although most advice was still offered on a commission basis, a few independent advisers and planners—mostly defectors from brokerage firms—began offering *fee-based,* no-load mutual fund advice. This meant that they charged no commissions, but instead collected annual fees from their investors. These former money movers—now managers—fanned investors' suspicions about the old commission system by pointing out that it depended on creating as many transactions as possible.

By the early 1990s, Wall Street knew it had problems. Discount and online brokers were killing their commission business, and most investors' perception of "full-service" brokers (who provide research and personal attention to investors' accounts) ranged from mild suspicion to contempt. A 1996 investor survey found that 70 percent of the respondents preferred to pay for advice either by a flat fee or by an asset-backed fee which is calculated as a percentage of the customer's assets. Only 23 percent still favored commissions. So Wall Street decided to go with the flow: If that's what investors wanted, instead of selling them stocks, bonds, and mutual funds, they'd sell them advice. The transformation was under way.

Advice Replaces Commissions

But the transformation is far from over. In a May 2000 CBS "MarketWatch.com" column on the brokers' "paradigm shift . . . from commissions to fees for the amount of money under management," Dr. Paul Farrell presented a jaundiced view. He believes that "Wall Street . . . hired some rather ingenious spin doctors who invented a rather clever marketing ploy—brokers would identify themselves as independent advisers, wearing these new nametags, to reflect this fundamental shift in the industry. One can't help wondering, however, that perhaps the new nametags are no more than a cosmetic change, especially when insiders admit that it's 'business as usual' on The Street."

Farrell is critical of how Wall Street wants to establish a . . . "new public identity of a financial adviser . . . without living up to the same ethical standards (as financial planners)." He continues: "Wall Street is refusing to be regulated as financial advisers, in spite of the fact that Wall Street is unquestioningly morphing from a brokerage industry into a financial advice industry and is also engaged in a massive ad campaign to position Wall Street as a one-stop source of financial advice." The confusion caused by this broker-"morphing" is intentional, and effective, but you can keep your bearings if you zero in on one simple consideration: costs. And you can keep your costs down by fully exploring your options for securing financial advice and information, among them: full service stockbrokers, investment advisers, savings and loans, mutual fund distributors, banks, financial planners, discount brokers, insurance agents, online brokers, mutual fund companies, and even CPAs.

Eliminating Possibilities

Since there are so many potential providers of advice, you have to eliminate some. Starting with the broadest categories, begin by excluding those that have relatively less to offer and/or are the most costly. The process is somewhat arbitrary and eliminates many thousands of organizations that have talented and dedicated people in their ranks. But you have to start somewhere, so here's the first round of potential advisers that you should cut from your list right from the start:

- *Insurance agents* They are involved in many businesses, but their principal focus is insurance, not investing. Also, they are likely to be a captive sales force, working for one company, and offering only one family of funds or only a limited selection of expensive, load funds.
- *Mutual fund distributors* These are usually small companies, often with only one office, that also distribute only a limited selection of load funds.
- *Banks or savings and loans* Once again, these have a limited selection and offer only load funds.
- *CPAs* Some certified public accountants have caused controversy by going into the mutual fund sales business. Traditionally viewed as objective financial counselors, CPAs who get into selling load funds, and pocket commissions, can no longer be objective if their advice can have a direct impact on their incomes; there is a clear conflict of interest. Further, while CPAs may seem to be investment savvy, many have limited investment experience. There is a notable exception, however; some CPAs offer fee-based advice about no-load funds and within this small population there are some very talented professionals.

Considering the Remaining Possibilities

Once you've eliminated the least likely advice candidates, you still have several options. These choices can be broken down into three types, defined by the way the advice is structured and presented:

1. Continuous management.
2. Periodic advice.
3. Published advice.

Overview of Continuous Management

Unsurprisingly, continuous "wealth management" has traditionally been the province of the wealthy—think Rockefellers, Carnegies, and Waltons. First, they have sizable assets that require considerable attention, and second, they can afford it. Service providers receive ongoing fees based not on specific transactions, but on specific services, such as accounting, management and custodianship of your holdings and of the returns on managed assets.

If you have assets of $100,000 or more, this arrangement has obvious advantages. First of all, you don't have to be any more involved than you want to be, other than keeping score. Further, you have the comfort of knowing that you have a knowledgeable steward watching over your affairs—one whose self-interests are aligned with yours. particularly when their remuneration is tied to your returns.

For the adviser/manager, this arrangement also has advantages. Importantly, the helper gets paid whether there are transactions or not. If market conditions, or your investment objectives, are such that "doing nothing" is the best course of action, the manager will not be tempted to make transactions simply to gain commissions. Another advantage is that the adviser can focus on a single issue: maximizing your investment returns.

Two for the Price of Two

If you've decided to hire someone else to manage a portfolio of mutual funds, you are not alone—many investors do. David Clay, a Sonora-based mountain climbing guide who leads expeditions all over the western United States, says, "I just don't want to devote my life to that stuff—it's scary. Let somebody else do it." Scary, of course, is relative. To some, spending the night in a tent buffeted by 30-knot winds on the face of a sheer 4,000-foot cliff, as David does, might be scarier, but it's his money.

Before proceeding, though, there are two negatives: The first is that a managed portfolio of mutual funds is cost-*in*effective because it incurs two layers of costs: those incurred by the funds in your portfolio, and those charged by the adviser you hire to manage the funds. The other negative is that if you have only a modest amount to invest, say $50,000 or less, your choice of advisers is limited.

Continuous Management: Less than $100,000

At the less-than $100,000 level, your situation is similar to that of most Americans: The size of the average household's investment account is $74,000. But remember: If done right, with compounding, even a "modest" portfolio should be "substantial" in not too many years, opening up many more alternatives for you.

While there appears to be a mind-numbing number of choices for personalized, continuous management, with limited capital, there are really only a few good ones. Discount brokers are out because while they will help you establish a portfolio; they won't provide personalized, ongoing management. Full-service broker/advisers offer "mutual fund wrap programs," where they manage no-load funds on an ongoing basis. While this may appear to be a good possibility, and some have even lowered their minimum initial investment levels to below

$100,000, the fees are very high and the possibility of negotiating lower fees is unlikely. Here are choices that make better sense:

FEE ADVISERS

Consider hiring an adviser who charges on an hourly basis instead of on the basis of transaction commissions. The biggest advantages to this choice are the adviser's objectivity and his or her ability to recommend the broadest range of no-load funds, including index funds. The disadvantage is that you might have difficulty finding an adviser willing to work by the hour, and that you'll probably have to initiate periodic checkups. *An elegant possible compromise: Request that the adviser structure a fund of funds (FOF) portfolio* (see below) that will require minimal ongoing management. You will probably find that once it is up and running, this type of portfolio needs less personal attention than you anticipated.

MUTUAL FUND COMPANIES

Invest in a fund of funds (FOF) portfolio. This alternative doesn't offer much personalized hand-holding, but it does provide continuous management, and in many cases, it incurs low overall costs.

An FOF owns a portfolio of several mutual funds, much as a regular mutual fund owns a portfolio of stocks or bonds. The FOF manager buys and sells mutual funds according to the FOF's objectives. The FOF can end up incurring two layers of expenses, as mentioned earlier, but this is not always the case—it depends on the type of FOF. FOFs that are run by a manager who invests in funds from many sponsors can incur expensive fees, but FOFs run by fund families that invest in a portfolio of their own funds have lower expenses—some charge none. Their only expenses arise from the expenses of their own portfolio funds.

FOFs would seem to be a good idea, and the concept is not new. While some have done well, however, their overall record has been disappointing. One reason is that so many of them do incur two layers of expenses because of double management. The other is that many have been launched near market peaks and pulled together a collection of funds whose similar investment styles went from hot to cold, leading to heavy redemptions.

Morningstar's Principia Pro database tracks the records of more than 120 FOFs, and the results suggest that this good idea has more often than not suffered from poor execution. However, there are some notable exceptions. The following FOFs invest in their own fund family.

Fidelity Funds

- *Fidelity Four-in-One Index Fund* This recently launched fund is a good all-around offering. It indexes all U.S. stocks and some international stocks, and has a modest stake in bonds. It combines Fidelity's Spartan Market (S&P 500) Index Fund (55% of its holdings), Spartan Market International

(15%), Spartan Extended Market (15%) (mid-cap stocks), and the U.S. Bond Index Fund (15%). Its minimum dollar investment of $10,000 allows you to invest even though you can't meet the minimums of each fund within its portfolio. Annual expenses for FOF management: 0.10 percent.

- *Fidelity Freedom 2000, 2010, 2020, 2030 Funds* These funds bundle Fidelity's managed funds so you don't have to keep reallocating your portfolio as you get older—they do it for you: The prospectus explains the philosophy this way: "[The funds] will continue to invest, becoming increasingly conservative over time." A comparison of Fidelity Freedom 2000 with Freedom 2030 shows how their asset allocations progressively become more conservative:

	Equity Funds (%)	Fixed Income Funds (%)	Money Market Fund (%)
Fidelity Freedom 2000	43	45	12
Fidelity Freedom 2030	85	15	—

When the funds reach their target date, instead of terminating, they will convert to the Fidelity Freedom Income Fund, which is made up of U.S. stocks (20%), bonds (40%), and money market (40%). Minimum investment is $2,500, and expenses are 0.08 percent.

T. Rowe Price Spectrum Fund

- *T. Rowe Price Spectrum Growth, Income, and International Funds* Morningstar calls these T. Rowe Price funds a "solid, affordable way" to get diversification, although their equity funds are a bit more conservative than those offered by many large fund sponsors. Their international FOF debuted in 1997, the other two are more than a decade old. Since inception, Growth—because of the more conservative tilt—has lagged the average annual return of funds in its Morningstar category by a slim margin. The other two FOFs have beaten the average in their respective categories: Income by almost 1 percent annually and International by over 2 percent. A low minimum investment of $2,500 makes this an affordable choice even for the small investor, and there are no FOF expenses to siphon off returns.

Vanguard Funds

- *Vanguard Life Strategy Conservative Growth, Moderate Growth, Growth, and Income Funds* As with all Vanguard funds, expenses are very reasonable, with no FOF layer of expense and very low expenses of the portfolio's funds. Compared with their respective categories, funds have either tracked their average peers or lagged slightly. Minimum investment is $3,000.

- *Vanguard STAR Fund* This is a solidly performing, balanced fund with 55 percent invested in stocks and 35 percent in bonds. It has beaten its average Morningstar peer by a slight margin since its inception in 1985. Its minimum investment is low, at $1,000, and there are no FOF-layer expenses.

You have a similar plethora of choices if you decide you'd like to explore FOFs that pull together mutual funds from outside a particular fund family. The following are some good options in this category.

Schwab MarketManager Portfolios

- *Schwab MarketManager Growth, Balanced, International, and Small-Cap Portfolios* Unlike most FOFs that invest outside their own fund families, these four Schwab funds have historically given investors their money's worth for the extra FOF expenses. Since their debuts in 1996, with the exception of a 2-year period for the MarketManager Growth Fund, none have lagged badly and most have outperformed, in some cases, by impressive margins. FOF expenses are a maximum of 0.50, but have been partially waived until February 28, 2001. Minimum investment is $1,000.

Masters' Select Funds

- *Masters' Select Equity and International Funds* Technically, the two Masters' funds, launched in 1997, are not FOFs—they don't invest in other funds. Instead, they are more accurately described as "multimanager" funds. They employ five (Equity) and six (International) portfolio managers, each of whom picks his or her 15 to 25 "best ideas." The Masters' concept is simple: "Assemble some of the brightest minds in the business and give them free rein to pursue only their most compelling ideas."

  The structure, in theory, should result in superior performance:

- Managers are selected because they have histories of outperformance.
- Each manager can concentrate on his or her "highest conviction" ideas.
- Managers invest across most styles and sectors, which should result in more consistent performance over time.
- Even though each manager's picks are concentrated, aggregating their combined selections results in a good diversification.

  Expenses resulting from the two-tiered management structure have been above average—Select Equity: 1.38 percent; Select International:

1.29 percent. In addition, a 2 percent redemption fee is charged if an investor holds shares for less than 6 months; proceeds of this fee go to the funds. Size efficiencies have been achieved as the funds have grown and are bringing fees down. An added bonus is that the funds vow to fight "asset bloat": "Funds will be closed to new investors to protect the integrity of the concept."

Despite its elegant structure, the domestic fund had a short rough spot in the beginning that can be attributed to its mild bias toward value (when growth was in vogue), but it has since recovered as the market's obsession with large-cap growth stocks subsided. Select International has consistently bested its category by a wide margin. Minimum investment is $5,000. Management launched a third fund—a value fund—in mid-2000. The performance of the Masters' Select International and Equity funds can be compared with the performance of their Morningstar counterparts as follows:

Masters' Select Funds Cumulative Return since 1997 Inception— Period Ending 06/30/00*

Masters' Select International	102.73%	Morningstar Foreign Stock	56.70%
Masters' Select Equity	98.66%	Morningstar Large Blend	86.31%

* *Source:* Morningstar Principia Pro 06/30/00.

Buying a Load Fund through a Full-Service Broker—If You Must

No matter how much is written and how many consumer and personal finance magazines rail against it, a lot of people still buy load funds from commissioned stockbrokers/soon-to-be-advisers. Briefly put, load funds are funds for which you pay a commission at the time of initial purchase. This is a very expensive proposition and, in most cases, a waste of money. The discussion of this choice is included here with less than a ringing endorsement, solely in the interest of completeness. Most load funds sold this way, in addition to sales loads, pay "trailing" or ongoing distribution fees that, in theory at least, are designed to motivate your broker to stay in touch with you and keep you invested in the fund. They also should provide ongoing monitoring and service, should you need it.

The ABCs of Share Classes

If you're buying a load fund, the first thing you're going to have to deal with is understanding different "share classes." Wall Street obfuscation has no finer example than the bewildering multiple share classes (A, B, or C and others) assigned to load funds.

Mutual fund loads used to be charged pretty much one way: You paid them up front and you were done with it. The modern version of this is found in today's front-end "A"-class shares. But once no-load funds began making serious inroads into the industry, investors began resisting paying sales loads, fund disitributors realized that they had to give investors at least the illusion of choice. New share classes were created to camouflage their charges, each assessed differently—but the load is still there.

Of the most common classes, as noted, for "A" class shares the commission is charged up front, at the time of purchase. On the other hand, "B" shares charge no commissions when you first invest, so all your money is immediately put to work. But, "B" shares impose higher annual fees that are amortized over 5- to 7-year periods. If you don't stay with the investment during the entire amortization period, you'll also be charged redemption fees (called "contingent deferred sales charges"—CDSCs); based on the earliness of your withdrawal. The "B" shares are said to be "back-end loaded." A third alternative, "C" class (level-load) shares, have no front- or back-end sales charges, but they charge higher ongoing annual expenses that go on forever.

The A-B-C complexity distracts investors from what should be their main focus: the underlying investment. A more insidious problem is that they cause confusion. It is not at all unusual for investors to believe that they bought a mutual fund without paying any sales charge. Invariably, it turns out they were sold load-camouflaged "B" or "C" shares.

Lightening the Load

If you are still interested in buying a load fund, here are some suggestions:

- Insist on funds from large sponsors, so that future switches between funds can be made within that family to avoid paying additional commissions. Also, avoid *all* broker-sponsored in-house funds—their fees tend to be the highest, and partly because of those high fees, their records have been mediocre to poor.

- If you're looking for a broker/adviser, don't just walk into your nearest brokerage office. You'll just be turned over to the "man (woman) of the day," who may know very little about funds—many brokers don't. Instead, call the office manager ahead of time and ask to be put in contact with an experienced (10 years or so, at least), funds-savvy broker.

- Alternatively, try networking in your community for a well-regarded, fund-savvy stockbroker. Don't ask for recommendations from folks who don't know any more about investing than you do. Call the money-smart people in your circle of acquaintances, and usually, they'll be glad to make recommendations.

Continuous Management—$100,000 Plus

Once you've passed the $100,000 threshold, even more choices become available to you. Among these are mutual fund wrap programs, also known as managed asset accounts; fee-based advisers; and trust and management services provided by mutual fund sponsors.

Mutual Fund Wrap Programs

In Chapter 12, these programs are discussed in detail, but for now it's only important to have a general sense of what they are and how they work. Wrap programs have grown substantially in recent years. Cerulli Associates, a Boston-based consulting firm, estimates that for the 12 months ending March 30, 2000, assets invested in wrap programs increased by over 52 percent to $118 billion. If these managed asset accounts continue to grow at the present rate, Cerulli projects that "the total annualized growth rate for 2000 could hit 69 percent."

Participation in one these accounts provides you with continuous personal contact at the firm that offers it. It stands to reason, then, that they are also the most costly option available to you. Providers of this level of service include large wirehouse (full-service) and regional brokerage firms. Independent advisers and planners also offer these accounts, placing their clients with discount brokerage firms such as TD Waterhouse. Costs are based on a percentage of your investment. A $250,000 account invested in managed equity mutual funds would incur total annual costs (direct and indirect) as follows:

ANNUAL EXPENSE CATEGORY	TOTAL ESTIMATED ANNUAL COST (%)	(%)
Mutual fund expenses	1.4	$3,500
Funds' transaction costs	0.8	2,000
Wrap fee	1.5	3,750
Total	3.7	$9,250

If you have a fund wrap account, you may find the total costs shown here to be surprisingly high. That's because, on your broker's account statements, only one of the three costs is shown—the $3,750 wrap fee, usually deducted in quarterly increments. Although expense ratios are shown in each of your funds' financial statements and in prospectuses, they are not reported to shareholders on a per account basis, nor do they turn up on the wrap provider's statements. And fund transaction costs that accrue with every purchase or sale they make are not shown anywhere, although they are very real.

Costs totaling 3.7 percent of your investment are very high. However, many people are determined to use a fund wrap program, because they want or need continuous personal service. If you are one of them, there are some ways to reduce these costs. For example, you can usually negotiate a lower wrap fee if you're willing to do a little haggling. It appears that a 40 percent discount (of the wrap fee only) is possible with most firms—the decision is usually up to the branch manager where you do business. Still, even a 40 percent discount reduces the total by only 0.90 percent—you're still going to be paying fees totaling 2.8 percent. That's still very high calculated against 10 percent expected returns from stocks over the long term.

While fee advisers' wrap fees are usually lower than those charged by wirehouse brokers—around 1 percent—the average fund costs still bring the grand total to 3.2 percent. Fee advisers, however, commonly use (or should use) index funds, which can lower costs substantially. For example, a half-indexed portfolio's costs would be:

	ANNUAL EXPENSES (%)
50% Managed Funds	2.20
50% Index Funds	0.30
Average fund expenses	1.25
Adviser fee	1.00
Total annual costs	2.25

Additional transaction fees are charged for trading some no-load funds through discount brokers, but these are nominal.

But how much "management" do the unmanaged index funds in your portfolio require, particularly after establishing the account the first year? Since it's little or none, the adviser's fee should be reduced to 0.75 percent or even 0.50 percent, which would make the grand total 2 percent or less, improving the economics somewhat.

Broker Referral Programs

Some brokers like Charles Schwab have formalized programs that refer you to advisers who charge a fee for their service. Total costs are comparable to the 40 percent-discounted brokerage firm wraps previously mentioned. Schwab charges an annual fee to registered investment advisers to participate in the referral program.

When you're investing at the $100,000 to $300,000 level, you may find that an all-managed mutual fund program makes you feel comfortable. However, there is no escaping that the comfort/cost trade-off places a heavy ongoing cost burden on your portfolio's returns. As discussed in Chapter 12, you are probably better off in wrap programs that buy individual stocks—rather than a mutual fund or funds—for your account.

Continuous Management—$200,000 to $300,000 and Up

Once your investments climb above the $200,000 level, more choices become available; and costs, as a percentage of the amount invested, begin to decline. But again, because of inflexible mutual fund fixed costs, the mutual fund wrap concept remains relatively cost-inefficient:

- *Wirehouse wrap programs* Although mutual funds' costs remain relatively fixed, wrap fees are more negotiable at this level. On a $400,000 account, for example, the wrap fee might be negotiated down as low as 0.75 to 0.9 percent.

- *Fee advisers* It's hard to generalize, but at this level, the "standard" 1 percent fee seems to be more negotiable, particularly on investments that exceed $250,000.

Specific programs for investors of $200,000 or more are offered by a variety of providers. Here is a sampling:

- *Fidelity Portfolio Advisory Services—Minimum $200,000* Fidelity will establish an account, identify a model asset allocation strategy based on your needs, and actively manage a portfolio of Fidelity funds or one that blends Fidelity and non-Fidelity funds that are available through their mutual fund supermarket (approximately 4,000 funds). A personal contact is assigned to your account. Fees are lower than either wirehouse or fee-adviser wrap programs, starting at 1 percent on the first $200,000, and declining as the size of your investment increases. Fidelity handles all kinds of accounts, and they are probably your best bet if you want yours to be aggressively managed.

- *TIAA-CREF Trust Company—Minimum $300,000* The Teachers Insurance and Annuity Association-College Retirement Equities Fund (TIAA-CREF) is the largest private pension system in the world. Established in 1918 as a nonprofit foundation, this organization, which manages assets of over $300 billion, began offering mutual funds to the public for the first time in 1997. Since then, their funds have outperformed most comparable funds. On an ongoing basis, management is currently limited to investing in 11 TIAA-CREF funds, but others may be added in the future. Two of the funds combine both active and passive management.

When accounts are established, new clients are provided with complimentary access to the TIAA-CREF legal department for will and trust development. The cost of TIAA-CREF's services are very reasonable, considering the relatively low account load handled by each personal manager—approximately 70—and the free legal services provided to investors. Annual fees start at 0.80 percent and decline thereafter. TIAA-CREF is particularly attractive for investors who are looking for a program that is relatively conservative, offers low-cost asset management, and provides some legal help and trust services.

- *Vanguard Asset Management Services—Minimum $500,000* Although Vanguard will take some non-Vanguard funds and stock in when they accept an account, the goal is to get you to invest all assets in Vanguard funds. With 80-plus funds to choose from, that shouldn't be a problem. Each account has a portfolio manager, each of whom handle approximately 50 accounts. Costs are very low, starting at 0.65 percent annually for accounts totaling up to $1 million and declining relatively quickly above that, falling to 0.20 percent for accounts of over $2 million. Considering the low expense ratios of Vanguard's funds, overall costs are slightly lower than those of TIAA-CREF.

- *Fidelity PAS Special Option—Minimum $500,000* This program is an enhanced version of the Fidelity Portfolio Advisory Service discussed earlier. It offers more personal services, notably customized, tax-sensitive management that can help shield investors from the year-end tax burden associated with most mutual funds. Annual fees start at 1.1 percent and decline thereafter.

- *Consultant Wrap Programs* Also called wrap or individually managed accounts (IMAs), these are programs where money managers—sometimes the same ones that manage mutual funds—manage individual securities for investors. The resulting portfolio is almost like having your own private microfund. In recent years, consultant wrap program assets have grown much faster than mutual fund assets because they offer some significant advantages, such as personal service, and sensitivity to individuals' tax situation. However, they also have some drawbacks. Because of their growing importance, though, a separate chapter (Chapter 12) is devoted to a detailed discussion of how they work.

Periodic Advice

For decades, periodic advice was the most common practice in the investment industry. Today's brokerage firms are moving away from this service. Normally, the client makes transactions after receiving advice from the expert: A stockbroker recommends a fund, for example, that the investor then buys. If you want to be actively involved in your investments, this structure should suit you. If you don't want that much involvement, however, you won't want to go this route because it requires you to be directly included in each transaction and every act of portfolio management.

In one respect, the arrangement is flawed: The adviser gets paid up front, regardless of the outcome. This provides the adviser with less reason to identify closely with your own investment interests. Also, trades may be made without calculating their impact on an investor's entire portfolio; and this drawback is exacerbated if investors deal with more than one broker/adviser, as is commonly the case.

From the standpoint of the broker/adviser, transaction-based compensation also has drawbacks, not the least of which is having to serve two masters—you and the brokerage firm. At one extreme, if there are no transactions, brokers don't "keep their desk," which means they lose their job. At the other extreme, if they make numerous transactions—called churning—they have to be careful not to get themselves and/or the firm in trouble. The broker does an ongoing balancing act on a high wire, stretched between you and the firm.

Sources of Periodic Advice

You have several options if you go the periodic-advice route:

- *Full service stockbroker/advisers* Even though stockbroker/advisers are moving out of this business, they still buy and sell stocks, bonds, and mutual funds "the old fashioned way"—on commission.

- *Fee advisers* Periodic advice is an anathema to a typical fee adviser—it's opposed to how most want to structure their businesses. Typically, they charge an ongoing fee calculated as a percentage of assets under management. Some, however, will agree to consult with you on an hourly basis.

- *Mutual fund companies and referral programs* As the democratization of Wall Street continues, nowhere is it more obvious than in the impressive array of services and tools that mutual fund companies and discount brokers will provide to help you set up and manage your own mutual fund portfolio. If you are establishing your first account or want assistance analyzing the one you have, they offer diagnostics and analyses that you can explore online or in discussions with a representative in person or over the phone. Most of them will provide one-time analyses, asset allocation assistance, and projections based on your personal circumstances via their Web sites. You are guided through the information-gathering phase during which you input your financial circumstances, and within seconds, their recommendations and conclusions appear.

This is a huge improvement over years past, when insurance and mutual fund salespeople ceremoniously unveiled computer-generated summaries of this same information at your kitchen table, and you knew you were in for a very long evening. The Schwab site's "Beginning Investor's Guide" provides a fine example of this new type of service. It lets you complete an investor profile that is tailored to address the following objectives:

- General Goal Planner.

- Retirement Planner.

- IRA Analyzer.

- Estate Tax and Probate Planner.

- College Planner.

- *One-time written planning tools* If you want more personal attention, Schwab, Fidelity, Vanguard, and others provide written, one-time portfolio advisory services. You complete a questionnaire (if you have difficulty, you get help over the phone or at one of their offices; Fidelity has 70 and Schwab has over 360 walk-in offices), and in about a week, you receive written evaluations and recommendations that you can then discuss with one of their representatives. Schwab charges $400 for this service, Vanguard's fee is $500, and Fidelity will provide the service for free, but requires a $100,000 minimum initial investment.

While there are subtle differences, all three firms offer roughly comparable service. They all request the same information from you: your age, tax bracket, income, investable assets, present investments, and so on. The outputs and conclusions, therefore, won't be markedly different since they're calculated from essentially similar compound interest tables, tax rates, mortality tables, inflation and asset-class rates of return projections, and so forth. Their assumptions and recommendations will be orthodox and, very importantly, impartial. They won't be biased in a direction that favors the sale of any particular product—life insurance, variable annuities, or particular mutual funds, for example. These organizations aren't primarily interested in what you buy—but they are vitally interested in that whatever you buy, you buy from them. Their financial smorgasbords are likely to include the funds you'll finally settle on. And if you want something they don't have, they'll get you to rethink whether you really need it.

While you might balk at writing a $400 or $500 check for a written analysis, remember that it's the rough equivalent of the sales load you'd pay when buying $10,000 worth of a load fund. And it can't be emphasized enough that the information and recommendations are objective and impartial.

General Published Investment Advice

It is said that an important role of many investment advisers is to be "validators"; that investors, having made a decision, need someone to motivate them to act on it. You may feel that you don't need any personal help whatsoever. But whether you are a rugged individualist or want the help of an outside adviser, you can't make decisions without information. In today's mutual fund universe, whatever your appetite, the amount of information available is almost limitless—and it ranges in quality from valuable to downright dangerous.

If you decide to make do with published advice, you're on your own—you receive it only in your mailbox or over the Internet. What you do with it is up to you. Paid-for published advice comes from subscriptions to magazines, newsletters, newspapers, rating services, and password-protected Internet Web sites. Mammoth quantities of free investment advice are also available all day long from the experts that appear on CNBC, CNNfn, and the radio. If you are interested—or even fascinated—in investing, and want to control your own destiny, there are oceans of information to navigate.

Morningstar Services

The headwaters of mutual fund advice begin at Morningstar, the most widely used and quoted tracking service. There is ongoing dispute, however, about the Morningstar star ratings. Competitors and critics have made much of the fact that the ratings have little or no predictive value for future performance. Some studies have even concluded that there is an *inverse* correlation between star ratings and subsequent performance, that the higher the current Morningstar rating, the poorer the fund will do in the near future. Much of the misperception occurs because of the way that funds use high star ratings in their marketing. Ads frequently imply that a four- or five-star rating is a guarantee that above-average performance is likely to continue.

Morningstar, however, has never claimed that high star ratings can predict above-average returns. In the March 2000 issue of *Money,* John Rekenthaler, Morningstar research director, told Jason Zweig, "The odds are stacked against you if your buy a one- or two-star fund. But beyond that, I wouldn't worry a lot about whether a fund has three, four or five stars." Still, if you are going to get deeply involved in mutual funds, you'll ultimately have to do some original research, and for this the *Morningstar Principia Pro* program is the best resource available. It's designed for financial advisers, however, so it may be more than you need. Morningstar offers several other resources:

- *Morningstar Mutual Funds* (24 issues/year $495) This is Morningstar's flagship published mutual fund service. It has much of the same information that is available through Principia Pro. It provides excellent ongoing statistics and commentary. A 3-month trial subscription costs $55 and makes a fine mutual fund starter kit.

- *Morningstar FundInvestor* A monthly newsletter, it provides commentary, insights, and ongoing coverage of a select 500-fund universe that includes "analyst picks." A year's subscription costs $99.

- *Morningstar.com* This is a general investment Web site with an extensive section on mutual fund investing. *Mutual Funds* magazine calls their free fund screener, "kickbutt."

- *No-Load Fund Analyst (NLFA)* At $225 per year (3-month trial: $55, 1-month trial: $18) because of its in-depth analysis, you have to have more than a passing interest in analyzing funds. NLFA provides extensive and ongoing research on a relatively small universe of approximately 40 thoroughly researched funds in nine fund categories. The funds discussed span asset classes, from taxable and high-yield bond funds to large- and small-cap funds and real estate. NFLA publishers Ken Gregory and Craig Litman are widely respected in the industry, and most of their subscribers are professional investment advisers. In addition, they handle private accounts and manage three Masters' Select Funds (discussed earlier).

  Although it's not a prerequisite, some previous fund background would be helpful to make the most of the NFLA. Unless you have been knocking around the investment business for a while, you might find some of the lingo heavy going.

  Unlike most fund advisory services that provide ponderous lists of recommended funds—many more than you could ever realistically own—the NLFA includes only a handful of recommended funds in each category. Detailed, comprehensive reports of meetings and interviews with fund managements provide considerable insight into what makes them tick.

  NLFA also maintains four model portfolios that are periodically adjusted to achieve a variety of objectives: "Conservative Balanced,"

"Balanced," "Equity-Tilted Balanced," and "Equity." NLFA's *most* aggressive model portfolio is pretty tame in comparison to many: It "seeks the maximum return consistent with a low probability of a loss in excess of 20% over a 12-month period." On a risk-adjusted basis, returns enjoyed by this model since 1990 have been excellent.

One of the NFLA's strengths is in spotting young, well-managed funds. If you had cherry-picked among those identified by NFLA during the past decade, you would have captured some dramatic gains, many occurring before the selected funds became widely known.

- *Mutual Funds magazine* If you subscribe to only one magazine on funds, *Mutual Funds* is the one to choose. Since funds are the only subject covered, you won't have to wade through stories about other topics that don't interest you. The magazine provides insights and commentary on funds, the industry, recent developments, and general investing in a balanced and lively manner.

Other Internet Web Sites
- *Brill's Mutual Fund Interactive* (fundsinteractive.com) offers general fund information, including manager profiles and fund basics.
- *CBS MarketWatch* (cbsmarketwatch.com) is an excellent source of financial news, fund news, and commentary by columnist Paul Farrell.
- *CEF.com* is maintained by the Closed-end Fund Association and offers profiles of over 500 closed-end funds and information on closed-end fund investing.
- *IndexFunds.com* (indexfunds.com) is a good place to learn about index funds and the happenings in the indexing world.
- *Investinginbonds.com* (investinginbonds.com) offers everything a serious bond investor needs to know.
- *Investorwords* (investorwords.com) provides visitors a database of over 5,000 investment terms and concepts.
- *MaxFunds* (maxfunds.com) offers lively, somewhat irreverent coverage, with an emphasis on small, lesser-known funds.
- *Money.com* (money.com) is maintained by the personal finance magazine of the same name. It includes columns by Jason Zweig, one of the best fund observers in the business.
- *NAREIT.com* is maintained by the National Association of Real Estate Investment Trusts. It provides news, commentary, and profiles of most REITs.

- *SmartMoney.com* (smartmoney.com) is the Web site for the Dow Jones personal finance magazine, *SmartMoney,* produced by the publisher of the *Wall Street Journal.*
- *Undiscovered Managers Funds* (undiscoveredmanagers.com) offers scholarly research by academics that may be of interest to fund nerds and professionals.
- *Vanguard.com* (vanguard.com) is a great site with educational information, archives of terrific material, calculators, and just about anything you would want to know about investing and, more particularly, the advantages of index funds.

If you're serious about mutual fund investing, you can avail yourself of some, or all, of the resources mentioned here. But even after you've gotten started in your basic research, you still must accomplish one more important step before you can truly take control of your mutual fund investments. You've already been introduced to this step: We've repeated it often enough in these first three chapters. That's right—asset allocation. In Chapter 4, you'll learn just what this fundamentally important step entails.

CHAPTER 4

Asset Allocation— The Most Important Investment Decision

> Most of the time
> I don't have much
> fun. The rest of the
> time I don't have any
> fun at all.
>
> —Woody Allen

What's the difference between "good" investors and "bad" investors? Bad investors don't have any plan, other than "to make money." They take fliers, rely on experts promising unrealistic returns, ignore costs, jump in and out of the market, and invest in whatever is in fashion. If you want to be a good investor who sees your investment decisions earning great returns, you want to avoid that route. So what do you do? In this chapter, you will learn how to use asset allocation—the backbone of good investing.

Asset Allocation 101

So what is asset allocation? The phrase is Street-speak for how you divide up your money into the different investment categories—stocks, bonds, convertible bonds, real estate trusts, and so on. And then, it's how you decide on subcategories: large-, mid-, or small-cap stocks, for example. It's based on the assumption that more than anything else, your investment success will depend on sector-driven returns and your ability to devise, and stick with, a solid investment plan. If you have a sensible plan, stick with quality investments, are selective about advisers, and control your costs, you'll never be a bad—and certainly not an average investor.

55

The Folly of Tactical Asset Allocation

At its simplest definition, asset allocation simply means where you plan to put your assets, and when. In fact between asset classes, a whole cottage industry thrives on the promise that moving money around will provide the highest future returns. But this approach to investing—commonly called "tactical" asset allocation—is usually unsuccessful and a waste of money. Why? For the same reason that market timers and forecasters end up looking silly: Success relies on accurately predicting the future. And nobody can predict the future with consistent success.

To prove this point, take a look at Figure 4.1, which shows J.P. Morgan's Periodic Table of Investment Returns. The chart shows the returns achieved by the most common asset classes over the past two decades and provides strong evidence that *there is no discernible pattern to these investment returns over time.* For a year or two, international stocks led the parade. Over the next several years, large-cap growth stocks took over, followed the next year by small-cap growth stocks. You get the idea—you simply can't predict what's going to happen next. So what do you do instead? You skip the whole idea of tactical allocation and think *strategic* instead.

Strategic or Personal Asset Allocation

While tactical asset allocation doesn't work, "strategic" asset allocation can—and does. Strategic asset allocation, perhaps better called "personal" asset allocation, is the right way to divide up your money among your investments. It is the foundation, or plan, on which you will build your investment choices.

All personal asset allocation plans (and there are lots of them out there) share certain basic principles. They all recognize that when you're young you can take more risk; you've got lots of time to recover if something goes wrong. And they all realize that, as you grow older, you'll want to gradually shift toward less risky, income-producing investments. When you first begin investing, and at every step along the way, they also assume that you will adjust your investments to suit your individual risk tolerance, goals, and circumstances.

There are many variations on the theme, but as far as the basic framework, that's it. Asset allocation plans are available on just about any major fund family Web site. Among your many options, Fidelity's is excellent and Morningstar's ClearFuture (hidden in the 401(k) section) is particularly helpful. And, we provide our own plan at the end of this chapter. All the plans work roughly the same way: You plug in the amount you have to invest, how much you intend to be adding, your tax bracket, years to retirement, anticipated future returns, and risk tolerance. Once you click on "Accept," the programs grind out your

Annual returns for selected asset classes (1980–1999)
Ranked in order of performance (best to worst)

JPMorgan

Rank	1980	1981	1982	1983	1984	1985	1986	1987	1988	1989
1	Russell 2000 Growth 52.26%	Russell 2000 Value 14.85%	LB Agg 32.65%	Russell 2000 Value 38.63%	LB Agg 15.15%	MSCI EAFE 56.14%	MSCI EAFE 69.46%	MSCI EAFE 24.64%	Russell 2000 Value 29.47%	S&P/BARRA 500 Growth 36.40%
2	S&P/BARRA 500 Growth 39.40%	LB Agg 6.26%	Russell 2000 Value 28.52%	S&P/BARRA 500 Value 28.89%	S&P/BARRA 500 Value 10.52%	S&P/BARRA 500 Growth 33.31%	S&P/BARRA 500 Value 21.67%	S&P/BARRA 500 Value 6.50%	MSCI EAFE 28.26%	S&P 500 Index 31.69%
3	S&P 500 Index 32.50%	S&P/BARRA 500 Value 0.02%	S&P/BARRA 500 Growth 22.03%	MSCI EAFE 23.69%	MSCI EAFE 7.41%	S&P 500 Index 31.73%	S&P 500 Index 18.67%	S&P 500 Index 5.25%	S&P/BARRA 500 Value 21.67%	S&P/BARRA 500 Value 26.13%
4	Russell 2000 Value 25.39%	MSCI EAFE -2.27%	S&P 500 Index 21.55%	S&P 500 Index 22.56%	S&P 500 Index 6.27%	Russell 2000 Value 31.01%	LB Agg 15.30%	S&P/BARRA 500 Growth 3.68%	Russell 2000 Growth 20.38%	Russell 2000 Growth 20.16%
5	S&P/BARRA 500 Value 23.59%	S&P 500 Index -4.92%	S&P/BARRA 500 Value 21.04%	Russell 2000 Growth 20.14%	S&P/BARRA 500 Growth 2.33%	Russell 2000 Growth 30.97%	S&P/BARRA 500 Growth 14.50%	LB Agg 2.75%	S&P 500 Index 16.61%	LB Agg 14.53%
6	MSCI EAFE 22.60%	Russell 2000 Growth -9.23%	Russell 2000 Growth 20.99%	S&P/BARRA 500 Growth 16.24%	Russell 2000 Value 2.27%	S&P/BARRA 500 Value 29.68%	Russell 2000 Value 7.41%	Russell 2000 Value -7.12%	S&P/BARRA 500 Growth 11.95%	Russell 2000 Value 12.43%
7	LB Agg 2.71%	S&P/BARRA 500 Growth -9.81%	MSCI EAFE -1.86%	LB Agg 8.19%	Russell 2000 Growth -15.84%	LB Agg 22.13%	Russell 2000 Growth 3.59%	Russell 2000 Growth -10.48%	LB Agg 7.89%	MSCI EAFE 10.53%

Rank	1990	1991	1992	1993	1994	1995	1996	1997	1998	1999
1	LB Agg 8.96%	Russell 2000 Growth 51.18%	Russell 2000 Value 29.15%	MSCI EAFE 32.57%	MSCI EAFE 7.78%	S&P/BARRA 500 Growth 38.13%	S&P/BARRA 500 Growth 23.97%	S&P/BARRA 500 Growth 36.52%	S&P/BARRA 500 Growth 42.16%	Russell 2000 Growth 43.09%
2	S&P/BARRA 500 Growth 0.20%	Russell 2000 Value 41.70%	S&P/BARRA 500 Value 10.52%	Russell 2000 Value 23.86%	S&P/BARRA 500 Growth 3.14%	S&P 500 Index 37.58%	S&P 500 Index 22.96%	S&P 500 Index 33.36%	S&P 500 Index 28.58%	S&P/BARRA 500 Growth 28.25%
3	S&P 500 Index -3.11%	S&P/BARRA 500 Growth 38.37%	Russell 2000 Growth 7.77%	S&P/BARRA 500 Value 18.61%	S&P 500 Index 1.32%	S&P/BARRA 500 Value 36.99%	S&P/BARRA 500 Value 22.00%	S&P/BARRA 500 Value 31.76%	MSCI EAFE 20.00%	MSCI EAFE 26.96%
4	S&P/BARRA 500 Value -6.85%	S&P 500 Index 30.47%	S&P 500 Index 7.62%	Russell 2000 Growth 13.37%	S&P/BARRA 500 Value -0.64%	Russell 2000 Growth 31.04%	Russell 2000 Growth 21.37%	Russell 2000 Value 29.98%	S&P/BARRA 500 Value 14.69%	S&P 500 Index 21.04%
5	Russell 2000 Growth -17.42%	S&P/BARRA 500 Value 22.56%	S&P/BARRA 500 Growth 7.40%	S&P 500 Index 10.08%	Russell 2000 Growth -1.55%	Russell 2000 Value 25.75%	Russell 2000 Value 11.32%	Russell 2000 Growth 12.93%	LB Agg 8.70%	S&P/BARRA 500 Value 12.73%
6	Russell 2000 Value -21.77%	LB Agg 16.00%	LB Agg 5.06%	LB Agg 9.75%	Russell 2000 Value -2.44%	LB Agg 18.46%	MSCI EAFE 6.05%	MSCI EAFE 9.64%	Russell 2000 Growth 1.23%	LB Agg -0.83%
7	MSCI EAFE -23.45%	MSCI EAFE 12.14%	MSCI EAFE -12.18%	S&P/BARRA 500 Growth 1.68%	LB Agg -2.92%	MSCI EAFE 11.21%	LB Agg 3.64%	LB Agg 1.78%	Russell 2000 Value -6.46%	Russell 2000 Value -1.49%

Legend:
- Russell 2000 Value Index
- Russell 2000 Growth Index
- S&P 500 Index
- S&P/BARRA 500 Value Index
- S&P/BARRA 500 Growth Index
- MSCI EAFE Index
- Lehman Brothers Aggregate Bond Index

FIGURE 4.1 Periodic table of investment returns (Source: J.P. Morgan).

answers—sums and income streams from your various alternatives. The answers you'll get from these programs will be pretty similar, differing only in details depending on the variables you've provided.

You can do this on your own, too—if you don't mind doing the math. It sounds simple, to be sure, but don't confuse simplicity with irrelevance. The most important lesson you can take away from this chapter is simple too: *Your investment returns will be more a function of your allocation decisions than any other factor.* Simple as it is, judged by the mutual fund industry's money inflows and outflows, the average investor ignores asset allocation; and the average investor's returns, sadly, reflect this, year in and year out.

To repeat our ongoing theme, if you want to be successful, you can't invest like everybody: You can't be satisfied with being an average investor because, while average investors may know about asset allocation, few practice it. The lesson: Establish a sensible plan and stick with it!

Let's say that you are retiring soon and you don't have much put aside for the day when you leave your job. The program (or your manually calculated plan) will take into account the time frame you're facing in which you need to grow your investments, the amount you have to invest, and the results you're expected to achieve depending on the type of investment you choose (e.g., growth funds or bonds). These programs still contain one major potential flaw: They, too, involve at least a little bit of crystal ball gazing. They can't accurately predict future inflation rates.

Why is this important? If inflation should accelerate much faster than the reasonable inflation-rate projections built into the programs, stock valuations will implode, interest rates will soar, and the effect will so disrupt any suggestions based on them that the results will be rendered virtually meaningless. But, you have to start somewhere, and without a privileged view of the future, the allocation and planning tools are helpful. You need some kind of a road map to keep you from getting lost as you invest your way into the future. Whatever you settle on, *what is most important is that you start with, and stick with, a plan.*

Establishing the Basics of Your Own Plan

Developing a good asset allocation plan requires that you figure out three things right from the start. First, you need to define your investment goals: Are you building wealth for retirement? Are you trying to prepare for big expenses in the future, like college tuition for your kids or buying your first house? These are specific goals that your investments are intended to help you realize.

Next you need to figure out your time horizon: Are you just out of college? If so, you're in great shape; you've got lots of time to make your money grow to meet your future needs. On the other hand, are you in your 40s and only now getting around to paying attention to what you'll need after you retire? Are your kids still quite young, so you have 10 years or more to build toward their college funds? The amount of time you have for your investments to grow makes a big difference in the investment vehicle you choose.

Finally, you really need to understand yourself and your own emotional response to risk. This is what's commonly called "risk tolerance," and it will make a real difference in determining the kind of investment plan that you can live with. If you're highly risk tolerant, for example, you'll be better able to take the day-to-day movements of the market in your stride, whereas a risk-aversive person may find them terrifying and be tempted to overreact. A risk-intolerant person won't be happy with a high-risk investment, no matter how great the potential returns might be, and therefore will be unlikely to stick with an asset allocation plan that exposes the investor to a lot of volatility.

The Life Asset Allocation Plan

We've developed an approach to asset allocation that has broad general applicability and addresses each stage in an investor's lifetime. The "Life Asset Allocation Plan" begins with many of the same assumptions found in the other plans mentioned earlier: the general guidelines parallel those provided by almost any large fund family, brokerage firm, financial planner, investment adviser, bank, or insurance company. However, we have incorporated several improvements, such as giving real estate investment trusts (REITs, Chapter 9) and convertible bonds (Chapter 10) meaningful—rather than just token—percentages. There is really nothing truly new under the investment sun; it's basically the same information that "everybody already knows."

However, if everybody already knows it, why isn't everybody *doing it?* How was it that in early 1999, almost everybody invested in one or more of only 25 funds—nearly all of them large-cap growth funds. As mentioned in Chapter 2, those funds took in a stunning 96 percent of all net fund inflows. Could it be that everybody had exactly the same investment style and needs, so that all their plans called for exactly the same strategy? Of course not. And at the same time, "everybody" was pulling money out of REIT funds—shrinking their assets by one-third in just two years. More likely, "everybody" was simply chasing hot performance—or being chased by poor performance—and ignoring asset allocation entirely.

Throughout this book, many detailed examples show how chasing hot performance works rarely, if at all, and why it is sheer folly to make it your long-term approach to wealth building. Before you turn to the actual allocation plan we recommend, however; look at the elements that make our recommended, graduated approach to asset allocation different from most others.

- We include REITs, giving them a 10 percent constant percentage, because they appear to be misunderstood and underappreciated by most investors. With many REIT funds providing bondlike yields of 7 percent and moderate growth prospects, they should be a part of your long-term portfolio.

- Convertible bonds are recommended for the entire fixed income allocation until age 50 because they offer a big increase in returns when compared to the returns of straight bonds, and also have a relatively lower risk profile compared to stocks. At age 50, "straight" bonds are introduced, and their allocation increases sharply over the next 20 years, with the convertible allocation reduced accordingly.

- While you obviously have to have an emergency reserve, cash (money market funds or T-bills) is not recommended in our plan, although many plans do include a cash portion to your overall asset allocation. We find it hard to understand why an investor with a 20- or 30-year time frame would benefit from keeping an ongoing investment in cash.

Figure 4.2 shows our recommended model for a lifelong asset allocation plan.

A few caveats are in order. First, any plan projecting *anything* for decades has obvious limitations—we don't have any crystal balls, either. REITs, because they are not in favor and pay high yields, could conceivably provide higher future total returns than stocks the next few years. If they come back into favor, however, we would want to reconsider the way they're currently figured into the plan. It's because they're not in favor right now that they are most likely to provide particularly favorable returns. Increased popularity would lessen that advantage (as explained in Chapter 9).

Convertible funds are another example of how the current plan might need adjustment in the future. Convertibles are invested in almost exclusively by the pros, which contributes to their attractiveness at the moment. If they become popular with the public, they would be less attractive (see Chapter 10 for more details). Increased popularity would probably mean higher conversion premiums, lower yields, longer maturities, resulting in risk profiles closer to stocks than bonds.

At the start of this chapter, we mentioned that a sound asset allocation plan is the foundation of good investing. But the two preceding observations underscore our second important point: There is *no* asset allocation plan that doesn't need periodic reassessment. Circumstances, responsibilities, needs and resources change, as does the investment climate. That's why investors should revisit their plans periodically, and certainly whenever a major change occurs.

And there's one other thing to remember. Whether you adopt a plan from one of the Web sites or follow our plan, neither they nor we can offer a plan that is perfect for your circumstances. You may not want—or need—to *ever* own

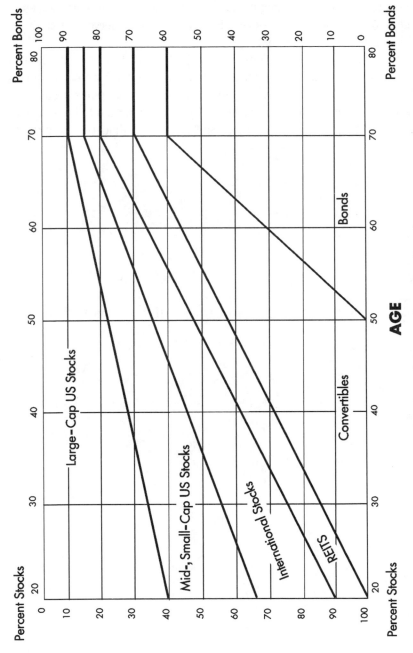

FIGURE 4.2 Life plan asset allocation plan.

bonds. You might not want to own REIT or convertible funds. Or you might want to allocate your assets between stock and bond funds differently from the way any general-purpose plan might suggest. Because your circumstances are unique, any allocation model—even this one—can only serve as a guide. You must tailor it to suit your needs.

Next, we talk about the various fund types. In Part 2, we look at the basic choice: between indexed and managed funds. In Chapter 5 we examine index funds, which should be your investment of choice if you want an extremely economical way to invest, but don't have the time or inclination to be a hands-on investor: You simply choose those that suit your asset allocation, and they do the rest.

Two Alternatives: To Index, or Not to Index?

CHAPTER 5

Index Funds

> You mean no
> management is
> better than
> professional
> management?
>
> —**John Bogle**
> *Bogle on Mutual Funds*

Index funds, got off to a slow start in the 1970s, but since then they have become an important force in the mutual fund industry. Why? Because they have consistently delivered superior returns over the years, beating the performance of most managed funds. Two big reasons are their low costs and their tax efficiency.

Index funds sound almost too good to be true. "Dumb" index funds beat most mutual funds run by smart managers most of the time. Their low costs are in stark contrast to managed funds where, as Rex Sinquefeld, vice chairman of Dimensional Fund Advisors, has observed: "Mediocre performance doesn't come cheap."

Index funds are particularly compelling if the investment process doesn't thrill you, because they require virtually no time and attention. You can be almost totally uninvolved, and over the long term, your returns will still beat the returns achieved by most other investors—including the pros. There is a towering irony that on Wall Street, something as perverse as indexing routinely provides higher returns than do the legions of highly paid experts and forecasters. Index funds are also durable; as the years pass, they stay on autopilot; they don't run out of fuel and are not plagued by the typical changes and disruptions that characterize the mutual fund industry.

So what is an index fund? It is a portfolio of stocks and/or bonds that replicates a widely followed market index such as the Standard & Poor's 500 Index, which tracks the 500 largest U.S. corporations, or the Wilshire 5000, an index of the total U.S. stock market. An index fund holds the securities or derivatives—options and futures contracts—structured to mimic stocks in the index. In

Street lingo, these funds are "passively managed." The fund's portfolio mix only changes in response to changes in the index it tracks.

Managed funds, on the other hand, are "actively" managed; their portfolio managers select securities to buy and sell and when. Managed funds want *to beat* the market, whereas index funds want *to be* the market. When there is an occasional change in their target index, which occurs as stocks are added and subtracted each year due to mergers and replacements in the index, the fund mimics the change. Thus, index funds are never called on to make investment decisions even as investors' money flows in or out—they simply buy or sell additional securities in the same proportion as those stocks appear in the target index. This is very different from what happens when money flows in or out of managed funds, which usually requires that the fund manager(s) decide what securities to buy and sell.

Why Indexing Works

Most index funds can't beat the market because they are, in effect, the market (they hold the same securities in the same proportion as their target index). As Burton Malkiel, author of the investment classic, *A Random Walk down Wall Street* (Norton, 2000), put it: "The market prices stocks so efficiently that a blindfolded chimpanzee throwing darts at *The Wall Street Journal* can select a portfolio that performs as well as those managed by the experts."

No matter how hard the experts try, most don't beat the averages. In any measurable human endeavor, if most participants' skills are roughly comparable, it is inevitable that most will achieve average or near-average results. If a hundred toddlers go on an Easter egg hunt to look for 1,000 not-very-well-hidden eggs, a bell curve graphing the average number of eggs in each returning tot's basket will peak at around 10 eggs. A graph of the distribution of major league batting averages, SAT scores, or golf tournament scores will not look much different: Adding up each participant's results and then dividing the resulting sum by the total number of participants gives average results—most scores will cluster near the bulge in the curve.

It's no different with stock returns. During any given period, most returns will approximate the overall market's return. The widely followed benchmarks for such returns, such as the Standard & Poor's 500 Index and the Wilshire 5000 Index or the Dow Jones Industrial Averages, reflect the "average" return of the stocks in them.

Indexing—Before Costs

However, if the question is asked, "What was the average investor's return last year?" the answer is quite different from the market's return. Investors' returns are lower—because they pay commissions, trading costs, and other fees that reduce their returns. Here's where you find the answer to the age-old question, "Where are all the investors' yachts?"

Let's return to our Easter egg hunt. Collectively, our toddlers, who don't have to surrender any of the eggs they find, still can't go home with more than an average of 10 each because there simply aren't enough eggs. No amount of enthusiasm, effort, or preparation will alter this fact: The law of averages does not allow *above-average returns by most participants.* And this law operates whether you're calculating Easter eggs or investors' returns.

In his book, *Bogle on Mutual Funds* (Dell Publishing, 1994), John Bogle explains what academics call the "efficient market theory": "Since all investors collectively own the entire stock market, if passive investors—holding all stocks forever—can match the gross return of the stock market, then active investors, as a group, can do no better." He further states, "An overwhelming body of data confirms that, on a long-term basis, the average investment adviser has been unable to outperform the stock market as a whole."

Why It's Hard to Be Average

Fund investors, however, are deluged with advertising and promotion that encourages them to reach a very different conclusion: They're led to believe that they can routinely garner market-beating returns if they will only invest with the "right" experts. What these promotional efforts fail to acknowledge, however, is the effect of costs. Because of this factor, most investors inevitably will be disappointed; even if they find a fund that achieves average investment returns before costs. After costs, it will deliver below-average returns. And, funds garnering below-average investment returns will deliver even lower after-costs returns.

"Professionals Have Fallen Well Short of Earning Their Keep"

Only the few funds that manage to beat the indexes *and* overcome expenses and trading costs provide added value for their investors. One of the acknowledged fathers of index investing, William Sharpe, Professor of Finance at Stanford University and Nobel Laureate in economics, in a recent interview with *indexfunds.com,* said: "The key issue is that past performance is a thin reed for how to predict future performance. Expense ratios and turnover are generally better predictors." Later in the interview, he said, "Some people who are really superior [at managing funds] could add enough value to offset the costs. The trick is separating the truly superior from the simply lucky."

"What chance does an investor have of finding that elusive needle in the now 3,500 stock-fund haystack?" Bogle asked in the April 2000 issue of *Mutual Funds* magazine. "History tells us: one chance in 27. At the end of 1984, there were 426 diversified stock funds. In the ensuing 15 years, only 16 of them beat (by as little as a single percentage point) the after-tax return on the stock market as a whole." The average after-tax return for the surviving funds was 13 percent per year, 4.2 percentage points behind the 17.2 percent after-tax return of the total stock market. "The average mutual fund grew [from $10,000] to $62,500 over 15 years; the index fund grew . . . to $105,000 . . . because fund managers as a group have failed to provide an excess return sufficient to overcome their heavy cost of some 2 percent per year. These investment professionals have fallen well short of earning their keep."

Vanguard's booklet, "Five Myths about Indexing," explains:

> Whether active funds as a group manage to outpace the S&P 500 Index in any given year is largely irrelevant for the long-term investor. Why? The primary strength of the index approach is a sustainable advantage: low costs. The 0.2% annual costs of a low-cost index fund compare extremely favorably to the annual costs of about 2.2% (a 1.4% expense ratio plus estimated portfolio transaction costs of 0.8%) for the average equity fund. In other words, the net "handicap" of 2.0% (2.2% minus 0.2%) makes it virtually impossible for traditionally managed mutual funds—as a group—to outpace low-cost index funds over time.

Vanguard may be a bit biased, but its calculations are not—stocks' historic returns in the past century have approximated 10 percent before taxes (more on taxes later). Over longer periods, after-fee returns of 9.8 percent (after 0.2% costs) versus 7.8 percent (after 2.2% costs) make a huge difference in ending sums.

History

John Bogle, Vanguard's founder, is generally regarded as the "father" of indexing, and has earned his well-deserved recognition because he brought the concept of index fund investing to the public. The first index fund debuted in 1971, launched by William Fouse at Wells Fargo Bank in San Francisco. With $6 million from the pension assets of Samsonite (the luggage maker), the fund invested equal amounts in all the stocks listed on the New York Stock Exchange. Two years later, Wells Fargo launched the first S&P 500 index fund. Bogle's fund, First Index Investment Trust, appeared later, on August 31, 1976, with only $11 million in assets. Bogle had hoped for much more money, enough to mimic the S&P 500 and its stock weightings. He could only approximate the index's holdings until the following year, when he finally had enough money to own all 500 stocks in the weightings equal to the index.

Morningstar's Principia Pro shows that only 13 index funds were available in 1990; by 1995, their number approached 100, but they were still garnering less than 5 percent of cash inflows into mutual funds. Indexing only really caught on with the public in the late 1990s, and cash inflows started to accelerate, as investors were attracted by the large-cap dominated S&P 500's torrid string of returns during the 1995–1999 period: 37.58, 22.96, 33.36, 28.58, and 28.25 percent.

In May 1996, Charles Schwab, as part of a panel at a fund convention, was asked what he was doing with his own money. The *Wall Street Journal* reported that Schwab was "sticking to mutual funds, mostly passive index funds, having sworn off market-timing in his 20s after finding it a 'loser's game.'" Warren Buffett, in a 1997 shareholder letter, told Berkshire Hathaway investors, "Most investors, both institutional and individual, will find that the best way to own common stocks is through an index fund that charges minimal fees." Fidelity, the mutual fund giant, caved in to market pressures in 1997, when it doubled to six the number of its index funds. The chief of their retail unit told the *Wall Street Journal*, "We have to offer what the consumer wants. There is no choice."

Rightly or wrongly, indexing became synonymous with the S&P 500. By 1999, as their number approached 300, over 40 percent of all new money flowing into equity funds was going into index funds. Bogle ranked them right up there with other modern inventions like the "electric light bulb, the tank, the telephone, the airplane." While their impact on humankind may not be as profound, there's no question that he proved his skeptics (most with self-serving interests) wrong. In the early 1990s, critics carped that indexing was "guaranteed mediocrity"; but by the end of the decade there were few fund managers who wouldn't have loved records that equaled indexing's "mediocrity." John Bogel's conclusion: Trying to beat the market is "the triumph of hope over experience." Burton Malkiel's conclusion: "There is no question about it, indexing has triumphed."

FUNDamental Facts

Up to Par

In a *Dow Jones Asset Management* interview, Burton Malkiel talked about indexing and realistic expectations about investments: "You won't be able to boast on the golf course about all of the great winners you had. However, you'll play the round at par each time. How many golfers can play each round at par? That's what you're going to do with an index fund."

What's a "Good" Index Fund?

The definition of a good index fund is simple: one that tracks its target index most closely and consistently. In May 1999, on the Motley Fool radio show, John Bogle was describing the no-load Vanguard S&P 500 Index Fund, with its 0.18 percent annual expense ratio. Asked about the Morgan Stanley Dean Witter Index 500 Fund with its 5.25 percent sales load and 1 percent expense ratio, he answered: "It stinks."

Learning about the major indexes (see Table 5.1) is important. If you own a managed fund, it is almost always trying to *beat* a specific index. As Vince Lombardi once said, "If you're not keeping score, you're just practicing." You should know how well your managed funds are doing compared to their target indexes. If the benchmark (the index) routinely beats the fund—rather than the other way around—it's time to trade up to an index fund that so easily eliminates the underperformance risk.

Table 5.1 lists the most widely followed indexes.

Stupid Indexes?

Although many index funds collect more than their fair share of returns every year, thoughtful observers have raised questions. One, in particular, deserves serious consideration: As good as index funds are at tracking their target indexes, how good are the indexes themselves? Might they be poorly constructed, or heading in the wrong direction? Might an index fund investor like a driver in the fog, be following the taillights of the car ahead—off a cliff?

Take the S&P 500 Index, most often used by the media as the proxy for stock market returns and by market professionals as their performance benchmark. In 1990, technology stocks represented approximately 9 percent of the index. In January 2000, the technology weighting was a "record 30%, up from about 13% just three years ago," according to the *Wall Street Journal.* By February, as tech stocks continued to soar, CNBC reported that by Merrill Lynch's calculations, the percentage was over 34 percent, and by their reckoning, the weighting needed to be increased. In the early 1980s, it was felt that the S&P was also overweighted, but by another sector: energy. At year-end 1980, energy stocks represented 29.7 percent. As energy stocks lost favor, their percentage of the index shrank to between 6 and 7 percent by the late 1990s.

Another example is the most widely followed international index of all major foreign stock markets—the Morgan Stanley Europe, Austral-Asia, Far East Index, commonly called the EAFE. December 31, 1989, when Japanese stocks were at their "bubble top," their weighting in the EAFE was 58.1 percent. When the bubble burst, Japanese stocks declined 65 percent, taking the EAFE down

TABLE 5.1 Major Benchmark Indexes

INDEX	DESCRIPTION	FUNDS USING BENCHMARK
U.S. STOCKS		
Dow Jones Industrial Average	Large industrials (30) General Electric, IBM, Merck, Coca-Cola	Dow Jones Industrial Average Index Funds only
Dow Jones Utility Average	15 electric & gas utilities AEP, Duke Energy, PG&E	Utility funds
Standard & Poor's 500 Index (S&P 500)	500 large U.S. industrial & utility companies (approx. 75% of U.S. stock market)	Large-cap stock funds
Standard & Poor's 400 Index (S&P 400 Mid-Cap)	400 largest U.S. companies excluding the S&P 500	Mid-cap stock funds
Standard & Poor's 600 Index (S&P 600 Small-Cap)	600 largest U.S. companies excluding S&P 500 & 400	Mid-cap/small-cap stock funds
Russell 1000 Index	Largest 1,000 U.S. companies	Large- and mid-cap stock funds
Russell 2000 Index (Russell Small-Cap)	Small U.S. companies, excluding Russell 1000	Mid- and small-cap stock funds—Widely followed small-cap benchmark
Russell 3000 Index	3,000 U.S. companies, includes Russell 1000 + 2000 companies	Total U.S. stock market funds
Wilshire 5000	All U.S. companies, approx. 7,000	Total U.S. stock market funds
Nasdaq Composite Index	All Nasdaq listed stocks, approx 5,000 companies	Aggressive, technology over-the-counter funds
Nasdaq 100 Index	Nasdaq's 100 largest companies Heavy technology weighting	Index, leveraged, technology funds

(continued)

TABLE 5.1 (Continued)

INDEX	DESCRIPTION	FUNDS USING BENCHMARK
INTERNATIONAL STOCKS		
Morgan Stanley Capital International Europe, Austral-Asia, Far East Index (MCSI EAFE)	All major foreign markets, international	Diversified funds, excluding EAFE emerging markets funds
Morgan Stanley Capital International Europe Index (MSCI Europe)	All major European companies	Diversified European funds
Morgan Stanley Capital International Pacific Free Index (MSCI Pacific)	All major Pacific Basin stock markets	Diversified Pacific Basin/Asia funds
Morgan Stanley Capital International Select Emerging Markets Free Index (MSCI Emerging Markets)	Many emerging country markets	Diversified emerging markets funds
Dow Jones World Stock Index	2,900 companies in 34 countries, including 730 U.S.	Global funds investing in foreign and U.S. stocks
Wilshire REIT Index	105 owners, operators of commercial real estate—no healthcare, mortgage REITs	Equity REITs, REIT funds
BONDS		
Lehman Aggregate Bond Index	Combines Lehman government corporate, mortgage-backed, asset-backed indexes	General bond funds
Lehman Corporate Bond Index	Investment grade corporate bonds	Corporate bond funds
Lehman Government Bond Index	Tracks U.S. Treasury, agency bonds	Government bond funds

with it; and by 1999, their weighting had shrunk to 23 percent. Managed international funds that had trailed the EAFE for 15 years by an average annual margin of 5 percent, outperformed the index for the following 10 years by an average 2.5 percent per year. The reason? On both the way up and the way down, managed funds were underweighted in Japanese stocks compared to the target index.

Too Much Technology?

A second example comes from the recent Wall Street passion for technology stocks. By the end of 1999, not only was the S&P 500 heavily weighted in technology, it was similarly dominated by large-cap growth stocks. This fact had not gone unnoticed by the folks at Vanguard. Despite the public's stampede into their flagship S&P 500 fund—Morningstar's Russ Kinnel confirmed what observers already knew: Vanguard management had been very vocal in "favoring (their) Total Stock Market (Fund—invested in all U.S. stocks) over (their) 500 Index (invested in the 500 largest U.S. stocks) all along."

In an April 2000 *New York Times* column, Gretchen Morgenson warned that index funds were becoming narrowly focused: "S&P 500 index funds are less diversified today than ever. [In 1999], only 31 stocks accounted for all the S&P 500's 21 percent gain. By contrast, in 1995, 341 stocks were responsible for the index's 37.6 percent climb. Put in a slightly different way, as of March 1, the 10 largest holdings represented 25 percent of the total market value of the S&P 500." Jonathan Clements, in his *Wall Street Journal* "Getting Going" column, countered the *New York Times* a couple of weeks later: "Criticisms of Indexing Don't Hold Up." To the contention that index funds were undiversified, compared with actively managed funds, he provided the following Morningstar statistics:

	PERCENT INVESTED IN 10 LARGEST HOLDINGS (%)	PERCENT INVESTED IN TECHNOLOGY COMPANIES (%)
S&P 500 Index funds	25.3	31.1
Managed diversified funds	36.2	29.1

Clements commented: "Whether you index the S&P 500 or the Wilshire 5000, what you are getting is a fund that pretty much mirrors the U.S. market. If you think index funds are undiversified and top-heavy, there can be only one reason: The market is undiversified and top-heavy." He quoted Gus Sauter, Vanguard's managing director in charge of index funds: "'It's not that index funds are getting riskier and riskier in a vacuum. The market is getting riskier and index funds merely reflect that.'"

In theory, managed funds—in addition to protecting you from stock market drops—should also shield you from oversized sector weightings such as energy and technology. However, history shows that most active managers invest heavily where the action is—those sectors that are doing the best. The result is that they haven't consistently protected their investors from either bear markets or the risk of sector overconcentration, because as a group, they *are* the market: They can't outperform themselves.

This leads to our primary conclusion: If market sectors become overvalued or undervalued, overweighted or underweighted, the mother of all investment principles—asset allocation—will largely determine your final outcome. But within most sectors, compared to the more costly managed funds, the odds of higher returns are heavily stacked in favor of index funds.

Critic's Corner

In addition to questions about the indexes themselves, other anti-indexing arguments include:

- *Unlike managed funds, index funds offer no downside protection in bear markets.*

The reasoning behind this argument is that unlike managed funds, which usually hold varying amounts of cash, index funds are virtually fully invested at all times. No uninvested cash reserve is available to cushion a market slide. Additionally, since active managers are "on top of things," they will presumably be able to "get out" when market conditions worsen. However, while the criticism sounds reasonable, history doesn't bear it out. According to a *Wall Street Journal* comparison, "In five of the past seven market downturns [that occurred in the 1987 to 1998 period], S&P 500 index funds . . . actually turned in better performance than the average actively managed general stock fund."

Statistics show that managed funds' historic cash positions have been the opposite from what they should have been: Cash levels have been low near historic market tops and higher near bottoms. So you can't expect active management to provide consistent and meaningful downside protection. If your preoccupation is to minimize stock market risk, you should have a more conservative asset allocation, using REIT, bond, and convertible bond funds rather than expecting active stock fund managers to protect you from falling stock prices.

- *Index fund performance is self-fulfilling.*

The argument is that performance-chasing investors pump more and more money into index funds that buy more of the leading stocks, driving up their prices, thereby increasing returns, which in turn, brings in more investors—and so on. However, industry studies have found no relationship between index fund and managed fund inflows and their relative performance.

- *If everybody indexes, markets will be so efficient that indexing will cease working.*

Even with indexing's increased popularity, the vast majority of all money is actively managed. At the height of their popularity in 1999, S&P 500 Index funds were collecting over 40 percent of all fund investors' new money, but as large-cap stocks (which drove the S&P 500's returns) lost favor, the percentage declined as investors shifted their attention to technology and biotechnology. The idea that Wall Street is going to be turning out the lights any time soon is fanciful. As good as indexing is, it isn't perfect—there is no perfect investment or investment strategy.

Index "Improvements"

Regardless of whether they resisted in the beginning, once the index train got rolling, everybody began hopping on board. Whether the world needs more index funds (or "improved" versions like enhanced index funds, leveraged index funds, reverse index funds, or exchange traded index funds; see following section) any more than it needs 11,000 funds total, remains to be seen. But needed or not, they're here.

Enhanced Index Funds

The first "improvement" in indexing was the introduction of enhanced index funds. They arrived on the scene in the early 1990s, promising index-plus-a-little returns, using various strategies to achieve these results. On their Web site Morningstar's John Rekenthaler described them and their passage to obscurity:

> In the tame old days before Nasdaq dominated the galaxy (say, 1997), enhanced index funds were indeed the rage. Their vow was modest—to edge past the index year in and year out—but then again, so were our collective ambitions. Plus, the logic seemed sound. Since portfolio managers will generally perform poorly if they are missing the year's top sector (try competing in 1999 while being light in technology!), why take that chance? Why not copy the indexes' general characteristics and whip those blind, dumb animals [the indexes] at the stock-by-stock

Heard on the Street

The Securities Industry . . . Is a Manufacturing Industry
—Ralph Wanger, *A Zebra in Lion Country* (Simon & Schuster, 1997)

The securities industry, you know, is not a service industry. It is a manufacturing industry. If you want a stock, Wall Street will make it for you. Any business, any kind you want. Recently, the Internet being the rage, the investment bankers have worked overtime creating a stream of IPOs to meet the demand. And people love them, to judge by their P/Es some of which have soared into the triple-digit stratosphere.

Remember back in the early '80's when the hard disk drive for computers was invented? It was an important, crucial invention, and investors were eager to be part of this technology. More than 70 disk drive companies were formed and their stocks were sold to the public. Each company had to get 20% of the market share to survive. For some reason, they didn't all do it.

. . . disk drives were a good idea, the Internet is a good idea. They have to be good ideas or they would not become widely popular. Come up with a concept that's patently silly or harmful and people won't want it. So, only a good idea can become so popular that it becomes a bad idea.

level? That way, portfolio managers could show off their greatest strength, their in-depth knowledge of companies.

As is so often the case with theories, the logic was more convincing than the results. In aggregate, enhanced index funds haven't been. Sure, there have been a few winners . . . , but for every winner there has been a loser. . . . And even the winners have alternated good and bad years—an unpleasant trait for a fund category that promises above (all) else, the virtue of consistency.

So while we can't quite call the group a failure, we must also acknowledge that it didn't fulfill its promise. Quiet obscurity would seem an appropriate fate.

Souped-Up Index Funds

The next generation was souped-up index funds—structured not to provide index returns plus a little, but index returns plus *a lot.* Using derivatives, the funds were designed to provide "Betas" of 1.5 to 2.0 times their target index's gain. A Beta of 1.0 means that a fund's volatility (price swings) is equal to the S&P 500 Index—a 2.0 Beta is twice the volatility of the index—in either direction. The rationale is that since the market goes up more often than it goes down, you are likely to increase your overall return. If the S&P 500 Index gains

10 percent or 15 percent, a 2.0 Beta fund promising 2.0 would return 20 percent or 30 percent.

The same sponsors also launched contramarket funds designed to track indexes in reverse. These funds are structured to move in the opposite direction of the market so a 1.0 Beta contramarket fund should rise 10 percent if the S&P 500 drops 10 percent, while a 2.0 Beta reverse fund should rise 20 percent.

In addition to the new flexibility, these funds provide other innovations:

- For the first time, investors in tax-deferred accounts (such as IRAs)—where the rules forbid going on margin (investing with borrowed funds)—can, in effect, use leverage.
- While current regulations also forbid shorting stocks or funds (a strategy that profits from falling prices) in tax-deferred accounts, contramarket funds enable investors to accomplish the same thing.
- Investors in taxable margin accounts can buy 1.5 and 2.0 Beta funds on margin, which effectively leverages their accounts even more.

Leveraged Funds' Bottom Line

Since they first began being offered, in 1993, most of these funds have delivered returns reasonably close to their stated objectives. A more important consideration, however, is that, because of the added risks, they are not suitable for most investors. The added volatility will leverage the average investors' bad timing into very bad timing. However, if you are among the small minority who is equipped to handle the increased risks, you can check the sponsors' Web sites, which provide descriptions of their growing list of offerings: Potomac-funds.com, Profunds.com, and Rydexfunds.com.

Exchange-Traded Index Funds (ETFs)

Technically, ETFs are unit trusts—unmanaged portfolios of shares of stock held by a custodian (usually a bank). ETFs track their target index closely, like open-end index funds that can be redeemed at NAV daily. Also, like the open-end variety, they allow you to buy an entire portfolio of stocks in a single transaction. Unlike open-end index funds that are bought and sold once a day based on their portfolios' closing prices, ETFs, trade all day, closely linked to their fluctuating net asset values. In 1993, the first exchange-traded index fund, Standard & Poor's Depository Receipts (SPDRs, commonly called "Spiders"), was listed on the American Stock Exchange. It tracks the S&P 500 Index and has grown to $16 billion in assets.

Foreign funds have recently been added: Barclays Global Investors (BGI) listed the first 15 of their iShares ETFs in May 2000. Domestic funds have continued to introduce new ETFs as well. Late in the third quarter of 2000, Vanguard announced they were bringing out five new Vanguard Index Participation Equity Receipts (popularly known as Vipers), their first ETFs. Barclays and State Street have both announced their intention to offer dozens (Barclays plans 36 and State Street 9) of new ETFs in the near future, many of them tracking U.S. indexes.

FUNDamental Facts

Sector Smorgasbord

ETFs are on their way to dicing, slicing, and pureeing every investment sector and subsector in sight. Once completed, then what? Anybody who thinks that picking future sector outperformers will be any easier than forecasting stock or fund performance just hasn't spent enough time attempting it. But that won't stop folks from trying. Prediction: A whole new cottage industry will emerge— Wall Streeters proclaiming particular "sector expertise." You can avoid them if you stick with plain old indexing—the world's most powerful expert-avoidance mechanism.

Like open-end index funds, ETFs can expand or contract their asset size to fit the number of investors that hold them. Unlike open-end funds, though, redeeming shareholders cannot force the fund to sell portfolio shares. That's because when they redeem their shares, they sell them on the exchanges rather than back to the fund. Unlike listed closed-end funds (exchange-listed funds whose open-market prices have no close linkage to their NAV), listed index shares don't sell at deep discounts or premiums, because arbitrageurs (professional traders who profit from small price disparities) keep the prices of listed index shares close to their target index during trading hours.

Open-end index funds redeem shares once daily: Orders placed at any time during market hours receive that day's closing price. Exchange-listed ETFs, on the other hand, trade all day long like any other listed stock. Another difference: ETFs are traded through brokers who charge a commission for each transaction.

So far, traders account for most ETF activity. The *Wall Street Journal* reported recently that the average holding period for Nasdaq-100 Index ETF (called "cubes" because the symbol is QQQ) was only *four days*, compared to 400 days for the average mutual fund, according to Bogle Financial Markets Research, Malvern, Pennsylvania.

In an interview in Morningstar's online "Ask the Expert" segment, Gus Sauter, manager of Vanguard's index funds, was asked, "What advantages do SPDRs offer over index mutual funds?"

Sauter said, "There is no question that SPDRs offer greater flexibility than S&P index funds. You can trade a SPDR at any time during the day, and you can sell them short. The question is: What's the value of that flexibility and what are you paying for it?" He pointed out ". . . the flexibility offered by a SPDR is meaningful for market-timers, but meaningless for long-term investors."

Another view is offered by Mary Rowland, columnist for MSN MoneyCentral: "ETFs stay fully invested in the index. They are priced constantly, rather than once a day like mutual funds. They can be bought on margin, which means they can be bought with borrowed money. . . . I bought the Nasdaq 100 Index more than a year ago. I sold off half when it doubled in price a year later. But I don't consider myself a trader. I want to own the Nasdaq index for the long term."

Below is a list of the broad categories of exchange-listed index funds listed on the American Stock Exchange (so far the only exchange listing ETFs). The industry is estimating that by January 2001, there will be over 60 ETFs trading, including the possibility of fixed income (bond) and actively managed funds. The best way to keep current on this fast growing phenomenon is to visit the American Stock Exchange Web site: amex.com. The following are the most popular and actively traded ETFs:

- Spiders—Standard & Poor's Depository Receipts; SPY.
- S&P Mid-Cap 400—Mid-Cap Spiders; MDY.
- Diamonds—Tracks the Dow-Jones Industrial Averages; DIA.
- iShares—Country, indexes, sector indexes.
- Nasdaq 100 Index Trading Stock; QQQ.

ETFs do provide added liquidity and an extra sliver of cost savings (expense ratios are less than Vanguard's open-end S&P 500 fund). Also, in the event of a market meltdown, they are not forced to sell portfolio securities by redeeming shareholders, so they are less vulnerable to triggering capital gains. On the other hand, you have to pay commissions to buy and sell and the international ETFs' projected expenses are higher than Vanguard's foreign funds.

The bottom line on ETFs is this: Unlike indexing itself, which provided a significant improvement in the way you can invest, ETFs provide only a very small incremental gain. More important, they make it easier and quicker to bring out the worst in investors: frequent trading.

Every study has shown that the more people trade (the public—not professional traders), the more they degrade their returns or incur losses. While part of their poor results can be attributed to expenses, the other factor is bad timing. This has been confirmed by studies of no-load fund traders' returns, where there were *no* trading expenses. The combination of trading expenses and mistiming takes a deadly toll on returns. However, it's not deadly for those in the business. Every time money moves, Wall Street's toll takers get their tiny slice—the specialists from the spreads and the brokers from commissions. Immense trading volume multiplies those tiny slices very quickly.

Charting Your Course

If you're already a fund investor, the odds are high that your managed funds have delivered below-average returns. You have not beaten the market (read index), the market has beaten you. That's why, if you're new to investing, indexing is the best way to get started, because it eliminates the many mistakes that plague new investors. Indexing's advantages include:

- Saves you time. A critical advantage because of the effects of compounding. New investors often waste years through trial and error before they get firmly grounded with a sound strategy.
- Shields you from expectations of unrealistically high returns that the financial marketers prey on.
- Provides an ongoing reality check that you can use to track your other investment's performance—you can always compare your fund to the index it tracks.
- Eliminates expenses and costs that are usually wasted in the attempt to achieve above-average returns.

In addition to low costs and tax advantages, plain vanilla index funds are user-friendly. You don't have to be an investment expert; you only have to learn a few investment principles, such as how to allocate assets and track your returns, not all the minutia of the investment world. You can spend your whole life investing successfully without exploring the nooks and crannies in the stock and bond markets. Traditional index funds have superb records of serving investors well and they are hassle-free.

There is no question that the latest innovations—compared to old vanilla index funds—make index investing quicker, easier, more exciting, and sometimes, cheaper. The media is having a field day describing how Vanguard is "duking it out" with the sexy new ETFs. But the real question is, who really benefits from the innovations? So far, there seems to be measurable merchant benefits, but customer benefits remain elusive. In a perverse sort of way, it seems as if all the new flavors of index funds make it even easier for investors to make bad decisions; they facilitate self-destructive behavior. *Already, the average investor's biggest problem is that he trades too often.* Making it easier, quicker, and more "exciting" to pull the trading trigger—and then amplifying the consequences with leverage—doesn't represent real progress for the average mutual fund investor. Instead, it's just the opposite.

Indexing is really the biggest advance in improving returns for average investors in the past 25—if not 50—years. Used sensibly, it solves a major part of your investment "problem"; slicing it into sectors and torqueing it with leverage and frequent trading, however, largely defeats its purpose. Don't be distracted by the glamour merchants; stay on a sensible, reasoned indexing course and your returns will beat those of most investors, and the pros, most of the time. The question then, is not *whether* to index, it is *how much* should you index? And that's a question only you can answer, after you've come up with a good asset allocation plan. Once you have, you'll be better able to decide how much of your investment dollar to put to work in index funds. But, as mentioned, index funds aren't perfect. Selecting the right managed funds is also important. In Chapter 6, we'll show you how to select the top mutual-fund portfolio managers.

CHAPTER 6

Picking Winning Managed Funds

Indexing Is Giving Up.

—Dennis Delafield

*Portfolio Manager,
Delafield Fund*

Winning managed funds are those that will consistently outperform most of the other funds in their category and, hopefully, their target index for years. The odds of picking future winners are low, however, because it requires forecasting—an inherently risky business. And as illustrated with the Easter egg hunt in Chapter 5, the law of averages allows only a few above-average performers in any activity. But that doesn't prevent you from *increasing* your odds of winning.

A landmark 1986 study showed that most of a portfolio's results are determined not by specific security selections or market timing, but by asset class selection. Asset class refers to the type of fund: growth funds, value funds, blend funds, and so forth. The study, which sought to identify the factors contributing to a portfolio manager's success, broke down the relative importance of each factor as follows:*

Asset class selection	94%
Security selection	4%
Market timing	2%

Still, most investors insist on looking for a fund manager who selects securities. This is their first step in a backward investment strategy that doesn't work. And it's easy to understand *why* it doesn't work. If you're painting a room, you have to do the tedious scraping, patching, and sanding before you open the first gallon of Adobe White. Skip the preparation and the finished job will look lousy,

---

Source: Gary P. Brinson, L. Randolph Hood, and Gilbert L. Beebower, "Determinants of Portfolio Performance," *Financial Analysts Journal*, July–August, 1986.

and it will get even worse as time goes on. The same principle is true for your fund portfolio.

You Bet Your Assets

As part of the asset allocation plan, you have to decide where to use actively managed funds and where to use index funds.

Conventional wisdom recommends using index funds in the large-cap sectors and managed funds in the less efficient mid- and small-cap sectors. But just how good is that strategy? Comparing managed funds with their target indexes provides a pretty clear answer. We used Morningstar's Principia Pro Plus to analyze a variety of periods, all ending March 31, 2000, to generate Table 6.1, which shows the percentage of managed funds that beat their target indexes for the periods indicated.

For the periods measured, only one quarter of managed large-cap funds has beaten its index, so the conventional wisdom holds true: The large-cap sector is not where the odds of picking above-average returns are high. Since managed small-cap funds beat their index almost 60 percent of the time, the odds of picking future outperformers are much better in this sector. However, Table 6.1 only shows the frequency of outperformance in the various sectors. While this is useful, it is much more valuable if you also know the magnitude of outperformance—you need to know not just how often managed small-cap funds outperformed, you also need to know by how much they did so. Table 6.2 answers this question.

Tables 6.1 and 6.2 clearly show that managed *small-cap funds are most likely to deliver the highest average returns versus their index.* So, what do these results tell you? The conclusions can be summed up as follows:

- If you're investing in large-cap funds, your best choice is to go with index funds.

TABLE 6.1 Percentage of Managed Funds Outperforming Benchmark Indexes*

	PERIODS ENDING 3/31/2000				
	3-YEAR (%)	5-YEAR (%)	10-YEAR (%)	15-YEAR (%)	AVERAGE (%)
Small-Cap Funds	57.6	57.1	53.9	67.6	59.0
Mid-Cap Funds	42.7	35.7	26.0	26.6	32.7
Large-Cap Funds	38.0	12.3	25.6	18.3	23.6

* Small-cap funds versus Russell 2000 Index. Mid-cap funds versus Standard and Poor's 400 Mid-Cap Index. Large-cap funds versus Standard and Poor's 100 Index for 3- and 5-year periods; versus Standard and Poor's 500 Index for 10- and 15-year periods.

TABLE 6.2 Outperforming Managed Funds' Average Annual Return

| | MANAGED FUND RETURN % (OUTPERFORMANCE %) COMPARED TO INDEX RETURN % | | | | |
| | AVERAGE | | | | |
	3-YEAR	5-YEAR	10-YEAR	15-YEAR	AVERAGE % OUTPERFORMANCE
Small-Cap Funds	35.96 (+102.6)	25.64 (+48.7)	19.47 (+34.8)	15.96 (+24.9)	+52.70
Index	17.75	17.24	14.44	12.77	
Mid-Cap Funds	43.37 (+58.5)	31.51 (31.0)	22.29 (+16.7)	15.96 (27.5)	+33.30
Index	27.38	24.05	19.09	12.77	
Large-Cap Funds	41.14 (+28.2)	35.02 (+15.1)	21.47 (+14.0)	20.25 (+10.1)	+16.77
Index	32.08	30.43	18.83	18.40	

- With mid-cap funds, you can choose either indexed or managed funds.
- In the small-cap sector, managed funds have the highest probability of beating their index.

Beyond the Numbers—Who Is Going to Run *Your* Money?

In print, online, and in interviews, three highly respected and experienced industry sources have provided valuable guidelines for the selection of fund families:

1. *John Bogle*—Vanguard's Chairman and founder and arguably the most influential, and highly regarded, figure in the mutual fund industry.
2. *Morningstar's staff*—The most respected mutual fund research organization.
3. *Jason Zweig*—*Money* magazine's savvy and pragmatic mutual fund columnist.

Here's what these professionals have to say.

As John Bogle Sees It

In an interview published by *Morningstar Mutual Funds,* September 21, 1999, Vanguard's John Bogle was asked, "What other fund companies [besides Vanguard] do you admire, and why?" Bogle's reply:

> The Vanguard competitors I most admire: TIAA-CREF, Dodge and Cox, Nicholas, and Capital Research and Management—but only if you can sharply minimize the impact of their sales loads. Why do I admire them?
>
> 1) Management character and integrity. For me, that's where everything begins.
> 2) Intelligent long-term investment objectives and policies (thinking long term is key).
> 3) Clearly-defined fund objectives and policies.
> 4) Consistent returns vs. their peers (not very surprising in view of 1 through 3!).
> 5) Low portfolio turnover (less buying and selling in portfolio).
> 6) High tax-efficiency (minimize tax liabilities compared to other funds). And "last but not least," reasonable expense ratios (mostly below 0.75% . . . but I hope they're working to get them lower!).

Bogle's response is not exotic or complicated, and his list of admired qualities comes unsurprisingly close to a closet definition of Vanguard's index funds: He values low expense ratios, consistent returns, and tax-efficiency in particular. But one problem with using his suggestions is it's not very easy for the average investor to determine which fund managers ooze integrity and which ones are character-lite. Still, his recommendations provide a good starting point for evaluating managed mutual funds.

Morningstar Staffers' Selection Process

Another set of criteria comes from Morningstar, the industry's most influential mutual fund research organization. In the summer of 1999, they described how they selected managed funds for their own employees' 401(k) plan. First, they had to lay the foundation. According to Morningstar: *"The first step* in reviewing our 401(k) plan was to examine the asset classes that the plan's funds covered" [emphasis added].

To continue: "The criteria we used in our [fund] screening process were:"

- Length of track record.
- Manager tenure.
- Performance consistency.
- Expenses.
- Style consistency.
- Risk-adjusted performance rankings.

Understandably, because of their analytical tilt, Morningstar's criteria were more quantifiable than those used by Bogle: manager tenure and risk-adjusted performance rankings, for example. But like Bogle, Morningstar emphasized *performance consistency, low expenses, clearly defined objectives, and consistent returns.*

Morningstar and Bogle differ in one important respect: Bogle specified high tax efficiency, while Morningstar did not. This omission, however, does not signify a disagreement with Bogle because Morningstar was picking funds for its tax-deferred 401(k) plan, where tax efficiency didn't matter.

What is key to notice about both Bogle's and Morningstar's selection criteria, however, is that neither one makes any references to extraordinary returns delivered by an individual manager or fund family in the past. Fund veterans know all too well that unusually good performance is just that—*unusual.* They know better than to project them to the horizon and beyond—and so should you.

"The Best Mutual Fund Family in America"

That's what *Money* magazine's Jason Zweig called Southeastern Asset Management, manager of Longleaf Partners Funds, in his August 1998 column, "The

Fundamentalist." Zweig is one of the industry's most insightful observers, so his evaluation carries a lot of weight.

He starts big and at the top: "[Longleaf]'s chairman is O. Mason Hawkins, whom I've come to regard as the Warren Buffett of mutual fund investing." He goes on to explain further:

- "Of the more than 700 firms that run mutual funds, only a handful ... Longleaf among them—bother giving their shareholders the opportunity to attend regular meetings and get their questions answered."
- "The folks at Longleaf share a bedrock belief: Fund investing should be a partnership between the portfolio manager and the investing public. ... More than any other firm I know, Longleaf takes the term "fund family" literally, treating its shareholders as true partners."
- "Longleaf holds its typical stock for five years." This is unusual in an industry where the average stock in a fund portfolio is held for over one year.

Morningstar's Don Philips makes a further important point about Longleaf's management. "The people at Longleaf could have gotten rich a lot faster by running their funds the way most people do—by maximizing their own short-term profits. Instead, they have gotten rich slowly by making their investors rich. And that's exactly how it should be." Philips's comment, while praising Longleaf, is not an encouraging assessment of the mutual fund industry as a whole. And all three of these Street-wise participant-observers are in agreement on the problem. The underlying theme of all three of their comments: "Ask not only what mutual funds can do for you; ask what they can do *to* you."

The most strident of our three experts is Chairman Bogle. During his Morningstar interview, he was asked, "What is the biggest challenge facing the fund industry right now? His response:

1. Getting our own house in order. We've failed to deliver to our shareholders a fair participation in market returns, largely because of excessive costs, insane (and tax-devastating) rates of portfolio turnover, and an inadequate corporate governance system.
2. Deflating investor expectations, born of the Great Bull Market, of high future returns.
3. Returning to our roots as investment managers and stewards of our shareholders, and abandoning our self-appointed mission as product marketers and opportunists.

Bogle's advice and insights—and those of the other observers—don't paint a pretty picture of the mutual fund industry, but if you are beginning to wonder whether you might be better off investing in CDs, while the industry faces its challenges, think again. The biggest challenge is not the industry's, it is your own—the common mistakes that hobble the average investor. If you have conquered those, there are many fine funds where you'll get a good or maybe even a great deal.

More Considerations

- *Eliminate costly load funds* This may seem to be so obvious that it doesn't need inclusion, but a step-by-step approach would be incomplete without it. An exception to the rule can be funds that impose small (1% to 2%) back-end loads for the first 6 months of ownership. This penalty for selling within 6 months is easily avoided by holding on to the fund beyond the penalty period.

- *Don't buy four- and five-star rated funds simply because of their star count* As pointed out in Chapter 5, star-chasing usually leads to poor results, even though the industry mightily encourages you to do just that.

- *Don't think your fund picks are going to be managed by the same person forever* Circumstances change, and so do fund managers; they change an average of every four years. Keep that in mind when you're looking at advertisements that show a fund's 10-year performance. They fail to note that in the course of 10 years the average fund is on its third portfolio manager.

- *Don't expect the fund itself to last forever, either* Currently, 50 percent of all mutual funds disappear during a ten-year period, having merged or liquidated. If you want to "put it away and forget it," forget managed funds. Instead, invest your money in index funds that aren't nearly as subject to changes and disruptions.

Corporate Culture—How Fund Families Operate

We agree with Bogle—the core of corporate culture is "character and integrity . . . *where everything begins.*" These factors are hard to quantify, but the following six indicators provide strong evidence:

1. *The Fund's literature* Does the fund communicate with its investors only every 6 months—when it's required to do so? Is its literature a series of lengthy, impersonal, ivory-tower treatises brimming with mind-numbing statistics and remote economic babble? Are fund returns presented boldly and clearly, or submerged in oceans of fine print? Fund literature can give you a clue whether the investor is treated with respect or indifference.

2. *Fund advertising* Does the message boil down to breathless claims of hot recent performance and little else? Do the ads have more stars than your average planetarium? If so, to quote Bogle, you're probably looking at "product marketers and opportunists." You should be seeking "investment managers and stewards" instead.

3. *Articles and columns about the fund* In addition to, or if you don't have access to, online sources, spend a couple of hours in the library combing the alphabetized company and fund indexes (usually following "contents" or "features" indexes) in the back issues of personal finance magazines like *Forbes, Kiplinger's Personal Finance Magazine,* and *Mutual Funds.* This research will uncover articles providing "character insights"—clues to the way fund managements think and what others in the industry think of them.

4. *Manager-investors* If chefs have to eat their own cooking, they're likely to take extra care in preparing the food. The same is true for mutual fund managers and why you want your manager to have a significant personal ownership in the fund. Some sponsors refuse to divulge it, some describe it only in general terms. A few, such as Longleaf, brag about it. All things being equal, braggarts are preferred.

    In November 1999, *Financial Planning* magazine ran an article titled, "Surprise! Most managers with big stakes in their own mutual funds beat their benchmarks." The article disclosed that over the past 3- and 5-year period ending in June 1999, "85% of the 30 funds [we] examined in which the managers, employees, trustees and, in some cases, independent directors hold significant investment have outperformed the average fund in their categories. While this list is not exhaustive, the total the managers and employees invested is more than $1.5 billion."

5. *Fund asset size* Does your fund's management have a history of closing funds when "size becomes a problem?" The larger the fund gets, the more difficult it becomes to manage it effectively. Most studies have concluded asset size begins to become a problem at the following levels:

Fund Type	Assets
Micro-cap	$100 million–$150 million
Small-cap	$500 million–$1 billion
Mid-cap	$1 billion–$2 billion
Large-cap	$10 billion

There is no "right" number for when size begins to hamper performance. Although many funds never close, of those that do, the almost-universal practice is closing when "size *begins* to hamper performance."

The problem is, once size has already begun to hamper returns, it's usually too late.

The issue of size versus performance presents a big conflict of interest in the mutual fund business. Management increases its revenues from the fees it charges, which encourages aggressive recruitment of new investors. But funds that become too large to manage effectively reduce performance for their current shareholders. How fund managements handle—or don't handle size—is probably the best indicator as to their true priorities. "Us or them?" One way to avoid this problem is by investing in new funds (Chapter 7).

Management Type—What to Consider, What to Avoid

A key issue when choosing an actively managed mutual fund is the core business of the management company. Although consolidations within the industry are blurring the distinctions, the broad categories are mutual fund firms, investment counselors, insurance companies, securities brokers, and banks. Mutual fund companies are the most desirable fund managers. They are most likely to provide superior returns because they have the freedom to focus on one business—managing mutual funds. Importantly, they have are fewer conflicts of interests and distractions than the other management-company types. Investment counseling firms, which manage separate accounts in addition to managing mutual funds, come a close second because their core business is still money management.

Banks and insurance companies are less desirable because their other businesses, such as selling insurance or making loans, may be as, or more, important to their overall corporate goals. And, ironically, securities brokerage firms—also known as wirehouses—are the *worst* fund managers because they, like insurance companies and banks, are engaged in many other businesses, including underwriting, brokerage, and investment banking. Wirehouses usually trail the rest of the industry with depressing regularity and by hefty percentages. A sometimes exception to the preceding are small, relatively newer research/investment banking boutiques, like Robertson Stephens and Montgomery Securities, before they were acquired by banks.

In the August 1998 issue of *Kiplinger's Personal Finance Magazine,* the editors compiled a list of top-performing diversified funds in six categories for 1-, 3-, 5-, 10-, and 20-year periods. Of 288 top performers, only 13 (4.5%) were broker managed. Of those, most were institutional or research boutique brokers. Only two were managed by wirehouses, one each by Merrill Lynch and Smith Barney (now Salomon Smith Barney). Similar findings were reported in the 1998 *Forbes* Fund Survey. *Forbes* ran a study titled, "Which of the biggest fund families has the best performance?" Not *one* brokerage firm appeared on their list.

Lack of Investment Controls

The attitude of fund management toward investors can be extremely important, and in the big wirehouses, that attitude has seemed to be indifference. Merrill Lynch Asset Management Group is one of the five largest asset managers in the world; in the United States, only Fidelity Investments is larger. Yet their funds have traditionally been laggards that show up in the bottom quartile of money managers—and in some rankings, the bottom 10 percent—of fund family rankings. *Mutual Funds* magazine's "Family Performance Ratings," published in October 1999, ranked them in the bottom 20 percent—124 out of 146. In the 1999 edition of *Barron's* annual rankings, Merrill Lynch ranked dead last out of 55 fund families.

Investors have grown tired of paying more for less: They redeemed over $9 billion worth of Merrill funds in 1999, just as senior management admitted they had a problem and began attempts to fix it.

Follow the Money

While brokerage firms charge their fund investors' more, they pay their mutual fund managers less, another reason for underperformance. Annual surveys continue to show that only notoriously low-paying banks compensate their fund managers less than brokerage houses do. Mutual fund companies, on the other hand, pay their managers a startling 70 percent more than brokers—an average of $274,500 versus $160,000. The best and brightest portfolio managers are not attracted to brokers that pay less and whose expense structures penalize their investment returns.

Experience Counts

It's probably the most overused cliché in the fund business, but it's nonetheless true: If you're going to pay for experience, you ought to get lots of it. But getting that experience is not as easy as you'd think. Recent surveys show that the average tenure of a fund money manager is four years and the average age is 29. Long-established fund families enjoy an experience advantage and, obviously, a veteran portfolio manager is preferable to a rookie.

Size Does Count

Since active management—compared to indexing—exposes investors to the risk of way-below-average returns, minimizing this underperformance risk is important. While it may seem more imaginative or daring to place your bet on small start-up funds and fund families, these are even more risky than the

---

FUNDAMENTAL FACTS

There were reports in the press that Morningstar was considering initiating fund family rankings in early 1999, but when contacted, John Rekenthaler, Research Director, responded, "Sadly, this project has stalled. . . ." This was due, in part, to a "lack of agreement by the editorial staff as to the relevant measurement system. I haven't given up hope . . . but you shouldn't expect anything imminent."

---

average managed fund. One five-year study showed that the worst 25 performers each year were over 40 percent smaller than the average fund. But petite funds also tend to outperform—the top 25 funds were 60 percent smaller than the average fund during the same period (see Chapter 8).

This potential for outperformance attracts investors to small or new funds despite the risks, and one way to minimize the risk is to add a layer of management consistency by seeking out small funds offered by large sponsors. A substantial fund family with a hefty research infrastructure provides important support for fund managers. Otherwise, the managers have to rely on outside research, much of it coming from "sell side analysts": the brokerage community and investment bankers, whose research is often tainted by their bias in favor of marketing and sales. In-house fund family analysts can be more objective.

Reading the Ratings

While Morningstar does not yet offer ratings for fund families, they are an important resource when selecting individual mutual funds. If you use Morningstar, for example, you'll want to pay most attention to the Category Rating. This lumps together funds in the same category—growth funds are compared to other growth funds, value funds are compared to other value funds, and so on. The Star ratings, on the other hand, lump most funds together without considering cap size or management style and are largely sector-driven. This makes them less useful.

Other Important Considerations

- *Portfolio management teams* Although committees are notoriously bad decision makers, many team managed funds have been successful, possibly because they are more consistent.

- *"Bottoms up" versus "top down" stock pickers* Portfolio managers sometimes are divided into two camps: bottoms up and top down. Simply put, top-down money managers use grand prognostications about interest rates, the GDP, industry forecasts, and the like as the framework for their stock picks. They may decide that consumer durables are poised for an up-move and load up on stocks within that sector. Bottoms-up managers select stocks one at a time, based on their opinions about the prospects for individual companies. If they end up heavily weighted in consumer durables, it's because analysis has pointed to their individual attractiveness. Top-down managers' performances tend to come in streaks—they deliver impressive returns when they are right, and dismal results when they are wrong. Bottoms-up managers are usually a better bet because their returns tend to be more consistent.

- *New-fund effect* Since new funds tend to outperform their older peers, they are excellent choices to fill the mid- or small-cap stock fund portion of your asset allocation. They have structural advantages (see Chapter 8), and if you invest at their inception, you automatically solve the timing problem that plagues so many investors.

- *Expenses* We shouldn't even have to mention this again—it's been so much a part of our mantra: Look for funds with low expenses.

- *Investment style* Management style and cap size drive returns. Therefore, if you have limited capital, your best bets are "blend" funds that straddle the middle between growth and value. If you have enough capital to split your bet, tilt toward growth funds, because most studies have shown that the growth sector is where managers add the most value. Blend funds won't provide the hottest performance, but they won't leave you out in the cold either.

- *Sector stinkers versus real stinkers* Almost all studies have shown that while past performance isn't very useful in predicting future outperformance, it is helpful in avoiding underperformance. While good funds may not stay good, lousy funds *do* tend to stay lousy.

- *Portfolio turnover* According to orthodox wisdom—and John Bogle— high turnover is undesirable, and most of the time it is. However, more than a coincidental number of high turnover small-cap growth funds have delivered superior returns, and one study has found that in the small-cap growth sector, high turnover actually boosted returns. Don't automatically eliminate a fund from consideration because of high turnover.

The Final Round

There was a good deal of information in this chapter, and it needs to be condensed so you can use it to "cut to the chase." The summary/checklist that follows rounds up the most important criteria in managed fund selection: It will help you identify the funds that are most likely to outperform. You may not be satisfied that you can identify whether a fund satisfies all the criteria, but it should come close.

Checklist

MANAGED FUND SELECTION SUMMARY

(Criteria ranked in order of importance)

____ *Management style* If you have a limited amount of money to invest, blend funds are best.

____ *Cap-size* Small-cap funds are best—most likely to beat target indexes; mid-cap funds next best.

____ *Portfolio manager(s)' track record* Superior past performance is a plus.

____ *Sponsor type* Mutual fund families best (e.g., Fidelity, Vanguard) are best; independent money managers second. Avoid broker-sponsored funds.

____ *New-fund effect* New funds tend to outperform older peers. Stick with new funds from large, experienced sponsors.

____ *No-load or low-load.*

____ *Fund family corporate culture* Although you want to avoid "what can we sell 'em today" marketers, it's hard to quantify.

____ *Portfolio managers' personal investment in fund* This is important, but not always disclosed.

____ *Expenses* Look at fund prospectus for low annual fees.

PART 3

Mutual Fund Universe: The Basic Choices

CHAPTER 7

Bonds and Bond Funds—Picking the Winners

A Bond Fund Is Not a Bond.

—John Bogle
Bogle on Mutual Funds

Bonds are simply debt. When corporations, governments, states, and municipalities need money, they borrow it by issuing bonds (their IOUs), usually through underwriters who sell them to individuals and institutions. The issuer guarantees your principal—the money you use to purchase the bonds. Bonds thus provide a safe place for your principal and a stable, predictable income. For these reasons, they are usually anchors in conservative income portfolios. But not all bonds are created equal when it comes to security. When you buy investment grade bonds, for example, you are buying debt with some risk; but the risk level is still much less than you face when investing in stocks.

Although it may seem silly, investment professionals hear it at one time or another: "But I thought that you couldn't lose money on bonds." Yes, Virginia, you *can* lose money in bonds. They are riskier than savings accounts for several reasons. For one thing, your principal is not insured by the Federal Deposit Insurance Corporation (FDIC). For another, bond prices rise and fall, driven by changing interest rates. Bond funds lose value when interest rates rise, so your total return could be negative—even though your income from the fund remains relatively constant. We'll discuss how this happens later in this chapter.

Why Buy Bonds?

You may choose to buy bonds for a number of reasons. You may need more current income, you may wish to add a measure of predictability and stability to your portfolio, or you might feel that stocks expose you to more risk than you care to undertake.

But, as noted, bonds are not entirely risk-free. If you invest in individual bonds, there are three principal risks:

1. *Loss of purchasing power* The return on your bonds may not keep up with inflation. Since the mid-1920s, stocks have provided average annual returns of approximately 10 percent per year, beating inflation (3% per year) by 7 percent. During that period, bonds' average 5 percent return has beaten inflation by only two percentage points—pretax. But in the 1970s, when inflation surged to double digits, bond investors lost out on two fronts: (1) investors' dollars bought less goods and services, and (2) their bonds and bond funds dropped in value (see item 3).

2. *Investment risk* Issuers of bonds may default, paying interest and/or principal late or not at all. The higher the bond rating, however, the lower the probability of default.

3. *Market risk* Bonds, like stocks, are traded in active markets. Bonds can be sold before maturity, and when that happens, they may bring more or less than the original purchase price. If interest rates rise, bond prices drop; whereas when interest rates fall, bond prices go up. The 1970s provides an extreme example of how this works. During that period of high inflation, interest rates rose substantially, and many high-quality long-term bonds were selling at 30 to 40 cents on the dollar.

Wall Street Speak

Coupons refer to the interest payments on bonds. The term comes from the practice, common in the past but rare now, of bond issuers attaching individual coupons to the actual bond. Each coupon represented a single interest payment, and the investor would detach ("clip") the currently payable coupon and present it for payment. These days, people don't usually have to clip their own coupons this way—the process is much more automated—but the traditional term remains in use in the world of bond investing.

Playground Economics

Bond price fluctuations are sometimes difficult for new investors to conceptualize. Bond prices move inversely to interest rates: They rise when interest rates drop, and they fall when interest rates soar. Think of a seesaw, with bond prices at one end and interest rates at the other. When one end rises, the other falls. The degree of rise or fall depends on the length of time until the bond reaches maturity. Next, picture that seesaw with two seesawers way out at the ends and two more sitting close to the center. When rates change, those out at the ends—as in long maturities (20 to 30 years)—move up and down the most. Their playmates, sitting close to the center (short maturities, 5 years or less), aren't nearly as affected (see Figure 7.1). A moving graph of how this works is on the home page of *investinginbonds.com.*

If you are trying to minimize both investment *and* market risk, invest only in the highest quality bonds with the shortest maturities. They're least likely to default, and they're far less susceptible to changes in interest rates. For higher income, however, you'll have to make a trade-off, choosing lower quality bonds and/or longer maturities. Buying very low-quality bonds or highly touted "investments" promising unusually high income usually ends up badly. This is called "reaching for income," and too often we hear sad tales of income-seeking investors—those least able to afford it—taking dreadful losses. Too-good-to-be-true yields usually are just that.

However, if you invest in bonds issued by the U.S. government, government agencies, or highly rated corporate or municipal bonds—or bond funds (a

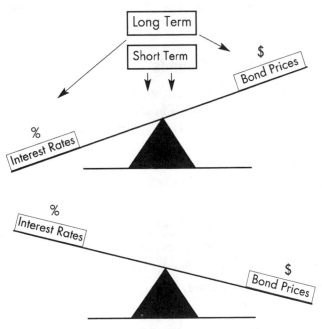

FIGURE 7.1 Visualizing bond-price fluctuations.

portfolio of bonds)—the likelihood is high that you will receive the interest you expect. These alternatives differ, in part, in the frequency with which they pay out income: Bonds typically pay income every 6 months, while bond funds usually pay income monthly. Bond holders receive their principal when their bonds mature, or prior to that if the bond is "called" (paid off before its scheduled maturity). Bond funds, having no maturity, in theory, are perpetual.

How Bonds Work

When the U.S. government borrows money, bonds are offered on the market through the Treasury Department and through authorized bond dealers, such as Goldman Sachs or Merrill Lynch. Treasury bonds (also called "Treasuries") issued by the federal government are purchased by large institutions (banks, mutual funds, insurance companies, etc.), and by individuals. Large, well-established corporations like IBM and General Electric also issue bonds that are thought to be less safe than the government's debt; they pay higher rates to compensate investors for the higher perceived risk.

Bond safety ratings are issued by rating services such as Standard & Poor's or Moody's. The average quality (in terms of safety of principal) of a bond *fund's* portfolio is disclosed in the prospectus, and can also be learned by consulting fund-rating services such as Morningstar. To help you understand the ratings given in these sources, a short version of Standard & Poor's corporate and municipal rating definitions is included at the end of this chapter.

Tax-Free Money Market Funds

If you are in the 28 percent federal tax bracket or higher and need some liquidity, tax-free municipal money market funds (funds that hold the bonds of municipalities) are a convenient—and tax-efficient place—to invest. If you live in a state with a high income tax, you would have to earn approximately 6¼ percent in a taxable money market fund to earn an equivalent after-tax return. The following list is a sampling of tax-free bond funds that are available.

TAX-FREE MONEY MARKET FUNDS	YIELD
Vanguard California Tax-Free Money Market	3.67
Vanguard New Jersey Tax-Free Money Market	3.93
Vanguard New York Tax-Free Money Market	4.08
Vanguard Tax Exempt Money Market Fund (national)	4.07
USAA Texas Tax Exempt	3.97
USAA Virginia Tax Exempt	4.01

Types of Bonds/Debt

- *U.S. Treasuries* Approximately $3.3 trillion in U.S. Treasuries are outstanding. These include bills with maturities of 1-year or less, notes with maturities of 2 to 10 years, and bonds, with maturities of greater than 10 years. Daily trading in Treasuries approximates $180 to $190 billion. The variety of bond instruments is very wide, including:

    Zero Coupon Bonds These are U.S. Treasury coupons or principal payments that have been "stripped" from Treasury obligations, so that there is no semiannual "coupon" payment. Investors buy them at discounts to the principal amount and receive payment at maturity equal to the principal amount (at par or $1,000 per bond). Their return is the gain from the discounted price to the full face amount. No periodic interest payments are made.

    Tips U.S. Treasury Inflation-Indexed (protected) Securities are bonds whose return is indexed to inflation—their purpose is to guarantee a real (after-inflation) return. Investors receive semiannual interest payments based on a fixed semiannual interest rate that is applied to the inflation-adjusted principal. The principal is indexed to the Consumer Price Index (CPI). If deflation causes the principal amount to decline, the investor will never receive less than the par amount of the bond when it was first issued. But if the CPI increases by 3 percent in a given year, that amount is added to your return. The amount accruing to principal is not paid out *although it is taxable.* Tips, therefore are more appropriate in tax-deferred accounts.

- *Federal Agency Securities (Agencies)* These are issued by various government-sponsored enterprises (GSEs) that were created to fund loans to borrowers such as homeowners, farmers, and students. Some of the largest issuers are Federal Home Loan Banks, Federal Farm Credit System Banks, Federal Home Loan Mortgage Corporation (Freddie Mac), Federal National Mortgage Association (Fannie Mae), and Tennessee Valley Authority (TVA). There is approximately $1.5 trillion in agency debt outstanding, which is an obligation (IOU) of the U.S. government.

- *Money Market Instruments* These include bankers' acceptances, certificates of deposit, and commercial paper (commercial loans issued by banks). Approximately $2.3 trillion in money market instruments are currently outstanding, and they are the obligation of the banks that issued them.

- *Corporate Bonds* These are bonds issued by corporations, and guaranteed by the issuing company, for operating cash flow and capital investment purposes. Approximately 150,000 issues, totaling approximately $3.0

trillion are currently outstanding. Their safety depends on the corporations' ability to pay.

• *Mortgage Securities* These bonds were created by savings and loans, commercial banks, and mortgage companies. Individual mortgages are "pooled" by issuers for sale to investors. As the underlying mortgages are paid off, investors receive interest and principal payments. The majority are issued by and/or guaranteed by federal agencies or government-sponsored enterprises such as the Government National Mortgage Association (Ginnie Mae) or the Federal National Mortgage Association (Fannie Mae). There is approximately $2.3 trillion outstanding in government-backed mortgage securities. "Private-label" mortgage securities, issued by investment banks and other private enterprises, total $300 billion—and the safety of principal is dependent on the financial stability of the issuer.

• *Municipal Bonds* These bonds are issued by states, local governments (county and city), and municipal agencies to build schools, bridges, highways, sewer systems, and so on. Interest is exempt from federal taxes, which allows municipal issuers to compete effectively for capital in the securities market. Currently, there is $1.5 trillion in municipal debt outstanding—obligations of approximately 50,000 issuers.

• *Asset Backed Securities* These certificates represent interests in pools of assets such as credit card receivables, and auto loans. Asset-backed securities have grown rapidly—there is now approximately $750 billion outstanding. The quality of these securities is determined by the quality of the assets that underlie them.

• *Repurchase/Securities Agreements (Repos)* Repurchase agreements are used as a source of financing by securities and banking firms, and others. Repos are agreements where sellers "sell" securities to buyers, simultaneously agreeing to repurchase them at an agreed on price at a future date. Outstanding contracts were estimated to be $2.4 trillion in 1999.

• *Foreign Corporate Bonds* These are similar to U.S. corporate bonds, but are issued by corporations domiciled outside the United States.

Investing in Individual Bonds

Bonds are rated according to their safety. The highest (safest) rating is AAA, the lowest rating is D, which indicates that the obligation is in default. Investing in individual bonds is a good strategy, particularly if you stick to quality issues—"investment grade" bonds—which are bonds with the four highest ratings: AAA, AA, A, and BBB. Fiduciaries—trustees, guardians, or other individuals with the responsibility of managing money for others—will not invest in bonds with ratings lower than BBB because lower rated bonds are generally considered to be speculative.

U.S. Government Bonds

U.S. government bonds are the highest quality; for safety, U.S. Treasuries are the clear choice. In addition, with only a few exceptions, there is no danger of your bonds being "called," that is, redeemed before their maturity date. This is important because premature redemption means a loss of the interest payments you would otherwise have collected. Because the U.S. government guarantees the safety of your principal, diversification of Treasuries is not necessary. You can buy individual bonds direct from the U.S. Treasury, free of commissions. If you have a small amount to invest, or need a monthly income check and are willing to sacrifice some yield for convenience, U.S. government bond funds are an alternative

Buying U.S. Treasuries

U.S. Treasuries are available directly from the Federal Reserve Bank nearest you, or you can purchase them online. Buying direct means you pay no commissions; brokers typically charge $50 to $75 per transaction. Once you have established an account, you can buy the following:

- *Bills* 3-month, 6-month, 1-year maturities. Minimum investment: $10,000.
- *Notes* 2-year, 5-year, and 10-year maturities. Minimum investment: $5,000 for notes with maturities of less than 5 years, $1,000 for notes with maturities between 5 and 10 years.
- *Bonds* Up to 30-year maturities. Minimum investment: $1,000.

Dealing with the Federal Reserve

You can:

- On maturity, you can the Federal Reserve Bank district office to instruct them to automatically roll over your investment into the next maturity. In other words, when your 1-year Treasury bill matures, you can ask them to issue another one with a new 1-year maturity.
- Have interest payments from notes and bonds wired automatically to your checking account after receiving the first payment through the mail.

You cannot:

- Buy Treasury securities, except at scheduled auctions.
- Buy zero coupon securities on your own (these are issued by bond dealers).

- Sell your bills, notes, or bonds through a Federal Reserve Bank. Securities must be transferred to a broker before they can be sold, which can be tedious and time-consuming.

Standard & Poor's Bond Credit Ratings—Short Version

The rating system measures the relative safety of your principal. These ratings are:

- *AAA* The highest rating.
- *AA* An obligation rated AA differs from the highest rated obligations only to a small degree.
- *A* An obligation rated A is somewhat more susceptible to the adverse effects of changes in circumstances and economic conditions.
- *BBB* A rating of BBB signifies that the investment has what is considered to be adequate protection. However, safety is more likely to be influenced by changes in circumstances and economic conditions than in bonds carrying any of the A-level ratings.
- *BB, B, CCC, and CC, C* Each of these ratings indicates a greater degree of insecurity, with BB being the least speculative of the group, and C being the most risky.
- *D* Obligations rated D are in payment default. The D rating is used when payments on an obligation are not made on the date due, even if the applicable grace period has not expired.

Sometimes you'll see plus (+) or minus (−) signs assigned to ratings from AA to CCC. These symbols are used to show relative standing within the major rating categories.*

The "Income Buyer's" Plight in a Period of Declining Interest Rates

In the early 1980s, 30-year U.S. government bonds were yielding an extraordinary 14 percent; the raging inflation at that time, made interest rates soar. Fifteen years later, inflation had subsided and bond yields were down dramatically, but investors who had bought individual bonds while yields were high continued to enjoy the high returns they had locked in, with noncallable Treasury bonds. Bond fund investors, however, saw their income continue to drop as their funds' ever-changing portfolios reflected lower rates. Money from newer investors, invested at lower yields, also shrank their income. "Income

---

*Description of ratings used by permission of *Money* magazine.

TABLE 7.1 Income from Long-Term Treasuries

YEAR	APPROX. LONG TERM INTEREST RATES (%)	ANNUAL INCOME	REQUIRED INVESTMENT
1980	14	$12,000	$ 86,000
1984	12	12,000	100,000
1985	10	12,000	120,000
1991	8	12,000	150,000
1998	6	12,000	200,000
2000	5.9	12,000	204,000

buyers"—particularly those investing in open-end bond funds—have been in a long, losing battle with interest rates.

While the effect on both the stock and bond markets has been salubrious for most investors, it has played havoc with income buyers who had gotten used to receiving a much larger return on their bonds. Table 7.1 shows the cost of a super-safe $1,000 per month income stream from long-term U.S. Treasuries. In 1980, the price tag was $86,000; by the late 1990s, the cost had risen to over $200,000.

Beat the Dealer—Buying and Selling Individual Bonds

Unless you invest in U.S. Treasuries, you have to have enough capital to get decent diversification in a bond portfolio, meaning owning 5 or 10 different issues, or more. Since it's inadvisable to invest in "pieces" of less than $10,000 face value, because they are difficult to buy and sell, one of the least democratized Wall Street practices has always been how bonds are sold. However, if you have the means, setting up a portfolio on your own is a good alternative.

Like some other Street near-monopolies, bond trading has been almost a closed club between professionals. Wholesale dealers (large Wall Street firms) buy bonds in big chunks called "round lots"; a block of bonds with a $1 million face value. (In the stock market, a round lot is 100 shares.) Bond dealers carve up their round lots into smaller units—often in $100,000 amounts—for sale to wirehouses and smaller brokerage firms. These, in turn, carve their units up into $10,000 to $25,000 pieces and sell them to the public. The problem is that thanks to all the middlemen, the small retail bond buyer pays an inflated price. The dealers buy bonds wholesale, inventory them, and add a profit markup when they resell them. But the markup isn't shown and individual investors paying retail prices can end up paying too much, which obviously reduces returns.

The picture for bond *funds* is a little different. While they have other structural disadvantages, enthusiasts point out that funds buy and sell bonds on the wholesale market, while individual investors pay retail. The result, they claim, is that investing in bond funds is better than investing in individual bonds. In that respect, they are right, but there are other disadvantages inherent in bond funds. If you know what quality of bonds and approximate maturities you are looking for, as well as their call features (if they can be redeemed early) and other features, there are compelling reasons for building your own bond portfolio. If you are so inclined, here are some hints to "beat the dealer":

- Buy bonds when they are underwritten and offered for the first time (if you have a broker, he or she can inform you of upcoming offerings). This way you will pay no more markup than the institutional buyers, whose bargaining power forces the underwriters to price bonds realistically.

- Shop the market. Call a few brokers and tell them what you are looking for: The quality, approximate yield, and amount you want to buy, *and make it clear that you are shopping.* Offerings are likely to be more competitively priced if your broker knows you are a comparison shopper.

Wall Street Speak

Laddering. This strategy is bond-speak for buying bonds according to a predetermined schedule of when they mature—every 1 year, 2 years, 3 years, or on whatever schedule suits your fancy. Laddering spares you from making heroic interest rate forecasts; you're admitting what the experts won't: that interest rates are unpredictable. With laddering, no matter where interest rates go, you have a predetermined schedule for the return of some of your money. As your bonds mature, you reinvest at the top end of the "ladder"—the longest maturity date—to continue the systematic investment program for as long as it suits your purpose. It's an uncomplicated strategy, and it allows you a fair measure of liquidity. You might want to invest $100,000 over a 5-year period, with $20,000 maturity for each year, so that each succeeding year you will have $20,000 come due—and you have the option to reinvest it in new 5-year bonds, each time.

- Shop the Internet. Some organizations are vowing to make the bond market more transparent and competitive by offering bonds on the Web; there's no reason they can't succeed.

- Assuming that you deal with reputable brokerage firms *and plan to hold until maturity,* leaving your bonds in their custody is a good idea as opposed to having them delivered to you. If bonds are going to be redeemed, or something else happens that you should know about, it becomes the broker's responsibility to inform you.

- If you have your bonds in your possession (not in a broker's custody) and you want to sell them, shop the market *and* the Internet. If you are selling a bond portfolio (as often happens with estate liquidations), ask brokers for *competitive bids.* This technique is used by experienced money managers and estate and trust attorneys.

- When you hold your bonds at a brokerage firm, some brokers figure they've "got you," and they don't have to bother to be as competitive with bids for your bonds. But they really don't have you, except in terms of convenience. You don't have to sell through your brokerage firm, and if you do, you could easily lose an extra $1,000 to $2,000 on a $200,000 portfolio. Check bond prices on the Internet to make sure you are getting fair bids before you approve a sale.

FUNDamental Facts

Investinginbonds.com

If you're inclined to invest in individual bonds, *Investinginbonds.com* is one whale of a Web site. It provides just about any information or resource you can imagine and more. The extensive glossary defines any bond term imaginable. If you want precise definitions of yield burning, or active or toggle tranches, you'll find them here. In addition, they tell you things you really should know, such as a yield calculator, where you plug in your state and tax bracket and it helps compare municipal returns. Maintained by the Bond Market Association, it includes links to dealers all over the country. *Investinginbonds.com* is a good place to get an idea of real bond price levels, very helpful if you are shopping for bids or looking to invest.

Bond Funds

Most bond *funds* are portfolios of scores or even hundreds of different bonds. They are usually categorized by types of issuers, such as government, corporate, or municipal bond funds. Structurally, there are four main types of bond funds:

1. Managed closed-end funds (see Chapter 11).
2. Unit investment trusts.

3. Managed open-end funds.

4. Index open-end funds.

Closed-end funds are covered in Chapter 11, and for the reasons described there, they have limited appeal for most bond fund investors. Unit investment trusts (UITs) have comparatively low annual fees but they typically have up-front loads ranging from 1½ percent to 3 percent. Compared to open-end bond funds, UITs are attractive in one respect: During periods of relatively high interest rates, investors are not subject to "income dilution" caused by fellow investors joining them as rates decline, so UIT investors can enjoy a more consistent income stream. Compared to closed-end funds (CEFs), UITs have another decided advantage—they can be sold at net asset value (NAV) at any time. Therefore they don't suffer from the discounts that can plague CEF investors.

The two remaining categories, open-end managed and unmanaged (index) funds, are similar, and can be evaluated using the same criteria. The major difference between them is that managed funds will generally have higher expense ratios. From your standpoint, however, the most important criteria should be their average maturity (interest rate risk) and quality (the risk of default).

1. *Maturity* Morningstar categorizes bond fund maturities as: short term (average maturities 4 years), intermediate (average 9.7 years), and long-term (16.2 years). Usually, longer maturities offer higher returns and fund prices are more sensitive to interest rate changes. Funds with shorter average maturities usually deliver lower returns and are less volatile. These rules of thumb apply when there is a normal yield curve (short-term rates of interest are lower than long-term rates). When there is an inverted yield curve (short-term rates are higher than long-term rates) better yields are available from short- and intermediate-term funds.

2. *Quality* Rating agencies assign quality ratings to individual bonds based on the financial strength of the issuer and their assessments of the likelihood of default.

Controlling Risk

If you are a bond fund investor, you have much more risk control than a stock fund investor; and to increase returns, you can make a reasonable estimate of the increased risk you are assuming. At the extremes of the risk spectrum, bond fund profiles are:

- *Highest safety/lowest yield* High average credit quality and short-term average maturities when the yield curve is "normal." Because the risks are low, yields on these bond funds are also relatively lower.

- *Lowest safety/highest yield* Low credit quality and long-term average maturities. Here, the prospect of high yields can offset the risks.

While the safety of individual bonds is assigned by the rating services such as Standard & Poor's or Moody's, the average quality of a bond *fund* is disclosed in the fund's prospectus, and by fund-rating services such as Morningstar.

Wall Street Speak

INSURED MUNICIPAL BONDS

There is a large market for insured municipal bonds, mainly from individual investors who are seeking increased safety of their principal. When bonds are underwritten by bond dealers, issuers like school districts purchase insurance for their bonds from private insurance companies. The insurers guarantee timely payment of principal and/or interest in the event of default. Seven major insurers provide coverage that automatically gets an AAA rating by the rating agencies. The advantage to bond issuers is that the high credit rating allows them to pay lower interest on their bonds. In addition to individually insured municipal bonds, you can also invest in insured municipal bond funds that only hold insured bonds in their portfolios.

Bond funds usually offer more safety than individual bonds of comparable quality, particularly for smaller investors, because of the instant diversification they provide; you own a proportionate share of *all* the bonds in a portfolio. If one or two bonds default, the diversification greatly reduces losses.

Absolute Safety, But . . .

If you are especially concerned with safety, a government bond fund is the best bet, and the lowest-cost funds are the best choice, offering diversification and convenience. Bond funds share certain structural problems, however. For example, bond funds, unlike individual bonds, have *no maturity date.* In theory, a bond fund is perpetual because it is continually replenishing its portfolio. A fund with an average portfolio maturity of 10 years might contain maturities ranging from 7 to 13 years. The 10-year average maturity will continue and in 7 years, the average maturity will still be 10 years.

For the same reason, a bond fund's stated yield is only an approximation made on the day you buy it. As time passes, as interest rates change, as the manager makes changes, and as other investors invest in or redeem shares in the fund, the actual income will fluctuate. For that reason, bond fund investors can only make a semieducated guess as to the amount of income they will receive in the future.

Bond Fund Costs

Ongoing fund expenses can be particularly burdensome for bond fund investors. In addition, sales loads (up-front, ongoing, or back-end charges) reduce the amount invested and/or the income, ultimately reducing returns which, compared to stocks, have not been that magnificent to begin with. No matter how and when they are assessed, loads reduce the amount invested, and the reduced principal generates less income and the amount returned when you redeem. Loads can be as high as 4 percent to 5 percent.

With managed funds, in addition to loads you have to consider the effect of the expense ratio, and annual fees that typically run to around 0.7 percent to 1.0 percent, but 1.25 percent is not uncommon. The higher the fees, the more they reduce your income. An expense ratio of 1 percent might not sound like much, but a reduction of your return from 7.0 percent to 6.0 percent translates into a hefty 14.3 percent reduction in your income. Measured against historical returns, bond fund fees are proportionately higher than those for stock funds.

Bond Fund Vagaries

Investing in an individual portfolio of high-quality bonds is a simple exercise; you pay a specific price, and you know your exact yield and when they will mature. If you invest in bond *funds,* however, there are more variables:

- *Possible income dilution* If you invest in a fund when interest rates are 8 percent, and rates later fall to 7 percent, new investors' money gets invested at the lower rate. The result: your income drops to less than 8 percent. In practice, this dilution works against bond fund investors more often than not, because investors tend to buy more when interest rates are falling—and prices are rising—and they stop buying or begin redeeming shares when rates begin to rise. Prior to 1994, investors had been buying bond funds in record numbers. Beginning with that year, rates began to rise and bond prices fell sharply. After prices fell, in late 1994 and 1995, net inflows to bond funds were practically zero. Investors didn't resume buying, on a net basis, until a couple of years later, when prices exceeded their previous highs.

- *Costs* As mentioned, the inverse correlation between costs and returns is even stronger than bond funds than for stock funds.

- *Unpredictability* Unlike investors in individual bonds, neither the principal amount nor the expected income can be predetermined.

Modest Expectations

Suppose you had invested in both an intermediate government bond fund and a small-cap (blend) stock fund 5 years ago. Suppose further, that you were omniscient and both your picks ended up with returns equal to the average of the top 10 percent performers in their respective categories. How would your two funds compare in terms of performance?

For the period ending March 31, 2000, the average return of the bond funds' top 10 percent (30 of 302 funds) was 7.06 percent, compared with 5.96 percent for the category as a whole. The best and brightest—and probably thriftiest—bond managers beat their peers by only 1.10 percent per annum. Meanwhile, the top 10 percent stock managers' (9 out of 93) returns averaged 30.61 percent versus 16.42 percent for their category, beating their peers by an average 14.19 percent a year. Winning stock fund investors (who paid average expense ratios of 1.55%) got much more bang for their management buck than did winning bond fund investors (1.09% average expense ratios). Conclusion: Since expenses are the biggest predictable determinant of returns, it is silly to waste money on a supposedly brilliant bond fund with high expenses and/or an expert to choose them for you: Even if you beat the odds, the "jackpot" is small.

Costs and Conclusions

There have been many studies showing the direct correlation between bond fund costs and returns, but one more can't hurt, particularly one that covers most categories. What is interesting is the wide range in costs along with its effects on final returns across all sectors and maturities.

Table 7.2 shows the average expenses and returns of Morningstar's major bond fund categories, along with low-cost Vanguard funds, where available, for the 10-year period ending December 31, 1999. Vanguard's funds (italicized) are used as illustration because they had the largest selection of low-cost funds available during the period. The results show that costs are a key determinant in performance.

There is no alchemy in the fact that the returns of 11 out of 12 Vanguard Funds beat their respective categories. The only fund that lagged, Vanguard High Yield Bond Fund—a junk bond fund—did so by only 14 basis points ($^{14}/_{100ths}$ of 1 percent). We couldn't help but suspect, knowing Vanguard, that their fund return lagged because it took less risk. While a "high quality junk bond fund" is an oxymoron, a look at the portfolios of Vanguard's fund versus that of the average junk bond fund (as of March 31, 2000) confirmed our suspicion: The average fund had 76 percent of its portfolio in single-B or below rated paper,

TABLE 7.2 Vanguard Expenses and Returns on $10,000 versus Morningstar Major Bond Fund Categories

CATEGORY	AVERAGE % EXPENSE RATIO	AVG. ANNUAL % RETURN— 10 YEAR	RETURN
GOVERNMENT BOND			
Short-Term	0.88	5.99	$17,897
Vanguard Short-Term Federal	0.27	6.59	$18,923
Intermediate-Term	1.09	6.55	$18,855
Vanguard GNMA	0.30	7.71	$21,020
Long-Term	0.78	7.18	$20,004
Vanguard Long-Term U.S. Treasury	0.28	8.15	$21,885
GENERAL BOND			
Short-Term	0.88	6.32	$18,457
Vanguard Short-Term Corp.	0.25	7.02	$19,701
Intermediate-Term	0.95	7.03	$19,730
Vanguard Total Bond Market Index	0.20	7.54	$20,679
Long-Term	1.07	7.48	$20,581
Vanguard Long-Term Bond Index	0.20	8.58	$22,784
HIGH YIELD BOND	1.29	9.95	$25,815
Vanguard High Yield Bond	0.29	9.81	$25,500
MUNICIPAL BOND (NATIONAL)			
Short-Term	0.69	4.98	$16,260
Vanguard Limited-Term Tax Exempt	0.18	5.33	$16,801
Intermediate-Term	0.96	5.91	$17,761
Vanguard Interm-Term Tax Exempt	0.18	6.66	$19,064
Long-Term	1.05	6.01	$17,927
Vanguard High-Yield Tax Exempt	0.18	7.07	$19,801
Vanguard Insured Long-Term Tax Exempt	0.19	6.84	$19,384
Vanguard Long-Term Tax Exempt	0.18	6.98	$19,632

TABLE 7.3 Comparison of High-Yield Funds

BONDS RATED	AVERAGE HIGH-YIELD FUND—% INVESTED	VANGUARD HIGH-YIELD FUND—% INVESTED
U.S. Government/Agency	0.00	6.70
BBB	2.00	7.90
BB	20.00	40.00
B	61.00	45.10
Below B	8.00	0.30
Nonrated	7.00	0.00

while Vanguard had only 45.4 percent, showing that, even in this lower quality category, Vanguard is a prudent manager. Table 7.3 shows how Vanguard's "low quality" fund stacked up.

Planning Your Portfolio

Using bonds to increase income (or provide a measure of predictability) is a relatively simple, step-by-step process. Starting with asset allocation, how much of your portfolio do you want to commit to bonds or bond funds? No matter what your age, if you have a low risk tolerance or need income, you might need more bonds. If you anticipate educational expenses, or other predictable obligations, investing in bonds that will mature when the money is needed is an alternative to leaving money in savings accounts or taking the risks of stocks. For example, you can buy bonds that will mature when your child reaches college age, and you can feel secure that the money will be there when you need it.

For your bond allocation, should you be investing in taxable or tax-free municipals? That depends on your tax bracket. Don't make the surprisingly common mistake of investing in tax-free bonds just because "tax-free" sounds so appealing. Base your comparison of taxable versus tax-free bonds net after-tax returns. *It's what you keep that counts,* and if your after-tax returns are higher with taxable bonds, that's the course you should take.

Additional bond research resources are available using major fund Web sites such as Morningstar, Vanguard, Fidelity, and T. Rowe Price. If you are cyberchallenged, a few hours spent with Morningstar at the library or reading the *Forbes* or *Consumers Report* annual mutual fund issues will provide all you need to know to make reasoned, sensible bond fund selections.

Just as when investing in bonds, consider laddering your funds' average maturities to dampen portfolio volatility. And don't pay hefty fees to experts to pick bond funds for you. If you have a sizable portfolio ($250,000 or more), they will siphon off hundreds or even thousands of dollars every year for something you can do yourself. All you need to do is you stick with low-cost funds, such as Vanguard's or Fidelity Spartan's, that invest in quality bonds, run by well-known sponsors. Bond fund selection is not that complicated— you really need to determine only four things:

1. Do you need taxable or tax-exempt bonds? (check your tax bracket for the answer).
2. What average portfolio quality do you want? BBB to AAA?
3. What portfolio average maturities do you want? 1 year, 5 years, longer?
4. How much are you going to pay in fees and expenses? Check the bond funds' prospectuses.

While you might prefer to spend a day at the beach, the time you devote to this simple research will save you many dollars in fees every year. Give yourself a reward—take a small portion of the saved fees and treat yourself to a luxurious weekend at a posh resort that you might not otherwise think you can afford. Suddenly, you *can* afford it. And you deserve it.

A Case Study

The following example shows what one woman, with no experience in finance, did to prepare herself for the future after her husband's death. It shows what you can do if you use common sense and are willing to spend some time learning what's available.

Anne, 60 years old and recently widowed, had no investment experience. She owned her home and had few expenses, but needed to invest $250,000 from her husband's life insurance and $240,000 in his 403(b) plan. Social Security income amounted to $950 per month.

One idea she kept hearing, appealed to her— she sought help from a fee-based financial planner, instead of a broker that typically relies on commissions. One of her friends who had been widowed a few years earlier recommended Susan, a fee-based planner, who met with Anne several times.

At their first meeting, Anne decided to hire Susan on an hourly basis ($120 per hour) because the program she envisioned was fairly simple and, once set up, would not require ongoing, intense management. Susan estimated that the total hours billed would amount to no more than ten, and that once Anne's portfolio was established, it would probably be advisable that they meet every two years thereafter to make sure that Anne's situation was proceeding according to plan.

Anne's situation was relatively simple. She had no liquid assets, other than the $250,000 insurance proceeds and the $240,000 in the 403(b) account. Withdrawals from the 403(b) plan (rolled over into her IRA) were going to be taxable income, so Susan helped Anne schedule them to minimize the tax liability, making sure that she would withdraw only what was needed each year.

Susan felt Anne needed a 6½ percent to 7 percent annual return on her investment for spendable income. However, she also needed some participation in stocks as protection against inflation, because at Anne's age (60), she had a life expectancy of over 20 years. Susan's solution: a portfolio of low-cost bond funds—$120,000 in each—with $35,000 in a money market fund that allowed Anne to withdraw money at any time, to cover possible emergencies. Anne also invested $95,000 (approximately 20% of her total assets) in Vanguard's Total Stock Market Portfolio, a stock fund indexed to the entire U.S. stock market, to provide growth.

Because of Anne's 20-year-plus life expectancy, Susan expressed concern about the relatively small stock allocation, but Anne felt that she needed that level of spendable income to support her lifestyle. In addition, it seemed likely that she might sell her home and move to a smaller home or a condominium at some time in the next few years, which would provide some additional capital.

After unanticipated 403(b) paperwork, Susan ended up billing Anne for 11 hours (a total of $1,320). While Anne was a bit shocked by the amount of Susan's fee, her daughter pointed out that it amounted to only $^{26}/_{100}$ of 1 percent of the amount invested. Put in these terms, the fee seemed reasonable—far less than she would have paid a brokerage firm. Her daughter also pointed out that it was very unlikely that a brokerage firm would recommend funds with expenses as low as those recommended by Susan. Overall, Anne was pleased with her portfolio:

	DOLLAR INVESTMENT	APPROXIMATE YIELD (%)	ESTIMATED YEARLY INCOME
USAA GNMA Fund	$120,000	7.09	$ 8,500
Vanguard Long-term Treasury Fund	120,000	6.41	7,692
Vanguard Long-term Corporate Fund	120,000	7.61	9,132
USAA Treasury Money Market Fund	35,000	5.34	1,860
Vanguard Total Stock Market Portfolio	95,000	1.00	950
Total Investment	$490,000	5.74	$28,134

Anne might not have totally understood how much of a bargain she got: Sound, impartial advice, high-quality bond funds managed by large experienced fund sponsors, and a relatively maintenance-free portfolio. Her cost: average annual expenses of about 27 basis points (slightly more than ¼ of 1%)—approximately one-third to one-quarter of what she would have had to pay to invest in the average no-load bond fund. Her savings worked out to approximately $3,000 the first year—including Susan's fee—and will be over $4,000 per year thereafter.

Compare this with what Anne would be facing if she had put her money in load bond funds, where their alphabet soup magic would eventually have extracted an additional $10,000 to $12,000, one way or another, during the first few years—in addition to higher ongoing annual expenses. As shown in Anne's example, if you have sufficient assets, you can use bond funds to create stability and income. They may not create excitement, but will provide you with a relatively secure future.

In Chapter 8, we travel to more exciting territory—the world of new-fund investing. Here's an investment strategy that can offer you remarkable growth potential, if you're willing to put in a little effort at the start and maintain a disciplined strategy.

CHAPTER 8

New-Fund Investing—
Betting with the Odds
and the Insiders

**People who like this
sort of thing will find
this the sort of thing
they like.**

—Abraham Lincoln

In the following pages, you'll learn about new fund investing. By new funds, we mean stock mutual funds that are being offered to the public for the first time. With the right combination of experienced managers, some of these new-comers have turned in excellent 1- and 2-year performances. We'll explain why this happens so you can decide if new-fund investing is a good strategy for you.

As discussed, there are few areas where managed fund investors have an above-average chance of consistently achieving above-average performance. The law of averages, costs, taxes, and the structural disadvantages (to be discussed) of open-end mutual funds inevitably grind most managed funds' returns down to below index-fund performance levels.

Above-average returns are primarily driven by sector and style. For example, if growth or technology or small-cap stocks are in favor, funds in those sectors will deliver the best performance, and little else much matters. If you're in the right place at the right time, you're in the clover; get it wrong, and you're in the soup. But forecasting sector popularity is very difficult, as the randomness of a sector's ups and downs shows (see Figure 4.1). However, there is a niche where you can boost the odds of above-average performance without sticking your neck way out into narrow sectors or leveraged funds (discussed in Chapter 4): a disciplined strategy of buying *diversified* funds when they are first offered.

Heard on the Street

Here's an interesting case for actively managed mutual funds over index funds. Performance numbers for the active managers would be a lot better if you looked only at nimbler new funds and left out the bloated old ones that are the real underperformers.

"Active funds that have been more recently invested outperform in a significant way the active funds that were long ago invested," Wharton School Professor A. Craig MacKinlay in an observation made during the Investment Management Consultants Association conference in San Francisco . . .

InvestmentNews, May 3, 1999.

New funds aren't for everybody: "Everybody" is preoccupied investing in four- and five-star funds. Compared with "proven" funds, new funds are harder to invest in because information is usually scanty. There are no Morningstar write-ups, star ratings, proven track records, article reprints, or glossy booklets; just a stark, usually black-and-white prospectus. New funds also aren't on anybody's recommended or approved list. Most gurus regard them as just idle curiosities—worthy perhaps of a revisit in a few years—but only *after* they've proven themselves.

Heard on the Street

What makes new funds so devilishly attractive? So mysteriously alluring? Like a blind date. A new baby. A surprise party. Your first trip to an exotic location. We long for adventure. New horizons. We're explorers. The unknown turns us on.

And yet. And yet. Inevitably. Something happens. "It" disappears. The magic fades. Romance cools. Babies grow up. Gifts wear out. And new funds eventually lose their edge. Like clockwork.

Dr. Paul B. Farrell, *CBS MarketWatch* May 8, 2000.

Orthodoxy, however, overlooks that:

- A disproportionate number of new funds show up regularly on the list of top performers, year after year.
- Industry insiders regularly invest in new funds.

Have you noticed how many top-performing funds lack 3-year track records, and/or how many you've never heard of, although you might recognize the sponsor? It's not merely a curiosity but the result of performance-boosting characteristics that are unique to new funds . They provide a legitimate opportunity to consistently increase your returns. The June 1999 *SmartMoney* cover story on new funds challenged skeptical readers: "Try these numbers on for size: In 1998, 11 of the top 20 domestic diversified stock funds were less than two years old. In 1997, nine of the top 20 were new, and in 1996, 13 of the chart-toppers weren't much beyond their first birthday."

Mere coincidence? Not likely. The article points out: "In Denver, home to such mutual funds giants as Janus, Founders, Berger, and Invesco, it's become something of a ritual for insiders to buy shares of the new funds." The public shuns new funds, but people in the investment business understand their edge. In addition to *SmartMoney*, studies and citations of new funds' outperformance have been reported in *Forbes, Barron's, Mutual Funds, Value Line Mutual Fund Advisor, Lipper Analytical Services, No Load Analyst, Fidelity Insight, InvestmentNews,* and *Kiplinger's Personal Finance Magazine*.

Characteristics of Top Funds

In 1998, using Morningstar Principia Plus, we analyzed the 25 top-performing diversified U.S. stock funds in each year during the 1993–1997 period. Since the top performers changed from year to year, the study yielded a total of 125 funds. During the period of our study, our "top 25s" delivered an average 40.77 percent return, compared with 20.25 percent return of the Standard & Poor's 500 Index and 16.17 percent of the average stock fund. Our objective was to identify characteristics common to top-performing funds that could be used to help predict above-average performance. Four criteria showed significant correlation to superior returns:

1. *Fund age* Eighty-two funds (66%) were less than 3 (calendar) years old. Sixty one (49%) were 1 year old or less.

2. *Asset size* The median size of the funds ranged from a tiny $7 million (1996) to $85 million (1993). Small funds had a clear advantage: No fund began with more than $2 billion in assets and 25 (20%) started with virtually none. With two possible exceptions, asset growth was not artificially restricted by limiting investors—all were generally available to the public.

3. *Manager category* Ninety-six funds (77%) were managed by independent managers (advisory and mutual fund firms), with the remainder variously managed by insurance companies, banks, and brokerage firms. Brokers' funds lagged by a country mile, with only a 5 percent showing.

4. *Investment sector* Eighty-five (70%) of our 125 outperformers were small-cap funds. This showing was particularly notable—and possibly surprising—because small-cap sector returns significantly trailed both the mid- and large-cap sectors during the period studied.

Analysis of our results turned up the following observations:

- If, at the beginning of each of the years studied, had you used Morningstar ratings to try and forecast which funds would dominate the list of top 25 performers, two thirds of the top performers could not have even been considered; they lacked the 3-year record necessary for a Morningstar rating.

- If you were investing through a "full service" (wirehouse) broker like Merrill Lynch or Paine Webber, the odds are poor that they would have invested in a top-25 fund; the odds are high that they would have steered you toward their own in-house funds, which had morbidly low chances of achieving top-25 (or even average) performance.

- If you were investing in funds that were currently popular—riding the wave of the large-cap sector's high returns—you could not have invested in 70 percent of the winners, because they were in the out-of-favor small-cap sector.

- Only if you were in the *very* small minority of investors who were actively searching for both new and small-cap funds, might you have invested in any of them.

In 1998 and 1999, we conducted a new top-25 analysis as defined earlier. The findings were similar to previous studies with one exception. In 1998, the market's obsession with large-cap stocks resulted in a 64 percent large-cap showing among the top-performing funds. In 1999, however, the long-term trend reasserted itself: Small caps represented 64 percent of the top 25.

New-Fund Effect Confirmation

In 1998, the Charles Schwab Center for Investment Research published a 5-year study, entitled "Do New Funds Offer Better Performance?"* Based on an analysis of the 100 top-performing funds in the Domestic Equity Fund Universe (which includes both load and no-load funds), the study explored the "new-fund effect." In it, Schwab compared the percentage of new funds (opened within the preceding calendar year) with the percentage of new funds among

---

* © 1998 Schwab Center for Investment Research. Reprinted with permission.

TABLE 8.1 New Funds (Opened within Preceding Year) in Top 100 and in Domestic Equity Fund Universe

	1993	1994	1995	1996	1997	5-YR. AVG.
Percentage of Funds in Top 100 That Are New	17	23	20	33	16	22
Percentage of Funds in Universe	17	16	13	12	13	14

Source: Excerpted and used by permission, "The New Fund Effect: Fact or Fiction?" *No-Load Fund Analyst,* November 1996.

the 100 top-returning diversified domestic equity funds during the 5-year period, 1993 through 1997. Their findings are summarized in Table 8.1.

Their observation: "If there were no new-fund performance advantage, those two numbers would be roughly equal each year. They were not." Put another way, *of all funds opened during the period, 50 percent more showed up as top performers than would have happened on a random basis.*

Companies' Sizes and Investment Style Affected Performance

Next, they asked the question, "Was the 'new-fund effect' concentrated among specific fund groups?" They found:

> The new-fund effect among small-company funds was stronger than for all new domestic equity funds (which included large-cap growth, value and blend funds, and small-cap growth, value and blend funds). In fact, the number of new *small-company* funds showing up in the top 100 funds . . . was almost *three times* as great as the percentage of new small company funds in the fund universe as a whole." (emphasis added)

Schwab also wanted to know if style made the difference:

> New small-cap growth funds, on average, outperformed their older peers fairly steadily over their first 18 months. The cumulative outperformance was just over seven percentage points after 12 months and about nine percentage points after 18 months. New funds in the other five categories (large-cap growth, large-cap value, large-cap blend, small-cap value and small-cap blend funds) were much less impressive, with cumulative outperformance after 18 months totaling just over one percentage point.

Schwab also determined, with one important exception, that new-fund outperformance was partly because the funds took greater risk—they were more prone to price swings. The exception: "Interestingly, new small-cap growth funds assumed the *least extra risk* (over the first 12 months) even though they provided the *most additional gain*" [emphasis added]. The study also provided another significant, and particularly useful, finding: "Irrespective of fund category, much of the outperformance was concentrated in the *first six months* of the new funds' existence. For example, in the small-cap growth category, new funds outperformed old funds by approximately 1% per month for the first six months. This rate of outperformance slowed to about 0.3% per month in months 7 through 18 and disappeared entirely after 18 months." This finding, and our own "real money" experience managing client accounts, is distilled in the recommended new-fund buy/sell timing strategy described later in the chapter.

No-Load Fund Analyst's New-Fund Study

The Schwab study confirmed the findings of other studies of new small and mid-cap funds' superior returns, including one reported in the November 1996 issue of the widely respected *No-Load Fund Analyst* (NLFA) newsletter. It is important to recognize that *No-Load Fund Analyst* uses a proprietary approach that categorizes funds differently than other analysts, such as Morningstar, Charles Schwab, or Lipper Analytical. We don't want to get tangled with precise category comparisons and definitions and how they differ from each other; suffice it to say that they are all looking at the same pizza—the mutual fund universe—and slicing it just differently enough to call it their own. NLFA's "emerging growth" category is a close equivalent to Morningstar's small-cap growth category.

The NLFA's analysis of the returns of all 303 small- and mid-cap new funds launched between January 1990 and June 1996 are shown in Table 8.2.

No-Load Fund Analyst summed up their findings:

> The table confirms our expectation that small-cap and earnings momentum funds would show a greater new fund effect. Specifically:
>
> 1. The greatest increase in returns from buying new funds was in the Emerging Growth category. Plus, these higher returns were accompanied by less downside risk. Buying every new Emerging Growth fund that came out in the '90s, rather than holding the older funds, would have increased annualized cumulative returns by 5%—almost a 30% increase in returns.
> 2. New Growth-At-A-Price funds, both small-cap and small/mid-cap and Small/Mid-Cap Earnings Momentum Funds also showed significant outperformance with less downside risk.
> 3. Buying new Small-Cap Value funds added nothing to returns, while buying new Small/Mid-Cap Value funds actually would have been an inferior strategy to holding the pre-'90s (older) group.

TABLE 8.2 Old Funds versus New Funds

	AVERAGE CUMULATIVE ANNUAL RETURN (%)		
	OLD FUNDS ONLY	OLD + NEW FUNDS	NEW FUNDS ONLY
Emerging Growth	17.0	19.1	22.0
Small-Cap GAAP	14.8	16.0	16.8
Small-Cap Value	14.0	14.2	14.1
Small/Mid-Cap Earnings Momentum	16.5	17.0	19.1
Small/Mid-Cap GAAP	13.1	13.9	15.4
Small/Mid-Cap Value	11.5	10.5	9.7

Source: Excerpted and used by permission, "The New Fund Effect: Fact or Fiction?" *No-Load Fund Analyst,* November 1996.

Again, although the precise categorizations differ and the time periods vary depending on who is doing the study, general conclusions are easy to draw:

- New funds outperform their older peers.
- Small-cap growth funds outperform most often and two studies found that they did it without increased risk relative to their sector.
- The new-fund effect is most powerful during a fund's first 6 months.

Compounded Advantages

If you are going to invest in new funds, it's important to understand, as industry insiders do, why they have advantages. There is probably no single reason for the favorable new-fund effect. More likely, it is the result of several positive factors working together, to varying degrees at different times. Without understanding the "new-fund effect," you might not have the necessary staying power, because you'll get little encouragement from experts. One (inevitable) misstep, and you'll be tempted to go on to something else. If that happens, you'll miss a great opportunity to allow the probabilities to compound your returns over the longer term. Here's what new funds have in their favor.

Widest Stock Selection

A small, new, small-cap fund is ideal because, compared with other categories, it has the largest number of stocks to choose from. Table 8.3 presents the "opportunity ratios" of the various types of funds (large-, mid-, small-cap, etc.), based on an average fund portfolio of 100 stocks—the higher the ratio, the greater the number of investment choices and opportunities for outperformance. This ratio

TABLE 8.3 Opportunity Ratio

ASSET CLASS	ASSUMING A 100-STOCK PORTFOLIO	
	NUMBER OF COMPANIES	OPPORTUNITY RATIO
Large-Cap	125	1 in 1.25
Mid-Cap	529	1 in 5
Small-Cap	1,106	1 in 11
Micro-Cap	5,106	1 in 51
Total	6,806	

Source: Kern Capital Management, LLC analysis of U.S. equities (market capitalization's $10 million or more) from Market Guide Stockquest U.S. Database, September 30,1999. Courtesy of Fremont U.S. Micro-Cap Fund.

takes the total number of available stocks in a particular size category (e.g., there are only 125 large-cap stocks) and divides it by the number of stocks in the average fund's portfolio (in this case, 100). Thus, a typical large-cap fund has a 1.25 opportunity ratio—by definition it *has* to own most of the stocks in the large-cap universe—100 stocks out of only 125. A small-cap fund, on the other hand, has over 1,100 investment possibilities and a much more favorable ratio: 1 in 11. It's clear that your chances for outperformance are much greater with small-caps.

As assets grow, the number of stocks to select from shrinks, because the smallest companies become impractical or impossible to invest in. One reason for this is liquidity: Purchase candidates are eliminated because they don't trade often enough to allow the manager to establish—or later sell—them, or they are too small to have a meaningful impact on the fund's returns. Another reason is regulatory: Diversified funds aren't allowed to invest initially more than 5 percent of their assets in any one company.

In addition to being forced to buy larger companies as their assets increase, larger funds can't be as selective in putting their money to work—they *have* to buy stock in more companies. Funds that must own larger companies, and more of them, dilute the effectiveness of even the savviest of stock pickers. Is it reasonable to expect a manager to be as enthusiastic about his second 50, 100, or even 200 stocks?

Traveling Light

New-fund managers start out with a clean slate, unlike their older-fund peers who are carrying the inevitable baggage of ideas-turned-sour, stocks that have turned doubtful, or stocks that have fallen too far to sell. New-fund managers can invest in the ideas that they, their analysts, and their sources like best right now, not many months ago.

Size Advantage

Small asset size doesn't drive performance, but it does *allow* for outperformance. The only runner in a race wearing running shoes is more likely to finish at the front of the pack if all of her competitors are wearing combat boots. John Bogle puts it bluntly: "Size can kill." But size is one problem most new-fund managers don't have.

This is an important advantage. When the "size problem" looms, it can overwhelm the effectiveness of even the best stock picker: Large orders can drive a stock's price up or down so much that it reduces returns. The manager of a $1.3 billion small-cap fund was quoted, "It would be disingenuous to say that it's just as easy to run a small-cap fund with $1 billion in assets as one with $50 million. With $50 million, you're probably going to do better." And Daniel Miller, an investment officer of the Putnam Funds, told the *Wall Street Journal,* "Anyone who tells you there are not diseconomies of scale is lying." New-fund investors, however, usually don't have to worry about size. If they invest near inception and fund assets grow because of superior performance, by the time the size problem looms, they're already selling to later investors who are attracted by the superior track record that the fund established in earlier years. New-fund investors pass the size problem to later investors.

Market Inefficiency Opportunities

A talented manager can add the greatest value (superior performance) in the relatively inefficient small-cap sector. Since small companies are followed by few analysts, their information is less widely disseminated, so opportunities for "outsmarting" the market are more plentiful. The *Wall Street Journal* told readers to "expect to see some of the best [stock] performances to come from companies you've never heard of. A report by Prudential Securities has found that the less a small stock is followed by brokerage-firm analysts, the more it rallies when it beats those analysts' expectations." And *Worth* magazine quoted John Spears, a Tweedy, Browne partner and fund manager: "The only way you can buy a company cheap is when it is obscure or in bad shape." Obscure

---

Heard on the Street

In the last few years, fund marketers have had considerable success launching funds with "special subscription periods"—pre-offering periods where investors send money in before opening day. Although it provides the certainty of a set price on day-one, it also allows assets to build up, in some recent cases to uncomfortably large amounts, thereby smothering one of the benefits of investing in new funds. It's "special" for the funds and distributors, but not for investors. What's new?

Charles Jaffee, SMARTINVESTING Columnist
The Boston Globe, March 1, 2000

---

generally means small- or mid-cap. An "obscure large-cap company" is an oxymoron; if a large-cap company is cheap, it's probably cheap because it has real problems, as bruised large-cap value fund portfolio managers have found in recent years. So, while it's never easy for fund managers to discover hidden gems, their odds are much improved in the relatively large universe of small companies.

Research Concentration

If the fund is part of a large fund family, such as Fidelity or T. Rowe Price, the manager has more opportunity to cherry-pick using analysis from the large research infrastructure of in-house ("buy side") analysts. Large sponsors are also likely to be the first to get fresh ideas from brokerage ("sell side") analysts and consultants because they can offer higher rewards (more trading commissions) for original or fresh research ideas.

Uniqueness Opportunity

Large-cap funds' sameness is the result of relatively few stocks to choose from, as shown in Table 8.3. The result is a significant overlap in their portfolios and a narrower range of their returns. Small-cap funds, on the other hand, can be *very* different from each other. Like size, uniqueness doesn't *drive* returns, but it does provide more room for a talented manager's ability to shine. It's one less obstacle to stellar returns.

IPO Funneling

In a rising market, a large fund sponsor funneling hefty IPO allocations into a small fund can provide pyrotechnic returns. IPO prices that "pop"—or spike up sharply in price, two and three times the opening price, and sometimes more—

in the first few hours of trading are an obvious bonanza for lucky (or well-connected) recipients. Further, their soaring prices are relatively predictable. It doesn't take a quantum physicist on staff to predict a big pop if 2 million shares are being offered and "preliminary indications" (the equivalent of preoffering "buy" orders that are not permitted) are for 18 million shares. The practice of IPO distribution is probably the least democratized on Wall Street; institutions and wealthy investors typically receive 70 percent to 80 percent. Institutions with the biggest clout—a number of mutual fund families among them—get the lion's share.

The use of "hot" initial public offerings to boost returns is a sensitive one with the industry and at the SEC. Periodically, the SEC grumbles about the methodology investment bankers use to allocate IPOs, and occasionally they have penalized investment bankers for improperly using IPOs to curry favor. The *Wall Street Journal* (September 9, 1999) reported, "The issue of fair allocation of IPOs among the myriad funds run by individual fund firms is an ongoing subject of discussion."

Occasionally, the issue gets beyond the discussion stage. In September 1999, the SEC fined Van Kampen Growth Fund $100,000 and its former chief investment officer $25,000 for boosting the performance (61.99% in 1996) of a tiny ($200,000 to $380,000) fund. It was not available to the public during its "incubation period," but then was opened, and according to the SEC, Van Kampen used the artificially induced performance record to market it.

SmartMoney cited an instance of how an IPO pop can boost fund returns: "In a small fund, the pop you get from a 475 percent gain can really make a difference. Invesco Endeavor's (up 38.5% its first two months in 1998 and 84.21% in 1999) tiny stake in MarketWatch.com—which it bought when the company went public in early January at $17—caused the fund to jump 1.05 percent when it turned around and sold the shares for $98. 'It hit our price target,' jokes manager Tim Miller."

Positive Cash Inflows

Like martinis, consistent and moderate cash inflow has salubrious effects. *Too much* inflow plays havoc with performance because managers can't find enough attractive opportunities for all the cash. Countless "hot" funds have turned tepid, then cold, as torrents of incoming cash swamped their managers' abilities to put it to use. Outflows, usually the result of falling stock prices, can make problems even worse. Managers who would like to be holding or buying stocks, are in a tug-of-war with shareholders who want to redeem their shares, forcing the managers to sell their funds' holdings. The ideal condition for a fund is a consistent cash inflow that allows a manager to take advantage of buying opportunities as they surface.

Self-Reinforcing Returns

There is a body of thought that some small-cap funds' inflows actually *cause* and reinforce their own good performance. According to this theory, the funds buy stocks with relatively small floats (i.e., stocks whose daily trading volume is small because there are few shares available for trading). Day-after-day buying drives up stock prices. As those stocks rise, so does the fund's NAV, which prompts investors to put more money in the fund, which increases the fund's stock buying, which drives up the NAV still further, which attracts more investors, and so on. If one accepts this notion, moderate and consistent cash inflows *could* actually drive positive returns. But others take a more moderate view. They suggest that, since most new funds start with few assets and without a boatload of expectant investors, steady cash inflows are likely, which will enhance performance. Take your pick.

Front-Running

Brokers have been charged with executing buy orders for themselves before executing large orders for others; which is illegal. It's a form of *front-running*, and it allows the broker (or other front runners) to get the benefit of a price increase caused by executing the larger order after his own stock purchase has already been made. Compared to the skeptical view of self-reinforcing returns, the idea that returns are boosted by front-running is downright cynical. In this view, a large fund sponsor might salt shares in a new small fund, and then enter buy orders for the same stock in their larger, established funds. Simple physics would explain how this behavior would allow the sponsor to boost returns for its "baby brother" funds. Obviously, it's not a topic of wide discussion; whether it happens is unknowable.

Management Attention

We've said this before, but it bears repeating: There is no time during its life when shareholders' and fund sponsors' self-interests are more closely linked than when the fund is first launched. To launch a fund, management invests in start-up legal, administrative, marketing, and advertising costs. They may also "seed" the fund—invest in shares. While actual start-up costs can be as little as $100,000, one mutual fund consultant opined that even "$5 million [in advertising and marketing expenses] doesn't give you much of a chance to be heard (by prospective investors)." Management's goal, however, is to turn a profit on *their* investment, and the only way to do that is to increase assets to a level where the fund's operating fees are big enough to provide a profit. Most observers peg that level at $50 to $100 million.

Since the surest way to attract assets and achieve profitability is to deliver above-average returns to investors, new-fund managements are likely to be almost as preoccupied with performance as their shareholders are. Management's increased attention to performance can take many forms: IPO funneling, concentrating the firm's best research efforts, devoting more time, assigning more troops to the fund—whatever seems necessary. Once the fund is up, running, and profitable, management's attention is more easily diverted in other directions.

Not all new funds enjoy all these uniquely favorable conditions in equal measure. The "new-fund effect" is the result of most conditions adding *some* incremental positive return *and* the absence of many of the unfavorable factors that reduce older funds' returns. New funds provide the best opportunity for a savvy manager to show his stuff. Their added incremental returns demonstrate that most of the time, they are successful.

A New-Fund Investment Strategy

At this point, it may seem that new-fund investing sounds much more complicated than, say, indexing. And you're right. However, the two approaches have very different objectives. The goal of indexing is to virtually guarantee near-average returns and eliminate the risk of below-average returns, but it will never deliver above-average returns. *Above-average returns* are the goal of new-fund investors, who aren't satisfied with just average returns, even though "just average" is pretty darned good, considering how few investors achieve them.

However, above-average returns don't "come cheap"; there's a price to be paid in terms of your time and effort. If your reaction to the investment process ranges between indifference and antipathy, load up on index funds and leave new-fund investing to others. On the other hand, if you are intrigued and challenged by the idea of doing your own research, increasing your returns, and "beating the system," you will be well rewarded. However, even if you are convinced that the new-fund phenomenon is the best thing since canned peas, you should approach it with caution. New-fund investing is an improved way to invest in small- and mid-cap funds, just as indexing is an improved way to invest in large-cap funds—it's not an either-or proposition—you should do both.

When to Hold 'Em and When to Fold 'Em

Since the "new-fund effect" is most potent during a fund's earliest weeks and months, it only makes sense that you invest on, or as close to, day one as possible.

"Watching it" or "seeing how it does" is just plain silly. The new-fund strategy is proactive: You're trying to anticipate performance, not react to it, as the average investor does. And since the new-fund effect dissipates over time, an expected holding period is 18 months for successful funds and 6 months for funds that do poorly during their postlaunch "honeymoon period." If the honeymoon is unhappy, the chances of longer-term bliss are greatly diminished.

It might seem heretical to advocate a holding period of only 6 to 18 months—after all, mutual funds are supposed to be long-term investments. New-fund investing doesn't change that core strategy for the rest (and most) of your portfolio, which should also include large-cap stock and investment-grade bond funds. In addition, whether it annoys traditionalists or not, the average holding period for present-day fund investors is admitted to be "between two and three years" by a spokesperson for one of the largest fund supermarkets. Even the most practiced optimist has to conclude that the "between" is probably a lot closer to two, than three years.

New-Fund Selection

Assume for the sake of argument that your small- and mid-cap allocation is somewhere around 10 percent to 25 percent of your total portfolio. Investing in new funds means this segment of your investment will experience relatively rapid turnover; you're hardly ever going to disturb the remaining 75 percent to 90 percent. On balance, your total portfolio turnover will still be below average (one of the very few instances where you should strive to be below average). The question is, How do you choose the funds that will make up that 10 to 25 percent?

There never seems to be a shortage of new funds. In 1999 alone, 630 new funds were launched. From that large a universe, you have to reduce the possibilities to the few with the best probability of outperformance. Since it has never been shown that load are any better than no-load funds, the first cut is to eliminate load funds—front-end, back-end, a-little-along-the-way-load, and whatever-loads. Some load funds are available on a load-waived basis at fund supermarkets if you go through a "financial intermediary"—an investment adviser or planner. Eliminating loads will remove about half of the contenders for your investment dollars.

Desirable New-Fund Characteristic to Look For

After cutting out load funds, you've got a more manageable universe to choose from, but you've still got a way to go before making your selection. To review, you are seeking funds that most closely resemble the "ideal profile," garnered

Wall Street Speak

SHORT-TERM REDEMPTION FEES

Some sponsors have begun to impose 1 or 2 percent back-end loads on purchasers who sell within the first 6 months or less. The purpose is to discourage short-term trading that harms all shareholders' returns. Since 6 months will probably be your minimum new-fund holding period, don't let the short-term redemption fee discourage you. If it keeps the crazies out of your fund, it will help performance—a good thing.

from our seven-year analysis of top-25 funds, and the Schwab and *No-load Fund Analyst* studies:

1. New.
2. Small-cap growth or blend.
3. Small asset base.
4. Independent manager.

In addition, although it was not examined in the studies cited earlier, our real-money personal experience over the past few years leads us to add a fifth characteristic: Funds sponsored by a medium- to large-sized well-known fund family (see also "future powerhouse sponsors," in Chapter 15) will increase the odds of avoiding a clunker. Although it's more fun to bet on the "little guy," in the new-fund game, it's better to stick with the heavies, for several important reasons:

- *Resources* A big fund family has a large research infrastructure that it can bring to bear on the small asset base.
- *IPO leverage* The math is undeniable: large sponsors get larger IPO allocations, which can be funneled into small new funds. We call it "IPO leverage."
- *Division of labor* The marketing, human resources, and administrative departments of large sponsors carry the burdens of managing the mutual fund's business. In a small shop, portfolio managers are more likely to be wasting time on administrative and marketing chores when portfolio management should be their sole preoccupation.
- *Management depth* At a small boutique management, where there are only a few people, if the portfolio manager gets distracted, for whatever

reasons, there may not be anybody qualified to take his place. At a large firm, there is always experienced talent to step in and take over.

- *Psychology* For some, investing in new funds is venturesome enough. Investing in new funds from large, well-regarded managers takes some of the anxiety out of the process, which may be just what you need to muster enough staying power to go the distance.

You will miss those soaring tiny new funds that come out of nowhere to chalk up wondrous first-year returns, but you'll also miss the many more that go nowhere. What you gain from the trade-off is a higher probability of consistent new-fund success.

Just for the Record

Not to be forgotten, look for a portfolio manager with a superior track record. The odds of good performance are improved if the new fund is to be managed by someone—or a team—with an established identifiable track record of above-average performance. Why hire somebody with certifiably below-average past performance?

In many cases, a new fund will provide historical results for its manager while managing other funds—particularly if these results were achieved at the same sponsor. Almost without exception, all large sponsors have toll-free telephone numbers and Web sites. At the least, they will provide the names of previous funds and when they were managed. The Morningstar Web site provides historical performance information as do most fund family Web sites. You can also get the manager's biographical information in the new fund's prospectus. And when a "star" manager moves from one family to another, or starts a new management company, there is usually commentary on the various investment and mutual fund Web sites that invariably includes historical performance data. One way or another, you should be able to fish it out of the vast sea of Internet investment information fairly easily.

While the desirable characteristics of a fund manager have not been ranked in order of importance, putting his or her previous track record near last is appropriate. Most investors make the mistake of making this their first step, ignoring that in most instances, the manager has been riding the wave of sector and/or style favor or disfavor. This often means comparing "apples to oranges": The manager's success in a large-cap fund tells you little if she's heading up a small-cap fund this time around. Instead, you want to look for an "apples to apples" comparison, like the one provided by Morningstar's category rating. It will tell you how the manager performed compared to managers of similar funds. If you're examining a small-cap fund manager's record, how he performed versus the large-cap S&P 500 Index (his star ratings) isn't very useful.

Be Sector and Style-Conscious

You could get everything right up to this point and still undo it all if you get the final step wrong: sector and style selection. If you've paid attention to the desirable managed fund characteristics described earlier, you have already targeted small-cap funds as best, with mid-cap funds being a toss-up. You're not considering large-cap funds. So you've taken care of the sector issue. Now it's time to look at style. Of the three investment styles, the best odds of new-fund outperformance, in descending order, are growth, blend, and value.

Style really does matter. In 1999, for example, if you had bet that small-cap stocks would return to favor, your sector choice would have been dead right—*if* you invested in small-cap growth funds. The small-cap Russell 2000 Growth Index soared 43.09 percent. But a small-cap value bet would have put you dead in the water: The Russell 2000 Value Index lost 1.49 percent. So maybe we should pause a moment and consider the difference between the two. *Growth* stocks are those perceived to be growing faster than the economy. *Value* means stocks that are selling at low prices that are less than their perceived intrinsic values, as measured by their P/E ratio, for example. Growth was "in style" in 1999. Value, unfortunately for investors who were heavily committed to that sector, was not.

Blends Are Smoothest

Style is an issue. Even with their advantages, new funds are going to struggle if they are out of style. So how do you avoid choosing the wrong style? The surest way is not to make any style bet by investing in blend funds, which invest in stocks that sit in the middle between value and growth investment styles. Like whisky, blend funds are smoothest, which means that they are particularly compelling if you have a limited amount of cash to invest. Because they straddle the two extremes, you can't get marooned at the wrong end of the style spectrum. If there is room for more than one fund in your small-cap allocation, spice up your bet with a dose of growth funds, since they benefit the most from the new-fund effect and, according to the studies, without increased risk.

New-Fund Selection—Reviewing the Criteria

To revisit our criteria for new-fund investing, here are the seven considerations to keep in mind before making your final choice (or choices):

1. Age of fund—new.
2. Sector—small-cap stocks.
3. Style—blend and growth.

4. Small asset base.

5. Independent manager.

6. Large manager.

7. Portfolio manager's above-average track record.

Without direction, managed fund selection is laborious because of all the pros and cons of thousands of funds. But you are looking only at new funds, so you've eliminated 98 percent of the thousands you might otherwise consider. Narrowing in on no-load or load waived independently managed, small, small-cap funds culls out most of the remaining 2 percent. You have the luxury of concentrating on the very few new funds that meet the criteria each year.

Finding New Funds

To find new funds easily, you probably need access to the Internet; that's the best way to stay ahead of fund launchings. Several Web sites alert you to new-fund registrations, including the SEC's EDGAR (Electronic Data Gathering Analysis and Retrieval system) site: sec.gov. This lists literally hundreds of filings that you have to investigate individually. Much easier to use is the listing of new fund SEC filings at the Web site edgar-online.com. New fund registrations are filed using N-1A and N-1A/A forms, so under "full search" in the "Enter Form" box, type N-1A. Once you see that there has been a filing, you can view the complete prospectus as filed with the SEC on another site, freeedgar.com.

Morningstar.com reports on new fund launches, often with very helpful commentary, on a regular basis, as does *Mutual Funds* magazine. Tweddell.com includes a list of all new open-end fund registrations with fund Web sites and toll-free numbers, when available, along with recent issues of *NewFund Focus* newsletters. Subscribers receive recommended new fund write-ups, sale recommendations, and ongoing monitoring of new funds' performance.

If you have an account with a large fund family, such as Fidelity or Vanguard, a telephone call every 30 to 60 days should keep you current on recent or upcoming fund launches of their own funds. Fund supermarkets are useful because you can keep all, or most, of your new funds in one place. TD Waterhouse is usually very prompt in carrying new funds. There are sometimes minor delays bringing new funds on board, and occasionally one company will handle a new fund that the other doesn't, but if you have accounts at more than one, you will cover almost all the bases. The databases used by the telephone representatives at these firms are updated frequently to include new funds.

New funds can't be offered until they are registered and approved by the SEC. "Approval" simply means that the prospectus of the fund presents a fair and reasonable picture to prospective investors; it doesn't mean that the SEC deems the fund to be good or worthy. Typically, funds file new-fund registrations 30 to 60 days before they hope to open. The registration period is elastic: If the SEC has questions or problems with the documentation, the registration period can be longer. If the fund filing is problem-free, on the other hand, the launch date can be accelerated.

Timing New-Fund Buying and Selling

Investing in a new fund on day one is preferable because, in rising markets, some new funds have had fairly startling increases during their first few weeks. Magazine information can be stale, particularly if a new-fund launch is accelerated. Timing new-fund buying and selling is straightforward:

- Once you've identified a new fund that meets all, or most of, the desired criteria, invest as close to the launch date as possible.

- At the end of the 6-month "honeymoon period," if the fund is achieving above-average returns, compared to other funds in its category, hold on for another 12 months. A good way to monitor your fund's performance is at the Yahoo! stock Web site. You input your portfolio and compare returns with other funds, indexes, and stocks. You won't be able to track your new fund directly until it gets a Nasdaq symbol, which can be delayed by weeks or months, depending on how quickly the fund grows assets to meet the Nasdaq minimum for a symbol. Until a new fund has a Nasdaq symbol, you can follow its daily NAV on its sponsor's Web site.

- As the end of the 18-month period approaches, unless the fund is providing exceptional returns, it's time to start shopping for a new fund to replace it. However, if your fund is a real sparkler, and you own it in a taxable account, and/or management has closed it to try to maintain performance, it might turn into a good long-term holding.

Because of the relative frequency of transactions, compared with index and tax-managed funds, this strategy is relatively tax *inefficient,* so using it in tax-deferred accounts, such as IRAs, is preferable.

Nontiming: Big Benefit

The semiautomatic buying and selling of new funds is probably the biggest plus of all to using this investment strategy. As shown in Chapter 2, timing, or more properly, mistiming, is the factor that defeats more investors than anything else. Buying funds at launch and selling them at the end of the honeymoon period (if they disappoint) or at the end of 18 months (if they delight), liberates you from the backward-looking methodology that defeats *most* performance-chasing investors.

As powerful as the new-fund effect is, not chasing your own tail may be as important as the performance boost the new-fund effect provides. You won't be wandering in the investment wasteland of market timers, procrastinators, and forecasters. You won't be stuck with the rest of the pack, waiting and "watching it for a while" until "things are more certain," or until "after tax-time," or until after "the holidays," or until after you "see what the Fed does." If you've been prone to market timing, it will probably be the first time you will have a reasonable timing strategy.

Looking Forward Instead of Backward

New-fund investing is a forward-looking strategy. It is proactive because "the system"—getting in at the launch and monitoring funds until they have aged to reach your predetermined (6 or 18 month) sell points—does most of the work for you. By definition, if most investors are doing something wrong, and you adopt a strategy that keeps you from duplicating their mistakes, you're already ahead of the game. If the improved strategy also provides additional incremental returns, you're way ahead of the game.

What Could Go Wrong—Future Forebodings?

Leaving aside discussions of the likelihood of future stock market crashes ala 1929 or 1973–1974, the worst thing that could happen to the new-fund investment strategy is that it catches on with too many investors. Remember the "Dogs of the Dow" fad, where it seemed as if everybody was buying the least popular stocks in the index because they were due for a rebound? Countless investment innovations and discoveries have shown that once a strategy goes from being unorthodox to popular—once everybody starts doing it—the strategic benefit disappears.

We may have had an ominous glimpse of that future for new-fund investing in February 1999, when the Janus Strategic Value Fund was launched. Even though the value investment style had been unfashionable for eons, Janus's other funds had been running far ahead of most funds and were wildly popular. Janus shareholders had watched previous fund launches that provided spectacular returns and they were ready-big-time for the launch of Strategic Value. Janus launched the fund with a "special subscription period," which piled up the money before the fund's debut. Its $1.5 billion in assets gathered by day-one negated much of the new-fund effect. If this happens regularly and investors' collective enthusiasm shifts from proven funds to new ones, the profit-boost provided by the new-fund effect will probably be lost. An era of new-fund popularity would also inspire sponsors to shovel them out to meet demand and quality would suffer. Old funds would suffer from withdrawal pains, and new ones from bloat. We hope this won't happen—for sure, the industry won't promote it. Meanwhile, enjoy, and profit, from the new-fund effect.

Whatever happens to affect the popularity of new-fund investing, however, it's not your only investment option. In Chapter 9 we look at another choice you can make: real estate investment trusts (REITs). These have been unpopular for a few years, but don't let that put you off. A strong case can be made that REITs have seen a cyclical bottom and now deserve to "get some respect" on a long-term basis. So if you're inclined to skip the next chapter—don't.

CHAPTER 9

Real Estate Investment Trusts: Funds with "The REIT Stuff"

Promoters are just guys with two pieces of bread looking for a piece of cheese.

—Evel Knievel

Although investor enthusiasm is impossible to predict, we can measure unpopularity with some precision by looking at how much they cash out of their funds. And real estate investment trusts (REITs), have been very unpopular for a few years. They've never been as "respectable" as some other sectors, and that presents you with opportunities, which is one of the reasons we recommended them. Many pay bondlike yields, so even if your timing is off, you'll be well paid while you wait for their return to favor.

REITs are publicly owned corporations that invest directly in real estate (equity REITs), real estate mortgages (mortgage REITs), or both (hybrids). They share a tax advantage: Unlike corporations, which pay corporate taxes on their net earnings and then pay dividends to shareholders, who are taxed once again, REITs escape corporate taxation as long as they pass at least 95 percent of their earnings on to their shareholders in dividends. In addition to generous income (4% to 8% annually), they offer moderate growth, and low correlation to stock and bond price fluctuations.

Real estate investment trust funds should be a part of your portfolio. They have gone through boom and bust cycles in the past, and because of these extreme cycles, most investors avoid them today. And because investors have been obsessed with growth and technology stocks, REITs have been largely ignored. But there are good reasons to believe that future commercial real estate cycles will be more moderate, which should attract more investors. If REITs become more of a mainstream category, they could provide total returns that would compare favorably to, or even exceed, stocks.

Some investors wrongly associate REITs with the dreadful history of highly leveraged, expense-loaded real estate limited partnerships that imploded after passage of the Tax Reform Act of 1986, wiping out many investors and sticking them with large tax liabilities. Others are concerned about liquidity: "What do I do if I want to sell—can I get out?" These fears are misplaced. REIT shares trade daily on the major exchanges, just like any other stock, but most investors don't understand this. The REIT industry still has a long way to go educating investors as to what they are and polishing up its image.

Buy the Numbers

It is estimated that only 10 percent to 12 percent of America's commercial real estate has been securitized; that is, only this small proportion is encompassed in REITs or publicly traded stocks. They can be categorized in many ways, perhaps the simplest being by *type:*

- *Equity REITs* (approximately 92%) invest in real estate properties. Income comes from rents.
- *Mortgage REITS* (5%) invest in real estate mortgages. Income comes from mortgage loans.
- *Hybrid REITs* (3%) invest in both real estate *and* mortgages.

Wall Street Speak

SECURITIZATION

Securitization is the term for converting large, concentrated private or institutional ownership from a few wealthy individuals or institutions into publicly traded securities (stocks or bonds) owned by the public. Before mortgages were securitized, almost all residential mortgages were owned by banks and insurance companies. The formation of publicly traded Government National Mortgage Association mortgage pools, commonly called "Ginnie Maes," was the first time that mortgages were securitized, providing the public with the opportunity to own them.

Most commercial real estate remains in the hands of private individuals and institutional investors. The real-estate industry as a whole has a boom or bust reputation—much of it richly deserved—which explains investor reluctance to get involved. But equity REITs have established a record of decent sector returns—the National Association of Real Estate Investment Trust's Equity Index shows an average annual return of 12.70 percent for the past 20 years and 11.98 percent for the last decade—so they're well worth considering.

Heard on the Street

Few are willing to plow through the paperwork needed to learn about REITs or have the stomach for the risk of picking them. With most REITs focused on a single region, it is essential to buy a score of them to get diversity. For many the best way to invest might be a REIT mutual fund.

Business Week, December 29, 1997.

One problem with REITs has been the timing of their formations. Most have been launched near real estate cycle peaks, which has caused considerable pain to investors who got into the sector too late to realize the most favorable returns. This has also been the case with REIT funds. As the 1990s drew to a close, returns from "The REIT Stuff" have been dismal, compared with technology and growth stocks in general.

Another problem with REITs is the general perception that real estate investments are dangerous. When real estate folks and Wall Streeters get on a roll together, as they did in the wild and woolly days of real estate tax shelters in the late 1970s and early 1980s, it has always seemed to end badly, partly because when real estate pros find they can't sell properties to other real estaters, they turn to Wall Streeters, who seem to be able to distribute product no matter now doubtful it is. The result is that while many investors go to Wall Street for most of their investment needs, when it comes to real estate, many are gun-shy.

Despite the trepidation felt by investors, however, *somebody* owns all those tall buildings and not because it's their hobby. Typically, the owners are very wealthy individuals, large institutions such as insurance companies and major pension funds. These large-scale investors allocate 5 percent to 15 percent of their portfolios to high-quality real estate because they recognize that it provides relatively high income, inflation protection, and appreciation. You too,

> **FUNDAMENTAL FACTS**
>
> If you are skeptical about New Era economics and its lofty stock valuations, REITs could be a safe haven. In its "Annual Investment Guide" (June 12, 2000), *Forbes* interviewed "New Economy" Merrill Lynch analyst, Henry Blodget (34 years old) and "old economy" money manager, Jeremy Grantham (61 years old). Even after the Spring 2000 drop in the Nasdaq, Grantham predicted, ". . . from their highs, the S&P 500 will decline 50%; the Nasdaq, 70%; and the nonearnings Nasdaq, 80%." Where is he investing his clients' money? Approximately 50% in government bonds, predominately inflation-protected, and of the remainder, 23% in REITs (including timber holdings). "No credit risk. No inflation risk."
>
> If you believe in hard assets and the old economy, few investments are harder and older than dirt.

should consider REIT funds as a practical and efficient way to add professionally managed commercial real estate to your portfolio.

Attractive Investment Characteristics of REIT Funds

What do REIT funds have to offer you? Here's a partial list of the advantages to investing in REITs:

- *Income* Bondlike yields (4%–8%) from good-quality equity REIT funds are common.
- *Increasing income* Rents are usually linked to the Consumer Price Index (CPI) or other cost of living indexes.
- *Appreciation potential* Though REITs enjoy nothing like the hypergrowth of technology or biotechnology sectors, they offer modest appreciation, enhanced by moderate leverage (mortgages).
- *Liquidity* Most REITs are listed on the major exchanges, and REIT funds are bought and sold like any other funds.
- *Increasing industry stability* Observers are pointing out that recent real-estate industry down cycles have been less severe than in the past—viewed as evidence that commercial real estate is becoming less cyclical.
- *REIT prices have lower correlations to interest rate changes than stock prices* Stock prices tend to suffer when interest rates rise, but REITs suffer much less, partly because higher interest rates discourage new construction. Thus, existing real estate properties usually hold their own in value, and might even increase.

- *Inflation hedge* Real estate prices and rents (often indexed to the CPI or other inflation indicators) tend to rise faster during inflationary periods.
- *Performance* "Since their inception, REIT market performance has been roughly comparable to that of the Russell 2000 Index (small-cap U.S. stocks) and has exceeded returns on fixed-debt instruments (bonds) or direct investments in real estate."*
- *Significant insider ownership* Average equity ownership by REIT managements of stock in their own companies is 12.5 percent.*
- *REIT mutual funds provide ownership in a wide variety of property types and geographical diversification.*

The REIT investment picture isn't entirely rosy, however. REITs also have negative characteristics:

- The real estate business has always been cyclical; returns for REITs and REIT fund tend to mirror the industry's ups and downs. Now, however, securitization and tightened lending practices may dampen the historical boom-and-bust cycles.

Heard on the Street

PORTFOLIO STABILIZER: LOW CORRELATION OF REITS TO STOCK AND BOND PRICES

REIT fund manager Rick Imperiale's *Uniplan, INC Weekly REIT Portfolio Summary* (May 12, 2000), published a study for the January 1989 through December 1999 period of the month-to-month total return for both the NAREIT Equity Index and two major bond indexes:

"The correlation coefficient was 0.26 for REITs relative to Long Term Government Bonds and 0.35 relative to [corporate bonds]. This was discernibly lower than the 0.39 coefficient of correlation (how often and the degree they move in the same direction) for the broader equity market as measured by the S&P 500 for the same period. Thus we conclude that REITs as an asset class:

1. Act as a hedge against inflation and perform well during inflationary periods.
2. REITs are not materially correlated to bonds or reflective of fixed income investments like in their volatility characteristics."

National Association of Real Estate Investment Trusts—NAREIT.com.

- Public investors are still gun-shy about the industry. Unless they develop more enduring confidence, REIT valuations may stay low compared with other sectors.

- In terms of total capitalization, REITs are very small and many are illiquid, making them unsuitable for many mainstream institutional investors. This may serve to keep REIT valuations low.

Ground Floor

Congress passed legislation in 1960 to enable small investors to make investments through REITs in large income-producing properties such as shopping centers, apartments, offices, and industrial properties. Before President Eisenhower signed it into law, ownership of commercial real estate by the public had not been feasible. However, the legislation required that at least 95 percent of REITs' net income be paid out to shareholders as dividends. While the single level of taxation on REITs helped produce income for shareholders, it also had a negative effect: There was virtually no income left over (retained earnings) that corporations normally reinvest in their business to finance growth.

Another restraint in the law was that while REITs could own properties, they couldn't operate or manage them—they had to farm out management to third parties. This unwieldy structure didn't generate much enthusiasm from investors, so the industry muddled through its first 30 years. REITs waxed and waned in popularity but made little real progress, even during the robust real estate market of the early 1980s. At that time, it seemed as if Japan, Inc. was about to become America's landlord, and tax-shelter investors were driving up commercial real estate prices far above their real or economic values.

The Tax Reform Act of 1986 decimated most of these shelter partnerships by limiting the amount of interest that could be used as a tax deduction, by lengthening depreciation periods for property, and by restricting "passive losses" generated, for example, by depreciation on the property. By 1990, in addition to failing as a tax shelter, real estate saw falling prices as a result of the savings and loan crisis and regulatory pressures on institutional lending. Most sections of the country were overbuilt and real estate prices dropped between 30 percent and 50 percent. However, while the Tax Reform Act speared tax shelters, it also relaxed regulations by allowing REITs to operate and manage their own properties for the first time.

Ups and Downs

The climate for REITs improved even further in 1992, with an innovation called the "umbrella partnership REIT" (UPREIT). In UPREITs, members of existing partnerships join together with new investors to form an operating partnership. This allowed UPREITS to acquire properties from owners whose tax basis was so low—or negative—that previously, they had been unwilling or unable to go public or sell for fear of incurring capital gain taxes.

A further tax change in 1993 removed a barrier against REIT investing by pension plans, and a 1997 change simplified REIT operations. The end result has been substantial growth in REITs. Ten years ago, the entire capitalization of all publicly traded REITs was only $8.7 billion, whereas today there are approximately 300 REITs with assets of over $130 billion, two thirds of which trade on the exchanges or Nasdaq.

As you'd expect, the REIT fund population has also grown: from only five funds, with $150 million assets in 1990, to 63 funds, with assets of over $8 billion by year-end 1999. Nevertheless, the REIT fund population is still relatively miniscule in an arena where many sectors are measured in the hundreds of billions.

As stated earlier, REITs can be categorized in a number of different ways. In addition to categorizing them by type—equity, mortgage, or hybrid—they can be broken down further, by property type:

Industrial/office	27%	Healthcare	7%
Retail	21%	Mortgage backed	5%
Residential	18%	Self-storage	4%
Diversified	9%	Specialty	1%
Lodging/resorts	8%		

Some REITs invest only in particular property types such as self-storage, residential buildings, or apartments. Others diversify and invest in a variety of property types.

Wall Street Speak

FFO

If you explore REITs, you will soon come across the acronym "FFO," which stands for Funds from Operations. FFO is the rough equivalent of most industrial corporations' EPS (Earnings per Share). EPS is calculated by subtracting depreciation on equipment and machinery from earnings. FFO, on the other hand, *adds* real estate depreciation back to earnings. The accounting method is practiced by the industry because real estate tends to hold its value better than equipment and machinery; in many cases, it actually *increases*.

Interview—Forward Funds' REIT Fund Manager, Richard Imperiale

Richard "Rick" Imperiale has over 15 years' experience in the commercial real estate field. As CEO of UNIPLAN, a Milwaukee-based money manager, he is portfolio manager of Jefferson Growth & Income Fund and Forward Funds UNIPLAN Real Estate Fund. His REIT fund is loosely correlated to the NAREIT Equity Index (the REIT industry's equivalent of the Standard & Poor's 500 Index). Jerry Tweddell interviewed him in his Milwaukee offices in May 2000.

Q.   Why invest in REITs?

R.I.   Big institutions have known for a long time that real estate is a great asset class. Take any good piece of property, add a modest amount of leverage and suddenly you're well into mid-teen type returns (income and appreciation) with modest risk. Big institutions have always had direct ownership of real estate in their portfolios because they have the scale to do it. The problem has been that the smaller investor has never been able to participate in those returns as easily.

Q.   Let's take a large institution such as an insurance company, for example. Typically, what percent of their portfolio will be directly invested in real estate?

R.I.   Typically 5 to 15 percent. One of the more successful insurance companies, right here in Milwaukee, is Northwestern Mutual Life Insurance Company; they have close to 25 percent of their portfolio in real estate. The problem is, even if you are a well-off investor, you're not wealthy enough to own a diversified portfolio of high-quality real estate. The traditional fallback is owning a home, but that's real estate that's consumed as a lifestyle issue. However, other than its being modest inflation hedge, it doesn't contribute to your portfolio.

  What we point out is that you can enjoy mid-teen returns by buying REITs and enjoy the quality of a portfolio the big institutions enjoy with landmark buildings, central district business properties which are diversified by geography and by property type for a small investment.

Q.   How big are REIT funds compared to other fund categories?

R.I.   Tiny—infinitesimal—around $8 billion. Part of the reason is that most of the product is retail oriented and people, for whatever reason, don't appreciate the value that real estate adds to their portfolio. It becomes real obvious as a way for small and mid-sized institutions to participate. The overriding factor for the small investor is the liquidity—you can get in and out of them when you want to, while it's an entire planning process for most big institutions. I would argue it's better than the direct ownership of real estate—the individual gets scale, quality of property, and geographical diversity you couldn't otherwise afford—and you get liquidity.

Q. But isn't it sort of a boom-or-bust business?

R.I. It's always been a cyclical kind of business; the 1970s were the most extreme examples, with construction and lending REITs (mortgage REITs that did very poorly) as a prime example. REITs that lend are in the category of mortgage REITs, and I would argue that if you want to own mortgages, there are probably better ways to do it than through REITs.

Q. You're not kidding—according to the NAREIT Web site (NAREIT.com), the mortgage REITs have been dreadful. Why?

R.I. I think it's the result of a number of factors, but the main reason is that they tend to invest in the riskiest sectors. . . . The other is that returns reflect the most recent periods, which were very poor (during 1998 and 1999, REITs were out of favor generally and interest rates rose in 1999), which makes them look even worse.

Q. So mortgage buyers should stick to instruments like Ginnie Maes?

R.I. Precisely. I would say take mortgage REITs out of the equation if you want to own real estate; equity REITs are those that get 65 percent or more of their earnings from the direct ownership of property—those are the ones you want to focus on.

Q. What about equity funds' risk?

R.I Depending on your portfolio, a 5 percent to 15 percent REIT stake provides the most benefit in terms of lowering portfolio volatility and increasing total return. If your portfolio is fairly conservative with a lot of bonds, 5 percent gets you there. If you're fairly aggressive, you've got to pull it up to 10 to 15 percent to help moderate [volatility].

Q. Should we look at income REITs as a substitute for bonds?

R.I. They're a great substitute for some of your bond portfolio. In terms of pure mathematics—getting the most return for the least amount of risk—they dampen volatility so a very conservative portfolio doesn't—quote—"need" as big a stake in REITs as an aggressive one would.

Q. We've talked about risk in terms of a portfolio, but what about the underlying investment risk of owning real estate, particularly during a down cycle?

R.I. The one thing you can observe about real estate cycles is that they are becoming less severe. What used to happen was that builders would continue to build until there was a glut of excess property. Then you'd have a downturn and rents would generally go down and then the market would clear and firm up again. You had a very dramatic cycle.

What [happens now] is, most lenders in the real estate venue won't give money to developers unless they have a tenant to go into a project—a major tenant. Unless I can go to the bank and say I've got this thing half full before I break ground [the bank won't lend the funds to start the project]. There's very little spec building going on because lenders were really the ones that got burned in the last cycle, and they have a long memory.

Q. When did the lenders start to "get religion?"

R.I. It started in the mid-80s—they had less willingness to lend and it continued through the 90s. Now the cycle is much more subdued because lenders won't throw a lot of money at spec building. There may be some spec building at the margin, but most developers, if they're bankrolling without a lot of leverage—with their own money—they tend to be a lot more conservative. The result is a moderation in real estate cycles. I'd make the observation that cycles are less severe—upturns aren't as dramatic, but downturns aren't as deep either. That's a good thing for the real estate community; there is a certain level of market discipline that's been imposed on them.

Q. Returns of the NAREIT Equity Index during the 90s weren't that good— compared to other sectors—just shy of 10 percent. What's a reasonable expectation for the future?

R.I. Over the long term—five years or so—with modest leverage, you should see commercial property returning mid-teen—14 to 15 percent—total returns on an ongoing basis. It's a very stable forward return, which is a real positive in terms of the value of the cash flow. The most recent period you're looking at (the late 90s), was a down cycle, which reduces the returns for the whole period. I think if you look back at periods ending during up cycles— like ones ending in 1997, the indexes actually outperformed the S&P 500.

Q. As with everything else, I assume that management is critical.

R.I. A good management can add what I call "intangible leverage"—they can take a marginal property and add a lot of value to it. Bad management can take a trophy property and just destroy the value. There's a classic example here in town—The Milwaukee Center, ultimately owned by Teachers' Annuity of Texas in a bankruptcy foreclosure. It's a spectacular monument to real estate development—marble and glass—a beautiful structure. But it was always about 70 to 72 percent full and it was never a real popular building.

Great Lakes (Great Lakes REIT) bought it—they're very savvy—at 50 percent of replacement cost (cost to build a similar property) and within a year it was 95 percent occupied—one of the shining lights of downtown.

Teachers' Annuity (the prior owner), because they got it in a foreclosure, wasn't managing it in the same way as Great Lakes would; they just didn't have the skill to run the building the way it should have been run; although they had a—quote, unquote—property manager there, it wasn't somebody who had a vested interest in making the building work the way it should have. The intangible leverage provided by high-quality management can provide huge added value.

Q. During the Dark Ages (during the 1950s and 1960s), utility stocks used to be thought of as good, reliable dividend payers offering moderate growth and increasing dividends. Is that a reasonable way to view REITs?

R.I. I think it's reasonable.

Q. Stock-fund investing in inefficient markets tends to benefit from a small asset base. Does the same principle apply with REITs?

R.I. Absolutely, although a really small fund has higher expenses (the average REIT fund's expense ratio in 1999 was 1.59%). In recent years, the size problem has been REIT managers' wildest fantasy, but if it became a problem, I'd probably recommend shutting our fund to new investors at around the $500 million level; assets between $100 and $500 million are probably optimal.

Q. Are there any questions we should have asked, but didn't?

R.I. One thing I make sure I point out is that real estate is really a local market; driven by the dynamics of supply and demand—that's going to dictate the fortunes of the REIT. If you own office buildings in Atlanta right now, although it's improving, it's still sort of a crummy market, with 11, 12, and 13 percent vacancy rates. Rents aren't going up and lots of new buildings are being built that are just coming on stream; it's not a great environment. On the flip side, if you own real estate in the San Francisco—or in most of California—Spieker's (Spieker Properties REIT) is an example—your performance has been breathtaking.

Q. Even though we preach against trading, it would seem that REITs might provide opportunities to trade them—buying when they are selling at discounts to their underlying property values and selling when they go to premiums. Unlike closed-end trusts, it seems like they trade at premiums with some regularity and that 15 to 20 percent isn't unusual.

R.I. While we wouldn't advocate it for obvious reasons, history shows that when REITs are at discounts—trading at 15 percent or more discounts to liquidation value—it's probably too much. However, two years ago . . . they were at that level, [and] the following year they dropped another 10 percent. At 15 to 20 percent premiums, that's where we get more defensive in the fund, increasing our position to convertibles—cash and such. That's probably not a bad strategy for investors. But again, it's inexact—the last peak was at 39 percent average premiums, so if you bailed out at plus 15 or 20 percent, you left some on the table.

Q. How would you know when they are selling at discounts—reading a bunch of REIT quarterly reports?

R.I. An easier way would be [to consult with] brokerage firm analysts. The major brokerage firms all have REIT analysts and it's amazing how closely their estimates are to each other as far as [gauging the] underlying value of REITs.

FUNDamental Facts

There has been considerable publicity about how brokerage firm analysts slant their reports to favor companies they are trying to curry favor with. Why? Because glowing recommendations increase the chances of their firm's investment banking department being chosen as underwriters the next time a company wants to sell stocks or bonds to the public. So while brokerage house analysts' estimates of underlying REIT property values are worth considering, they have to be viewed with some skepticism.

Q. Wouldn't another good—and maybe better—indicator be when there are a bunch of new REITs and REIT funds coming on the market—and when there aren't any?

R.I. (Laughs) It sure is—a real good indicator.

Historical REIT Returns

Judged from history, Rick Imperiale's advice to stick with equity REITs is well founded. Table 9.1 shows the historical performance of the various REIT categories, with equity REIT returns italicized. As you can see, mortgage REIT returns have been dreadful, which has skewed the overall returns of all REITs. As "bad" as equity REIT returns were (approximately equal to common stocks'

TABLE 9.1 Long-Term Historic Period-to-Date Measures of Performance

INDEX SECTOR	COMPOUND ANNUAL RETURNS THROUGH MAY 2000				
	1-YEAR (%)	3-YEAR (%)	5-YEAR (%)	10-YEAR (%)	15-YEAR (%)
All REITs	−3.22	0.58	8.55	9.93	6.84
Equity REITs	*−1.17*	*1.18*	*9.37*	*10.86*	*9.54*
Mortgage REITs	−39.99	23.66	−2.11	2.29	−0.50
Hybrid REITs	−27.53	−20.13	−5.74	2.37	0.12

average of 10 percent returns over the past 100 years), their results have to be viewed in the context of having been in a 2-year down cycle at the end of the periods measured.

Equity REITs—Growing Income and Appreciation

During the 1990s, on a total return basis, an investor would have done far better in the Vanguard S&P 500 Index Fund: On $10,000 invested, the total returns for the 10 years ended December 31, 1999 were $52,688 versus $19,281 for the Wilshire REIT Index. However, not everybody had the luxury of investing just for growth. For those who needed income, the S&P 500 Index fund would not have provided much; as the decade wore on, its yield shrank from 3.52 percent in 1990, to 2.86 percent in 1995, and only 1.25 percent in 1999. For those investing during this period, on a $10,000 investment, annual income wilted from approximately $352 to $125.

With the benefit of hindsight, it's obvious that an S&P 500 investor could have done very well by cashing in some capital gains periodically and using them as "income," but that's not a very reliable, or "sure," way to generate income. Most income investors want a more assured income stream. This is where REITs fit the bill: Their higher yields are a good compromise between pure bond investing, which provides little or no growth of principal, and the appreciation from stocks.

Table 9.2 shows how an income investor would have fared during the 1990s in the two largest REITs with 10-year records—Fidelity Real Estate Investment and UAM Heitman Real Estate Securities—compared to the Vanguard Total Bond Market Index Fund, which reflects the performance of the overall bond market. The table shows a $10,000 investment on January 2, 1990, with capital gains reinvested and income dividends taken in cash for a 10-year period. The bond fund investor started out receiving more income, but as time

TABLE 9.2 $10,000 Invested—Yearly Dividend Income

	FIDELITY REAL ESTATE	UAM HEITMAN REAL ESTATE	VANGUARD TOTAL BOND MARKET INDEX
1990	$531	$ 783	$847
1991	510	625	817
1992	448	557	749
1993	625	540	693
1994	656	752	672
1995	740	890	704
1996	750	914	693
1997	824	1,004	704
1998	836	782	674
1999	757	1,143	676

passed, the two REIT funds increased their annual income, while the bond fund's income actually *declined* because of falling interest rates. By the middle of the decade, the REIT funds were paying more income and the gap widened from then on.

While income tells part of the story, it's important also to look at what happened to the investor's original $10,000:

$10,000 Investment—Value at End of Period

Vanguard Total Bond Market Index	$10,424
Fidelity Real Estate Investment	$16,129
UAM Heitman Real Estate	$12,635

While both REIT funds were increasing spendable income, their values rose as well. By the end of the period, their values increased by over 25 percent and 60 percent, while the bond investor essentially broke even. And again, the REIT funds' returns shown were for a period that ended with a 2-year down cycle. The REIT cycle turned up again at the beginning of the following year, and by August 2000, the value of the Fidelity REIT increased to $20,435, UAM Heitman to $15,225, while Vanguard's bond fund increased very slightly, to $10,528.

If you are an income investor, equity REIT Funds provide good opportunities in a future environment, when stock returns might be less bountiful than they were in the 1990s. You start out with a good income stream that will grow and a good likelihood that the principal amount will increase in value also.

Equity REIT Funds for Capital Gains

Opportunistic investors who have been smart or lucky enough to invest near REITs' cyclical bottoms have garnered handsome returns from a relatively low-risk sector. "Catching" REITs close to bottoms has an added benefit that other sectors do not: generous income if your timing is less than perfect. Quality REIT fund yields of over 8 percent were common at the end of 1999, just before the sector turned up. During the 1990s, there were two 3-year up cycles; both times, cumulative (calendar year) total returns exceeded 65 percent, as shown in Table 9.3.

If you take an opportunistic approach to REIT investing, classic indicators have identified REIT cycle bottoms in the past:

- A period after one—preferably two—years of negative returns.
- Few or no new REIT formations.
- Few or no new REIT fund launches.
- REIT dividend yields at the higher end of their historical range.
- REITs selling at 10 to 25 percent discounts from underlying property values.
- Large number of REIT takeovers, management buyouts, and REITs buying back their own shares in the open market.

Pie in the REIT Sky

There is another profit-making possibility in the future: Equity REITs could begin to gain the respect that the industry insists is overdue. If so, they might shed their image as being cyclical and enter the investment mainstream. There are reasons the common, negative perception might change:

- Accumulated years of reasonably consistent dividends.
- Moderation of up and down cycles.
- Increased operating flexibility as the result of eased regulation.

TABLE 9.3 Morningstar Specialty Real Estate Fund Average Returns (%)

1991	33.25	1995	15.26
1992	13.77	1996	31.66
1993	18.23	1997	23.06
Cumulative Total Returns	65.25	Cumulative Total Returns	69.98

- More transparency due to securitization, providing more information to investors.

- Increasing regulation by the SEC as more real estate becomes securitized; improving business practices should lead to greater investor confidence.

- Increase in the number of REITs, allowing more institutions to invest.

Mainstreaming Main Street

If REITs become more of a mainstream investment, they might not get as cheap at the bottom of the next down cycle, and the bondlike yields they provide might be a permanent thing of the past. Andrew Davis, portfolio manager of Davis Real Estate Fund sums up the bullish case:

> Real estate in the form of REITs is becoming a necessary part of any well diversified portfolio. The class of REITs that started to come public in 1992 has high insider ownership, better management, superior corporate governance, and a more focused strategy than any prior class of REIT. Without getting too technical, the 1986 tax reform act removed many of the tax incentives that benefited developers and led to much of the overbuilding in the mid 1980s.
>
> Moreover, the large number of publicly-traded REITs in the marketplace has shone a light into the world of real estate ownership, development, and acquisition. This light has improved business practices, created more publicly-available data and has allowed a tighter grip on capital by banks, insurance companies and pension funds. In the end, *less capital means less overbuilding—a major positive for REITs*. Finally, the Federal Government seems to understand the role REITs should play . . . overbearing regulations [have been] lifted to ensure fair competition and a "level playing field" for real estate managers, owners and investors. (emphasis added)

If REITs "get some respect," they might be at a cyclical buying opportunity that could very well turn out to be a historic investment opportunity.

Like REITs, convertible bond funds are ignored and misunderstood by most investors. They too, provide both income, appreciation, and an added measure of safety. They should also be part of your portfolio, as discussed in Chapter 10.

CHAPTER 10

Convertibles: Smooth Rides and Safety Belts

More than any time in history mankind faces a crossroads. One path leads to despair and utter hopelessness. The other to total extinction. Let us pray that we have the wisdom to choose the correct one.

—Woody Allen

Convertible bonds offer flexibility, relative safety, and most of the growth potential of common stocks. They are hybrids, providing the relative safety of bonds but allowing their owners to convert to a fixed number of shares of stock whenever they choose. As an added bonus, they provide more income than common stocks. Convertibles offer both appreciation and risk protection when the market is volatile. This makes them a good choice when you're trying to maintain the balancing act between growing your assets and at the same time, protecting them. Be forewarned: The math can be intimidating. You'd be well advised, however, to make the effort to understand how convertibles work and why they belong in your portfolio. Once you understand the basics, you can leave the messy convertible bond math to the managers of your funds.

Three Possibilities

Investing is a balancing act between seeking high returns and not losing most—or all—of your investment. As you get older, you have to get more conservative because if you blow most of it then, you have less, or no, opportunity to replace it. Your situation is one side of the equation; the other is the future direction of the stock market. If you knew what the market was going to do, it would be a cinch—like reading the January 2, 2005, *Wall Street Journal* next Monday morning. We've mentioned that there are only three possible directions the market can go: up, down, or sideways. Convertibles can work for you in all three cases.

Optimists insist that current stock valuations, which are very high compared to most of the twentieth century, are nonetheless here to stay. They argue that the end of the Cold War, technology, the information revolution, and the Internet means that we have left the postindustrial age and entered the information age, causing a new-era paradigm shift that will allow valuations to stay high. Some compare today's conditions to the 1950s, when stock investors shook off their fears of another depression and began buying stocks for growth. Up to that time, investors had required higher dividend income from stocks than interest income from bonds because it was perceived that stock yields were less safe than bond yields, but in the 1950s they gave up this preoccupation with safety.

Today's pessimists, however, take a different view. They say that once again, we are hearing the most dangerous phrase on Wall Street: "This time, it's different." They feel that we are in a speculative bubble, and when it bursts—(as they insist it must), stocks will retreat to their average valuations of the past 100 years; the average stock would then be selling 50 percent below current prices.

In addition to boom or bust, there is a third possibility, that the stock market of the future market will go sideways. Warren Buffett calls this a "muddle-through" market, and he provided a 17-year example (from 1964 to 1981) in the November 1999 issue of *Fortune:*

Dow Jones Industrial Average
December 31, 1964: 874.12
December 31, 1981: 875.00

Looking at the 0.88 gain over 17 years, Buffett said, "Now I'm known as a long-term investor and a patient guy, but that is not my idea of a big move. . . . And here's a major and very opposite fact: During that same 17 years, the GDP of the United States—that is, the business done in this country—almost quintupled, rising by 370 percent." He continued, "If I had to pick [stocks'] most probable (future) return it would be 6 percent. . . . And if [I'm] wrong, I believe that the percentage is just as likely to be less as more."

Planning for Uncertainty

You can choose to avoid the stock market. Millions do—even those with the wherewithal to invest. Noninvestors usually dismiss stock investing as "legalized gambling." But if you take a look at the historic returns from investing in stocks over most long periods, it's clear that simply avoiding stocks is a flawed strategy. Risk control does not have to be an either-or choice between stocks and bonds. There is a third alternative: bonds that can be *converted* into stocks, called unsurprisingly, convertible bonds.

Unloved Convertibles

An intriguing fact about convertible bond *funds* is that, in 1999, they were one of the three *least* favored fund sectors, reported annually by Morningstar. Morningstar's "least loved" funds, as measured by amounts of investor cash flowing into and out of them, have a 12-year record of above-average returns, outperforming 78 percent of all funds and 89 percent (!) of the most popular fund categories in subsequent 3-year periods. One year, Morningstar's writer called their least favored sectors, "the closest you can get in the mutual fund business to a sure thing."

How Convertibles Work

Understanding the mathematics of convertibles is a bit of a challenge. And, to make things even more difficult, if you are investing directly, you really can't think in terms of one or two bonds. Holding anything less than 10 bonds is impractical because there is almost no market for less than 10 bond pieces. That having been said, however, we'll use a single-bond issued on January 15, 2001, by an imaginary company as an example to explain the mechanics of convertible bond investing:

CommTelData Corporation (CTDC) 4.50% 1/15/2006 Convertible Bond

$1,000	Face value
5 years	Maturity—bond will be paid off on January 15, 2006
$ 45	Coupon—4.5% yield, annual interest, paid semiannually
$ 24	Stock price when bond is issued
33 shares	Conversion ratio

What this means is that an investor who invests $1,000 in the CTDC bond on the day of issuance will receive $22.50 interest every 6 months—4.5 percent of $1,000 in semiannual installments. On January 15, 2006, when the bond matures, he will also get his $1,000 returned. These features are called the "fixed income characteristics" of the bond.

Investment Value

Because of the bond's fixed income characteristics, it can sell at a price that reflects its "investment value," which is calculated much like that of any other bond. This value, in other words, will be a function of its coupon rate (the income percentage paid annually), quality (high-, low-, or medium-grade, according to its safety ratings; see Chapter 7) and maturity date (when it will be paid off). But the bond's *investment value* is not the only factor that may determine its price. The other price determinant is the fact that it can be converted into a fixed number of shares of stock.

Conversion Ratio

Our mythical bond has a 5-year maturity. Any time during this period, at the bondholder's option, he can convert it to 33 shares of stock. On the day the bond is issued, the stock was selling at 24. Since the $1,000 bond was worth only $792 in stock, converting wouldn't make sense at that time. The difference between the face value of the bond (its par value) and its conversion value is called the *conversion premium.*

Investment	$1,000 value of bond
Conversion Value	$ 792 (33 shares × $24 stock price)
Conversion Ratio	41.66666 (Number of shares represented by the bond's par value: $1,000 / $24)
Conversion Premium	$ 208 (Investment minus conversion value)

The conversion premium can be expressed as a percentage calculated as follows:

$$\frac{\$1,000 - \$792}{\$792} = 26.3\%$$

Convertibles and the Three Possibilities

The beauty of convertibles is that they provide security in bad markets, income and growth in good times, and the flexibility to adapt to changing conditions that common stocks and regular bonds can't offer. During the 5-year life of the bond, there are three possible scenarios:

1. The stock to which the bond can be converted goes down, settles into the midteens, and stays there until the bond's maturity date—
   - Common stockholders lose 40 percent to 50 percent.
   - Convertible owners earn their 4.5 percent per year and receive their $1,000 investment back at maturity. (Or they sell their convertible bond at a price determined by its investment value.)

2. The stock goes sideways—
   - Common stockholders receive 0 percent returns.
   - Convertible owners earn their 4.5 percent per year and receive their $1,000 investment back at maturity. (Or they sell at a price determined by its investment value.)

3. The stock doubles to 48—
   - Common stockholders earn 100 percent returns.
   - Convertible owners can convert to 33 shares of stock worth $1,584, or they can sell the bond at its appreciated value, realizing a gain of approximately 60 percent ($33 \times \$48 = \$1,584$).

In actuality, the convertible owner's return would be a sliver higher than $1,584, because, as stocks rise, conversion premiums narrow, but they don't disappear. Most convertible investors would probably sell the bond, rather than convert, unless they wanted to be long-term investors in the stock.

Our single-bond illustration is oversimplified because we're trying to make a simple point: Compared with common stocks, *some* returns are more assured. If your portfolio is totally committed to stock funds and you're worried about risk, replacing some of your stock funds with convertible funds will provide you with a nonfinancial bonus—added piece of mind. There is a trade-off involved: While you get most of the returns that stock fund investors receive, you don't get them all.

"The Bond Crash Was Worse Than the 1929 Stock Market Crash"

We recently talked with John Calamos of Calamos Asset Management, and author of *Convertible Securities* (Irwin Library, McGraw-Hill, 1998). Calamos is arguably the father of convertible bond funds, having established the first continuously operating convertible fund in 1985. In addition to overseeing four convertible funds, his firm manages $5.5 billion, mostly for institutions.

Calamos talked of his experiences with convertible securities in the early stages of his 30-year career: "One of the things I found (in the early 1970s)—I had been studying various market instruments in graduate school—was their ability, if they're used correctly—to control risk. Volatile markets were characteristic of the 1970s—not only with stocks, where people expected a lot of risk. What also happened was the bond market crashed. There were people then who said that on an inflation-adjusted basis, the bond crash was worse than the 1929 stock market crash. The sad thing was that so much conservative money was lost—people's life savings."

During the period that Calamos is talking about, two things occurred: Along with falling stock prices (the Dow fell from 1,000 to 500), soaring interest rates also crushed bond prices. Even the highest quality long-term bonds fell to 30 to 40 cents on the dollar. Calamos' focus on convertibles as his primary investment vehicle was to try to prevent such devastating losses. Since it's difficult, or impossible, to predict the future of stock or bond prices, using convertibles as a hedge against bad judgment—or bad luck—is sensible at any time. Calamos points out, "convertibles allow me to control risk in volatile markets. The volatility of the 70s has never gone away, really. In the 80s it was still there and again in the 90s. And here we are in 2000 with different circumstances and a different economic background, but markets are as volatile as ever. It's difficult to get away from it."

If you buy a convertible bond near par ($1,000), you are buying a fixed income security that will give you the relative safety of a bond because you will get your money back when it matures. And the investment value of the bond, for which you can sell it at any time, provides additional protection. If the stock of the issuing corporation falls 50 percent or 75 percent, the convertible bond will only drop part of the way—until it is resting on its "cushion"—its investment value.

A Smoother Ride in a Convertible

As Calamos points out, "We want to be in there for the long term and we want to be fully invested, but how can we manage risk as these markets zig and zag and drive people nuts?" Volatility can be unnerving, which makes some investors try to protect their capital by moving back and forth between being invested and in cash. But investors who try to jump back and forth between conventional stocks, bonds, and cash make wrong decisions more often than right ones. Convertibles offer increased safety: They allow you to stay with your investments because they increase your comfort level.

How does buying convertibles help you to control risk? Through the bond aspects of the investment. The coupon (semiannual payments), the bond rating, and the payback of your initial investment at maturity (relatively secure if you buy a high-quality issue) mean that you protect your principal. And the potential for achieving a good rate of return on your investment comes from the underlying stocks. As Calamos says, "If the stock, in fact, goes up, it will drag the convertible bond with it. You can have significant capital gains—it can double, triple, or quadruple if the stock keeps going up."

The Role of the Mutual Fund Manager

Convertibles are more complicated than stocks, but unlike stocks, their risk profiles can be more easily estimated—if you know what you're doing. Calamos describes in simple terms how he thinks of the risk-reward relationship for convertibles:

> We measure that so we can say we have 75 percent or 80 percent of the upside of the underlying stocks, and if we get hit with a bad stock market, we may only get hit by 20 percent or 25 percent of the downside. So that's a favorable risk-reward—most of the upside and a limited downside. If we can keep that ratio intact—which is the portfolio management part of it . . . as time goes on, you kind of "staircase up" (increase the value of your assets). That's really what has happened with convertibles for the last 30 to 40 years.
>
> The other [favorable] characteristic about convertibles is that no one knows about them. There seems to be a real lack of sponsorship—they're complex, they're an institutional type of vehicle and there's a lot of numbers associated with them. The typical individual investor, unless he's a real student of the market, doesn't know the terms or when it's callable and so on—it really is a specialty area.

The Income Buyer's Trade-off

As pointed out in Chapter 7, until 1999, interest rates had generally declined for the previous 20 years, decreasing the yield available to income buyers. Bond fund yields have dropped approximately 30 percent since the early 1990s, from approximately 8.5 percent to around 6 percent. However, convertible bond fund yields have declined even more: from between 6 and 6.5 percent to between 2.5 and 3.0 percent, a more than 50 percent decrease. So compared with "straight" bonds, convertibles would seem to be relatively less attractive than they were a decade ago. They don't solve the problem of the investor who has to squeeze every last drop of current income from his portfolio. But as Calamos points out, everything is relative:

> Convertibles are not islands unto themselves—look how far interest rates have fallen. In my opinion [convertible yields] are generous right now—we're seeing current yields (of convertible securities, before deducting fund expenses) pushing 5 percent. That's very competitive—three or four times dividends on the underlying common stock, and probably only 150 basis points (1.5%) [less than]

straight fix income (bonds). With convertibles, you do sacrifice some yield—that's the trade-off. But by accepting a 1½ percent lower yield, I've got the right to buy the underlying stock. Is it worth it? We think it's a cheap trade-off because you can get a very significant capital gain.

Table 10.1 shows how cheap that trade-off can be. The convertible bond fund investor who accepted 2.73 percent *less* yield in 1990, *increased* his average annual total returns by 6.90 percent. On a $10,000 investment, with all distributions reinvested, the average convertible bond fund returned $39,847, almost double the $21,013 achieved by the average long-term straight bond fund.

Modern Maturities

While lower yields, compared to 10 years ago, might seem to make convertibles less attractive, another factor makes them comparatively more desirable: shorter maturities. Compared to the 1980s and early 1990s, when maturities averaged 15 to 20 years, today they are much shorter: The weighted average of the convertible bond funds tracked by Morningstar is 7.2 years, and Calamos says they are even shorter in his funds—5 years. As he says, "If things go to hell in a handbasket, I've got bonds coming due . . . I'd rather have shorter maturities anytime. When the market gets hit, the investment grade bonds hold really well on the downside." The reduction of the "money-back" waiting period from approximately 15 years to 5 years, greatly increases the attractiveness of convertibles compared with 10 or 15 years ago.

The Downside: The Japan and Asia Experiences

The safety net provided by convertibles can be shown by the experience of Japanese investors. If a Japanese investor retired in 1988, the two most obvious investment categories were stocks and bonds. Since Japanese stocks had

TABLE 10.1 Straight versus Convertible Bond Funds' "Cheap Tradeoff" between Current Income and Total Returns

	1990 CURRENT INCOME (%)	AVERAGE ANNUAL TOTAL RETURNS 01/01/90–03/31/2000 (%)
Straight Bond Funds	8.75	7.51
Convertible Bond Funds	6.02	14.41
	−2.73 Yield	+6.90 Total Return

Source: Morningstar Principia Pro Plus for Mutual Fund, July 2000: Average category returns for convertible bond and long-term bond funds.

provided wonderful returns over the previous 20 years and bond yields were averaging only 1 percent, stocks—or stock mutual funds—would have seemed to be the logical choice. But it would have turned out to be the wrong one: From its highest level in 1988, the Japanese stock market dropped by more than 60 percent, and 12 years later it is still down more than 50 percent.

What would have been a better choice? Calamos's answer:

> If you had [invested] in the convertible bond market of Japan instead of the stock market, that dollar you put in—that is now worth 50 cents—[would have been returned to you] eighteen months later, because those bonds came due. And that's not an example of what you might have been able to do in a small niche—the Japanese market was the largest convertible market in the world—larger than the U.S. After big drops, investors' typical reaction is to wait until you're even before deciding what else you might want to do. The convertible investor could have done that at the end of eighteen months. The other guy [who invested in stocks]—after twelve years, that sucker is still waiting.

Calamos sums up how he views the risks faced by the older investor: "Say I'm retired and I have this lump sum from an (IRA) rollover, and you know what? I can't replace it—I don't want to roll the dice. I don't want to ever be down 50 percent and have to explain how the wrong guy got elected or Congress or the Fed did something—the preservation of principal is very very important. *One day, maybe the market will come down and not come back.*"

For a more recent example of the safety net provided by convertibles, think back to the 1997–1998 meltdown of the "Asian miracle." Let's assume, like the poor soul who invested his retirement funds at the top of the Japanese stock market, that you invested in the average Asian fund (Pacific/Asia excluding Japan) tracked by Morningstar in August 1997, when the market was at its top. At the end of the 13-month meltdown that soon followed, you would have lost almost two thirds of your investment. However, had you invested instead in the Mathews Asian Growth and Income fund—*a fund that invests at least 65 percent of its assets in convertibles*—you would only have lost a little over one third (see Table 10.2).

TABLE 10.2 Asian Meltdown: August 1, 1997–August 31, 1998

	% LOSS	AMOUNT REMAINING $10,000 INVESTED ($)
Average Pacific Asia ex-Japan Stock Fund	−61.14	3,886
Mathews Asian Growth & Income Fund	−35.21	6,249

Source: Morningstar Principia Pro for Mutual Funds, March 31, 2000.

And how long would it have taken to break even on your investment? In the Mathews convertible fund, you were at the break-even point 15 months later (December 1, 1999) with $10,038, while the average stock funds' value had only recovered to $8,453.

The Upside

But concentrating only on the downside can get depressing. Convertibles not only help when things go wrong, they also are a good bet for when things go right; after all, the reason to invest is not how much you might lose, but how much you might make. As Calamos says, "Why should I lend my money to companies to make their stocks go up and not participate in the stocks?" Since Calamos hopes for convertibles to gain 75 percent to 80 percent of stocks' returns, it's instructive to see whether his funds, in fact, have delivered those returns. Table 10.3 shows that while the average convertible fund's returns fell a little short of his targeted returns (at 67.2% of the S&P 500 Index's returns), Calamos's funds actually exceeded his objectives: One delivered 87.2 percent and the other (shown in bold) actually beat the index, gaining 107.5 percent.

Looking Forward

In a way, the wonderful 1990s was "bad" for convertible bond funds: They lagged behind soaring stock fund returns. Compared to technology stocks and indexing, convertibles provided only three- or fourfold returns—pretty dull stuff, which explains the massive indifference to them shown by most fund sponsors and investors. If the future is less benign for stocks, the convertible safety net will be much more compelling. That, however, will become apparent to the average investor only *after* it's obvious: after a big stock drop. And as we know, once it's obvious, it will be too late to protect your assets.

TABLE 10.3 Ten-Year Returns for Period Ending December 31, 1999: Convertible Bond Funds versus Common Stocks

	AVERAGE ANNUAL RETURN (%)	RESULT OF $10,000 INVESTED	S&P 500 RETURN (%)
Standard & Poor's 500	18.20	$53,233	100.0
Calamos Convertible A	15.57	42,495	87.2
Calamos Growth & Income A	19.03	57,097	107.5
Average Convertible Fund	13.78	36,350	68.3

Convertible sector funds provide a way to invest in areas where you might not otherwise venture because of risk. As an investment opportunity, Asia, for one, isn't going anywhere, and it may be that the meltdown was really just a postponement of an inevitable economic miracle in the region. Mathews International Funds thinks so; their Web site carries a banner: "Our company, our Funds, and our investment philosophy are all predicated on our conviction that Asia will be the fastest growing region of the world in the 21st Century." They may be right, but in the aftermath of the meltdown, an Asian stock fund may seem too risky . If so, Mathews' convertible bond fund provides a safety net that may be enough to overcome your reluctance to face that risk.

Or take the technology sector: While you may believe that the technology is compelling, it too, may seem too volatile. In 2000, Calamos Asset Management filed an SEC registration for Calamos Convertible Technology Fund—the first convertible technology fund— that could be an answer. But, once again, keep in mind the first principle of good investing: Asset allocation should be the foundation of your investment plan. Here's where you can use convertibles to best advantage, because they allow you to fine-tune your asset allocation. If you just can't bring yourself to buy "boring bonds," even though you know you should, less boring investment grade convertible bond funds are an elegant compromise. Or if you don't quite have the stomach for the risk of stock funds, or volatile sector funds, convertible bond funds are an alternative.

In Chapter 11, we explore the final category of your basic mutual-fund options: closed-end funds. These, too, are often neglected by investors; but they can provide interesting opportunities because from time to time they sell at unjustified deep discounts to their net asset value. Although they are a little more complex than more common open-end funds, they are well worth taking the time to understand.

CHAPTER 11

Closed-End Funds

Wagner's music is
better than it
sounds.

—Mark Twain

Closed-end funds (CEFs) trade on the exchanges just like stocks. In this, they are unlike open-end funds, which trade once a day, with the price determined by their net asset value (NAV) at the close of trading. CEFs also differ from open-end funds in that their shares aren't continuously redeemed or issued by their sponsors based on their NAV. When a CEF is first formed, only a preset number of shares in the fund are sold to investors. These are first sold in an initial public offering (IPO), and the proceeds are invested in a portfolio of securities. After the IPO, however, the fund is "closed": No more shares are offered for sale and shares are not redeemed by the sponsor. From then on, closed-end share prices are determined by supply and demand as with stocks.

While most of your fund portfolio should be invested in open-end funds, closed-end funds occasionally make a good alternative choice. For example, a closed-end fund may offer opportunities to buy at a substantial discount to NAV, or it may provide you with the chance to invest in an area that open-end funds don't provide. And there's another enticement for investors: Conventional wisdom has it that nobody likes closed-end funds anymore, which is reason enough to explore them.

The most important "new" concept you need to understand is the relationship between closed-end funds' open-market prices and their underlying NAVs. When a CEF is selling at more than its NAV, it is said to be selling at a "premium"; when the price is less than NAV, it is at a "discount." While CEFs occasionally sell at premiums, most of the time they sell at discounts. This can be easily seen in Figure 11.1, which shows the average discount of the Herzfeld Closed-End Fund Average since December 1987. Established in 1987, when the Dow Jones Industrials stood at 1938, it is an average of 15 large closed-end

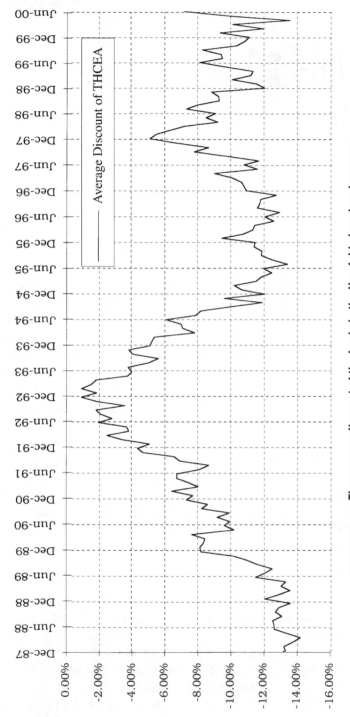

FIGURE 11.1 The average discount of the funds in the Herzfeld closed-end average.

Source: Thomas J. Herzfeld Advisors, Inc. (Miami).

funds listed on the AMEX and NYSE. Figure 11.2 compares the performance of closed-end funds with that of the widely watched Dow 30.

Figure 11.1 shows the average discount has fluctuated between approximately 14 percent at its widest points and 1 percent at its narrowest. As a group, however, CEFs never sold at a premium, although some individual funds in the average did. In May 2000, 94 percent of all CEFs were selling at discounts, and the average discount of the funds in the Herzfeld Closed-End Average was approximately 10 percent as shown in Figure 11.2.

Why Do Closed-End Funds Usually Sell at Discounts?

CEF discounts or premiums, which are expressed as percentages, are not difficult to calculate. If a fund is trading on the New York Stock Exchange at 10.75, and the NAV is $10, the $0.75 premium is 7.5 percent. On the other hand, if it is trading at 8.75, the $1.25 discount is 12.5 percent. While buying mutual funds at a discount sounds appealing, keep in mind that most CEFs sell at discounts most of the time, and for several reasons, including:

- They can't be sold back to the sponsor at NAV. Sellers are at the mercy of buyers who usually won't buy unless there is a discount. This is the biggest reason behind CEF discounts.

- Simply "because it's there" or, more importantly, because it's *usually* there. Since investors expect discounts, while they may narrow, they are unlikely to be extinguished.

- As a response to a shift in market psychology. When the market psychology sours, the risk that discounts will get even steeper is great.

Discounts can be grisly: During the 1973–1974 stock market debacle, some were as wide as 40 percent to 50 percent. In 1994, a year in which most open-end funds showed losses of 1 percent to 3 percent, the Herzfeld Closed-End Fund Average discount widened from approximately 4 percent to 12 percent, magnifying losses considerably. More recently, from December 1997 to the bottom of the spring 2000 sell-off, the discount widened from approximately 5 percent to almost 14 percent.

In addition to psychology, investors' perceptions are often colored by bad experiences associated with a particular CEF. For example, investors may feel that the initial public offering of a sector-specific CEF (say, the technology sector) was done at the wrong time. If such an IPO was distributed near the top of an investment fad that subsequently faded, early purchasers of shares would have suffered losses. This would make other investors less willing to buy into the fund unless they are offered a substantial further discount. Another problem: Rights offerings, where additional shares are made available to existing

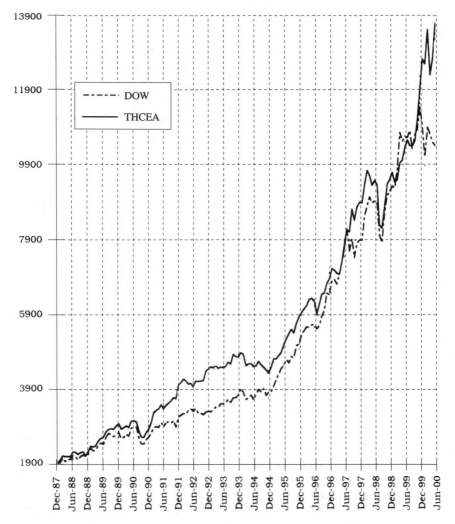

FIGURE 11.2 The Herzfeld closed-end average (THCEA).

Source: Thomas J. Herzfeld Advisors, Inc. (Miami).

shareholders at a slight discount, have often been ill-timed, when the NAV or share price was high diluting the value of existing shareholders who didn't subscribe to the additional shares. Because of sales charges on closed-end funds, IPOs are routinely distributed at premiums. After their IPOs, they typically sell at "business as usual" discounts. Obviously, IPO buyers have the cards stacked against them.

While brokers make significant distribution and marketing commitments to CEFs when they are first offered, after the IPOs, they move on to distributing other merchandise. CEFs become orphans, with minimal advertising or promotion—if they get any at all.

Why Do Discounts Vary?

As Figure 11.2 shows CEF discounts can vary widely. The largest discounts can have various causes:

- Equity funds often sell at deep discounts because compared to CEF bond funds, many provide little or no income.
- When open-end funds have had poor historical results, shareholders can vote with their feet and redeem their shares at NAV; but investors who want out of a poorly managed closed-end fund have to sell on the open market, where buyers are unlikely to be interested unless there is a wide discount.
- Out-of-favor investment sectors usually sell at bigger discounts.
- Large unrealized tax gains that pose a potential future tax liability for investors.
- Funds with a significant stake in illiquid securities (e.g., private placements, to be discussed) are discounted further because their holdings are not generally perceived to be as reliably valued as listed common stocks that trade on the exchanges.
- Unfavorable general market conditions.
- Leverage—over 80 percent of CEF bond funds use some kind of borrowing to enhance their yields, but this increases their risk. Discounts widen when buyers demand higher yield to compensate for the increased risk.
- IPO-burned shareholders sell depressed CEFs in order to move on, particularly late in the year to realize tax losses. Until their selling is exhausted, discounts tend to stay wide.
- Because of perceived risk, Third World country funds sell at deeper discounts than do industrialized country funds.
- Commissions reduce returns compared to "no-fee" no-load funds.
- Many investors don't want CEFs' added complexity and uncertainties, which also helps explain the usual discount.

Closed-End Cousins

Even though they are dwarfed by their open-end cousins that manage over $7 trillion in assets, CEFs are still a significant presence in the investment universe; there are over 500 funds with over $100 billion in assets. As a percentage of all funds tracked by Lipper, Inc., a mutual fund tracking firm, assets of closed-end funds have decreased from 7.92 percent in 1990 to 3.6 percent today.

It wasn't always so; in the 1920s, closed-end funds *were* the mutual fund industry. At that time, there were approximately 400 CEFs, with assets of $4.5 billion. Because most were highly leveraged, only a handful of the CEFs that existed prior to 1929 survive to this day—New York Stock Exchange-listed Adams Express, Tri-Continental, and Petroleum & Resources, being examples. CEFs languished in obscurity for decades until the 1980s, when closed-end bond funds became popular again because Wall Street marketed them as a way to "lock in" declining yields. A decade later, equity CEFs also regained some of their old popularity.

In the years 1992 through 1994, 273 new closed-end funds were launched. Typically, IPO underwriters added markups (effectively, premiums) of 7 percent over the funds' NAV, which generated approximately $3 billion in underwriting fees. These markups systematically vaporized shortly after the initial offering, as prices melted down to—and then through—the NAVs, ending up at discounts that endure to this day. Currently, two thirds of CEFs are bond funds, broken down as follows: taxable funds 30 percent, municipal (tax-free) single state 11 percent, and municipal-national 25 percent. Single-country stock funds represent 13 percent, domestic equity funds 16 percent, and growth and income funds 5 percent.

The Wrong Way to Invest in CEFs (The Right Way Follows)

The launch of closed-end Global Health Sciences (now called Invesco Global Health Sciences) in January 1992 is a classic example of how *not* to invest in closed-end funds. Global Health was marketed with an "almost track record"—its manager was the same one who had managed Invesco's open-end Financial Health Sciences Fund, which had been ranked the number one fund in the country the previous 5 years. The open-end fund achieved a remarkable 33.3 percent average annual 5-year return, with a 92.9 percent gain during the previous 12 months. While the new fund was going to be slightly different, it wasn't going to be *that* different—why would you want to be much different from the number one fund in the country?

Underwriters raised $345 million from investors, who plunked more money into the new fund in one day than had ever been invested in the old one during its entire 7-year life. Investors paid $15 per share—a price that included $24 million in underwriting fees—and watched the stock rise from the offering price of 15 to a high of 15⅛, and then roll over as it headed to a discount. Soon thereafter, the healthcare sector cycled out of popularity, and to make things worse, the Clintons trained their guns on the industry.

By year-end, Global Health Sciences was hovering just above $9 at a 10 percent *discount* to NAV (see Figure 11.3). In less than a year, investors had lost over $100 million—a third of their investment—and 2½ times more than the open-end sister fund's 13.8 percent loss. It took over 3½ years before Global Health Science investors broke even.

Global Health Investors' Mistakes

As stated in Chapter 2, the most common mistakes made by investors are mistiming (buying already hot sectors) and ignoring costs. In this case, although there were some technical differences, these errors were abundantly in evidence:

- *Performance chasing* Investors sank huge amounts of cash into the fund because the healthcare sector had delivered torrid returns for 5 years and prices and valuations were high.
- *Ignoring costs* Underwriters deducted 7 percent ($1.05) from the $15 per share offering price, leaving only $13.95 for investment (NAV).
- *Buying a CEF at a premium* IPO investors paid a 7 percent premium when 10 percent discounts are the norm.

A portrait of Global Health's IPO belongs in the lobby of the Wall Street Hall of Shame, along with scores of others. Even rookie brokers know that CEFs seldom trade at premiums. Yet, during the 1992–1994 period, thousands of financial professionals routinely sold premium-priced CEFs to their customers apparently without the slightest twinge of collective conscience, 273 funds "worth" $44.2 billion.

In 1994, of 39 CEFs launched, 37 were losers, dropping an average 13 percent in a year when the S&P 500 rose slightly. Then more CEFs glutted the market, and discounts became deeper and more widespread. While 63 percent of CEFs were selling at discounts at the end of 1993, by the summer of 1995 the percentage grew to 84 percent.

As disillusionment grew among investors, the discount of the Herzfeld Closed-End Fund Average widened from 2 percent at the end of 1992 to minus 12 percent in December 1994. As Wall Street wore out its welcome, the investor-destruction derby finally ground to a near halt. In 1994, 43 IPOs made it to market, down from 121 the previous year, and by 1995 there were only 5 debuts. More recently, in 1999, of the 33 new closed-end funds that went public, 31 were bond funds—only two were equity funds. By May 2000, 94 percent of

● Invesco Global Health Sci	Month-End Premium/Discount Time Period	%	Annual Average Premium/Discount Time Period	%
Highest Historical Premium	Jan 1992	7.45	1992	-3.71
Lowest Historical Discount	Jun 1996	-25.41	1996	-21.92

Current Premium/Discount is -12.67% as of 04-30-2000

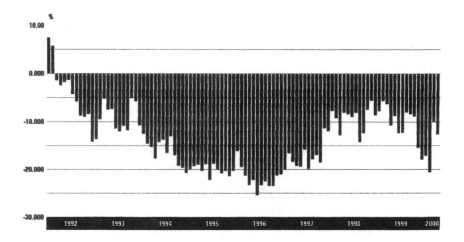

FIGURE 11.3 Month-end premium discount from 01-01-1992 to 04-30-2000.

all CEFs were selling at an average discount of 17.7 percent, according to Morningstar.

Reaching for Yield—Closed-End Bond Funds

As pointed out in Chapter 7, investment grade bonds—those unlikely to default—add the most predictability to a portfolio because you know exactly when interest payments are due and when the bonds will mature. Open-end bond *funds* have no maturity, so they reduce this predictability. In addition, their income is not totally predictable either as pointed out in Chapter 7.

While open-ended bond fund unpredictability is bad enough—their closed-end cousins take a step even *further* away from the certainty of direct investment in bonds. The additional unknown is the unpredictability of future premiums or discounts inherent in their closed-end structure. And if that weren't enough, still another level of uncertainty is that most closed-end bond funds (approximately 80%) use leverage—to varying degrees—to increase income to their investors. Leverage—borrowing at one rate with the expectation of being able to invest at a higher rate—usually results in increased income. However, when things don't work out as planned, instead of increasing income, leverage reduces it.

However, on the surface, the appeal of being able to buy—and receive income from—$10,000 worth of bonds for an $8,500 investment might seem compelling. Table 11.1 shows how long-term holders fared during the past 10 years in the 17 high-yield CEF funds that have been in existence for 10 years or longer, out of the 36 that are carried in the *Wall Street Journal* every Monday (market returns are shown because investors didn't receive NAV returns). Italicized entries are discussed in more detail in the bulleted list following the table:

Actual returns were disappointing:

- The average high-yield, closed-end bond fund, instead of garnering higher returns because of added risk, actually delivered lower returns than did the high quality, open-end Vanguard Long Term Corporate Bond Fund.

- Eighty-two percent—14 out of 17 funds—lagged Vanguard's *open-end* high yield fund. CEF investors who, in theory, should have gotten higher returns from investing at a discount, really didn't get a bargain at all. Most investors who paid full price (NAV) for the Vanguard fund achieved higher returns.

- Leverage, which, in theory, is supposed to increase returns, did not—or at least not enough to improve overall returns meaningfully.

TABLE 11.1 Market Returns—17 High-Yield, Closed-End Bond Funds
January 1, 1990–December 31, 1999

	ANNUAL RETURN %	$10,000—AMOUNT AT END OF PERIOD
Kemper High Income Trust	10.41	26,910
Pacholder Fund	9.91	25,724
High Yield Plus Fund	9.82	25,516
Vanguard High Yield Fund (open-end)	9.81	25,500
Cigna High Income Shares	9.75	25,343
High Yield Income Fund	9.20	24,108
Franklin Universal	9.01	23,704
Liberty-Colonial Interm High Inc	8.90	23,468
Zenix Income Fund	8.90	23,451
CIM High Yield Securities	8.78	23,209
Vanguard Long Term Corp (open-end)	8.58	22,784
Average Closed-End Bond Fund	7.95	21,795
Credit Suisse Asset Mgmt Income	7.92	21,425
New America High Income Fund	7.87	21,340
Van Kampen High Income Trust II	7.68	20,959
Van Kampen High Income Trust	7.67	20,936
MSDW High Income Adv II	6.25	18,336
MSDW High Income Adv	5.43	16,972
MSDW High Income Adv III	4.47	15,448
Prospect St High Income Portfolio	3.17	13,666

Conclusion: For long-term bond investors, compared to investing directly in bonds or open-end bond funds, closed-end funds have little appeal.

Trading Closed-End Bond Funds

For intermediate-term investors (24 to 36 months), CEFs can provide trading opportunities if you buy them when their discounts appear to be unusually wide. This is usually after periods when interest rates have been rising, causing stress and uncertainty in the bond market.

The first two columns in Table 11.2 show the average annual premiums and discounts of the same CEFs shown earlier, as well as the "month-end lowest historical discount," that is, the widest discounts during the same 10-year period. As you can see, at the extremes of pessimism, discounts were quite wide; 15 out of 17 traded at discounts of 15 percent or more and 8 were available at 20 percent plus, at some time during the 10-year period.

If, during the period, you had the patience and fortitude to invest only when discounts were unusually wide, your returns would have been excellent as prices recovered and the discounts narrowed. An added bonus would be that, as with equity funds, discounts tend to be widest after prices drop. Bond funds bought at already depressed prices and then discounted another 15 percent to 20 percent

TABLE 11.2 Average Annual Discounts and Premiums

	ANNUAL AVERAGE PREMIUM/DISCOUNT (%)		MONTH-END LOWEST HISTORICAL DISCOUNT (%)
	HIGHEST	LOWEST	
Kemper High Income Trust	+8.84	+1.69	−4.84
Pacholder Fund	+5.60	−12.42	−18.92
High Yield Plus Fund	+4.56	−7.36	−18.96
Cigna High Income Shares	+14.39	−0.40	−15.43
High Yield Income Fund	+10.19	−15.85	−24.24
Franklin Universal	+5.71	−14.28	−18.51
Liberty-Colonial Interm High Inc	+4.46	−7.02	−18.93
Zenix Income Fund	+13.92	−12.06	−14.61
CIM High Yield Securities	+3.94	−16.61	−26.15
Credit Suisse Asset Mgmt Income	+2.38	−12.88	−17.40
New America High Income Fund	+16.88	−19.14	−46.02
Van Kampen High Income Trust II	+16.99	−6.14	−24.52
Van Kampen High Income Trust	+23.53	−4.86	−11.59
MSDW High Income Adv II	+12.90	−13.78	−25.37
MSDW High Income Adv	+23.28	−12.73	−26.77
MSDW High Income Adv III	+19.30	−8.64	−20.00
Prospect St High Income Portfolio	+10.93	−11.25	−42.75

	Month-End Premium/Discount		Annual Average Premium/Discount	
● Credit Suisse Income	Time Period	%	Time Period	%
Highest Historical Premium	Jul 1987	8.45	1987	2.38
Lowest Historical Discount	Dec 1999	-17.40	2000	-12.88

Current Premium/Discount is -14.23% as of 04-30-2000

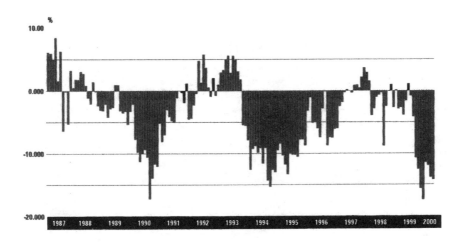

FIGURE 11.4 Month-end premium discount from 04-01-1987 to 04-30-2000.

because of a drop in underlying bond prices provide an extra income stream while you're waiting for prices to recover and for the discount to narrow.

Figure 11.4 shows the "Month-End Premium Discount of Credit Suisse Income Fund (CIK-NYSE) from 04-01-1987 to 04-30-2000," a graph from Morningstar Principia Pro for Closed-End Funds. As with most IPOs, the fund's discount deepened in 1989 and 1990 to more than 15 percent as disgusted investors dumped their shares after its 1987 IPO. The discount then gradually grew smaller, and by 1992, it sold at a modest premium. In 1994, another bad year for bonds, the discount widened to as much as 15 percent; then decreased again in 1995 and 1996. Investors who bought near the points when discounts were widest, at approximately 15 percent, achieved over 17 percent average annual returns (from "boring" bonds) during both of the 3-year periods that followed.

As bonds once again suffered in early 2000, the discount widened to more than 15 percent. It remains to be seen if investors who bought at that level will do as well as in the two previous cycles, but those who did, "bought" an approximate 13 percent current yield, which provides an excellent start. If history repeats itself, they can also look forward to some future price appreciation.

Christmas Shopping at Fire Sale Prices

Looking at CEFs when their discounts were widest after their IPOs—when disappointed early investors were taking their tax losses—provides you with an excellent buying guide. Table 11.3 shows that of nine offered during 1997 and 1998 tracked by Morningstar, the discounts of seven were widest in either November or December of the year after they debuted.

TABLE 11.3 Buying at Year-After, Year-End Discounts

FUND	INCEPTION	WIDEST DISCOUNT (%)
Blackrock High Yield	12/98	12/99 – 14.69
Chartwell Div & Income	6/98	12/99 – 17.29
Conseco Strategic Income	7/98	12/99 – 15.32
Debt Strategies	5/97	11/98 – 19.22
Debt Strategies II	3/98	12/99 – 18.89
Debt Strategies III	7/98	11/99 – 17.74
DLJ High Yield	7/98	12/99 – 16.36
Dreyfus High Yield	4/98	03/00 – 11.78
Managed High Yield	8/98	08/98 – 10.17

As the old saying goes: "If you keep your head while those around you are losing theirs . . .," you can profit from the average investor's mistiming. While pessimistic open-end fund investors have the assurance of selling at NAV, closed-end fund investors do not: They are forced to sell on the open market to other investors who are *equally* pessimistic, so it's easy to see how during periods of stress, CEF discounts widen. When the storm clouds clear and average investors decide it's safe to go back in the market, CEF discounts tend to narrow. If you have patience and discipline, you can profit from most investors' wrong-way investing patterns.

Revisiting Global Health Sciences

To demonstrate how the discount can work in your favor, a revisit to the beleaguered Global Health Sciences shows how it happens. At the end of 1994, investors were suffering from large losses caused by falling healthcare stocks. At that point, Global Health's IPO premium had been transformed into a discount of over 20 percent.

In 1995, healthcare stocks began a rousing 4-year recovery that boosted the NAVs of both the open-end and closed-end Invesco funds. In 1996, however, scalded investors in the closed-end fund were still depressed. As shown by Figure 11.3, the 20 percent discount persisted; and even widened at one point to over 25 percent, even though the fund's NAV had risen smartly. By 1997, most of the disappointed investors had apparently sold off their holdings, because the discount began to narrow; while the NAV rose 18.5 percent, the market price increased 31.0 percent. Finally, in 1998, the discount narrowed to an average 9.3 percent; in some months it was less then 6 percent.

Unlike the 1992–1995 cycle when the widening discount harmed investors, the narrowing discount in the later period boosted their results. Table 11.4 shows market returns which were even better than for the open-end fund.

TABLE 11.4 Growth of $10,000 – 01/10/95 to 12/31/98

	TOTAL RETURN (%)	ANNUALIZED RETURN (%)	AMOUNT AT END OF PERIOD
Invesco Global Health (closed-end)	265.06	38.23	$36,506
Invesco Health Sciences (open-end)	200.72	31.69	$30,072

Niche Opportunities

Because CEF investors are essentially locked into their funds, the fact that they can't redeem shares allows some managements to invest in opportunistic areas that are impractical or impossible for open-end funds to exploit. CEFs can use some of their assets to invest in illiquid markets (markets where there is very little trading) or in companies where there is no public market at all. Investing in nonpublic companies, called private placement or "venture" investing, can pay big rewards. An example of how this works can be found in two healthcare funds: H&Q Healthcare Investors and H&Q Life Science Investors.

Beneficiaries of "The Next Wealth Machine"

In their March 2000 cover story, "The Next Wealth Machine," *Worth* magazine made a bold journalistic bet on biotechnology. "Thanks to technology, medicine faces unprecedented change. For investors, this means unprecedented opportunity." It wasn't explained what "unprecedented opportunity" meant, but it might have referred to the success of the technology during the 1990s. Most investors would be delighted to equal returns of the technology funds: Their average annual 28.88 percent return provided early investors with a more-than 12-fold return: $10,000 grew to $126,431.

The decade began with just 12 open-end technology sector funds, with assets of less than $2 billion. By the end of 1999, they numbered 59, with assets up 80-fold to $103 billion. Today, the biotech "wealth machine" is not much bigger than technology was in 1990: There are five funds with assets of $2.8 billion.

If *Worth's* optimistic prediction comes true, the five open-end biotechnology funds will do exceedingly well; and there will, of course, be many more biotech funds by the end of the decade. However, there are two closed-end funds that might be better choices: H&Q Healthcare Investors (HQH) and H&Q Life Science (HQL), both listed on the NYSE, with more than one-half of their portfolios invested in biotechnology. A comparison between these two funds and their open-end counterparts reveals how the closed-end structure can have significant advantages.

HQH has assets of $209 million and was founded in 1987; HQL, with assets of $100 million was founded in 1992. Since inception, Alan Carr, whose previous experience includes managing a $300 million healthcare portfolio at Putnam Investments, has managed both funds. HQH's average annual 10-year and 5-year NAV returns for the period ending June 30, 2000, were 20.62 percent and 33.02 percent: HQL's 5-year return was 30.83 percent.

Venture Investments

Approximately 40 percent of both funds' assets are invested in private placements—venture capital investment in promising fledgling companies. Open-end funds cannot participate in a meaningful way in these types of investments because their unstable investor populations would preclude anything other than token amounts. For example, from 1991 to 1994, when biotechnology was out of favor, investors' redemptions depleted Fidelity's biotechnology fund's assets from $1.1 billion to $396 million. If the fund had had a large stake in illiquid venture investments, it might have been forced to suspend redemptions.

Partly because closed-end fund investors cannot redeem their shares as freely as their open-end counterparts, the H&Q funds' portfolio turnover averages less than 20 percent, compared to open-end biotech fund portfolio turnovers of 85 percent to 450 percent.

One disadvantage of such high turnover is that even if those funds invest in the next BioCiscos and BioMicrosofts, what good is owning them for only a few months? Funds with relatively small assets can invest in small stocks and own them for the long term. Here's where H&Q seems to be getting things right: As shown in Table 11.5, the median market capitalization (total value of a company's stock) of the stocks in H&Q's funds is only about one fifth the size of the average biotech fund—and that is just the publicly traded companies, not the venture investments.

While the H&Q funds enjoy the advantages of a small asset base now, it could be even more so if investors become more enthusiastic about biotechnology and open-end funds get deluged with cash. At the other end of the spectrum, if biotech falls out of favor, H&Q's funds won't have to liquidate their long-term positions at distressed prices because of redeeming shareholders. And the funds have other attractive aspects as well. For example, the latest SEC filings show Carr owning a combined position of over 40,000 shares.

TABLE 11.5 Assets and Median Market Capitalization

	OPEN-END BIOTECHNOLOGY FUNDS (5) AVERAGE*	HQH	HQL
Assets ($ml.)	562	209	100
Median Market Capitalization ($b.)**	3.7	0.8	0.8

* Dresdner RCM Biotechnology, Fidelity Select Biotechnology, Monterey Murphy Biotechnology, Franklin Biotechnology Discovery A, Rydex Biotechnology.

** Publicly traded holdings only—inclusion of venture investments would reduce median capitalization.

Managers of open-end funds may or may not have similar stakes in their funds, but there is usually no way to verify it.

Fidelity Select Biotechnology is the only other biotech closed-end fund with at least a 10-year track record, and is working on its fifth fund manager, whereas Carr has been at HQH's helm since inception. An evaluation would be incomplete of course, without performance comparisons (see Table 11.6).

Since Fidelity Select Biotechnology is pure biotech, and the H&Q funds are only 55 percent biotech, the comparison is inexact. Even so, based solely on past performance, Fidelity's fund would appear to be a better investment. However, that might not be the best strategy—if the biotech "wealth machine" delivers as promised, publicly traded holdings will boost NAVs for both H&Q and Fidelity, while strong forces could propel both H&Q funds past Fidelity's returns.

- During favorable conditions for biotechnology, more of H&Q's venture investments could go public, which would boost returns significantly. Fidelity won't have this advantage.

- H&Q's funds approximate discounts of 20 percent plus could narrow if enthusiasm for biotech increases; in the early 1990s, during the last wave of biotech enthusiasm, both funds sold at single-digit premiums.

- Premiums could also appear in anticipation of the IPOs of one or more of H&Q's venture investments, or discounts could narrow for the same reason.

- If unlike the past decade, small-cap stocks outperform large-cap stocks, public enthusiasm for H&Q funds' small-cap portfolios, compared to open-end funds' mid- and large-cap stocks, could narrow the discounts.

- In a period of small-cap outperformance, H&Q's insulation from asset bloat afflicting open-end funds could be a major plus.

For a better understanding, from the "inside," of the H&Q potential, we interviewed portfolio manager Alan Carr on June 19, 2000.

TABLE 11.6 Average Annual Return Based on Net Asset Value

	TEN YEARS ENDING 12/31/99 (%)	FIVE YEARS ENDING 12/31/00 (%)
Fidelity Select Biotechnology (open-end)	24.53	33.40
H&Q Healthcare Investors (closed-end)	15.55	18.94
H&Q Life Sciences (closed-end)	NA	22.53

Interview with Alan Carr, Portfolio Manager H&Q's Healthcare and Life Sciences Funds

Q. In a recent *Barron's* interview, you were asked whether "prospects [for biotechnology] rank up there with those presented by the Internet revolution." You said you felt, "From an investment standpoint, biotech is equally, if not more exciting." Anything to add?

A.C. I think the long-term outlook is extraordinary. As I pointed out, compared to the 80s, biotech has much more substance. There are 140 biotech industry products on the market and that number could double in the next 18 months, based on the number in the FDA (Food and Drug Administration) pipeline. Further, what may be even more exciting is that once [biotechnology products] are approved, they have a history of very strong sales early on as they fulfill a need that has not previously been met—$100 million sales the first year is not uncommon.

Q. In addition to the funds, do you run any private money?

A.C. No we don't. We are sharply focused—our funds get all our attention.

Q. While the closed-end structure has disadvantages, doesn't it give your funds the advantage of being able to do private placements that open-end funds can't?

A.C. [Open-end funds] aren't allowed to invest more than 15 percent in private placements and as a practical matter, they can't have a lot of their portfolio illiquid. Our structure allows us to accumulate relatively illiquid positions in publicly held companies.

Q. What has been the returns of your private placements versus the rest of the portfolio?

A.C. Private placement definitely contributed to returns—they added several percentage points to overall performance.

Q. The funds' fixed distribution policy—what is the intent?

A.C. Primarily to shrink the discount—although it doesn't seem to have had much effect. Also, it allows shareholders to invest at the discount to NAV, which should help over time.

Q. Your funds have a very low portfolio turnover compared to open-end funds—even accounting for venture investments. Any comment?

A.C. Historically, it's about 30 percent—which is indicative of what I feel is a realistic time frame [to try to anticipate developments]. I don't believe you can expect to look out any more than about two years.

Q. What about "asset bloat"—if biotech becomes hugely popular, won't that give you an advantage over open-end funds?

A.C. At the end of the quarter (3/31/00) we had about $650 million and we're had to modify our approach with venture capital—we've been able to take more of a leadership role with investments in the $5 to $6 million range. In some cases, we became the lead investor and had the clout to set price—so that has been a plus. However, do I think we could operate the same way with $2 billion? Probably not.

Bombed-Out Asset Class

In May 2000, a senior equity funds analyst for Merrill Lynch, told CNBC that foreign country CEFs were a ". . . bombed-out asset class." But he continued, "The good news is that the average discount is widening. . . . All things being equal, if you can buy, say, a closed-end Japan fund at a 22 percent discount, it's probably better than buying an open-end (Japan) fund (at NAV)." Merrill Lynch's "good news" obviously wasn't good for investors, who have previously invested at premiums or narrow discounts only to watch them widen, but it does provide possible future gains if for whatever reason, discounts narrow.

Very occasionally, for reasons that look silly with 20-20 hindsight, enthusiasm for a single-country fund soars. When the Berlin Wall came down in 1989, the Germany Fund rose to over a 50 percent premium, and it averaged 14 percent in 1990. However, as expectations dampened, the premium shrank and went to a discount in 1994 that has averaged over 10 percent every year since.

If you think that countries like Indonesia, Korea, or Pakistan—or Cuba for that matter—have bright prospects, CEFs are sometimes the only pure way to invest through a mutual fund. Some countries' economies have declined so much that the prices of their CEFs sell in low single digits; for example, Jakarta Growth Fund (1⅜), Thai Capital (3), Korea Equity (3⅝), and Herzfeld Caribbean (Cuba) (5¹¹⁄₁₆). It's appealing to think that you can "buy a whole country" at a steep discount for less than $10 a share, but when fund assets implode, as these have because of the poor economic conditions in the countries involved, expenses—which are relatively fixed—soar. Jakarta Growth Fund's recently reported expense ratio was 4.66 percent. Even so, they may be unprofitable for their sponsors. If sponsors decide to terminate their fund and distribute the proceeds, the funds' investments may be so illiquid that they cannot be sold at the prices used to calculate their NAVs. If so, the apparent discount might not be as wide as reported and realized proceeds could be less than you're counting on.

Discounts and premiums can change dramatically. After the early 1998 Asian economic meltdown, although the three Korean CEFs had fallen, they were still trading at over 40 percent premiums to NAVs. Investors were apparently antici-pating a quick recovery. As time wore on and the recovery failed to materialize, the premiums evaporated and soon became 30 percent discounts by the spring of 2000—percentage losses were huge. The lesson: *No matter how optimistic you may be, don't buy CEFs at premiums.* As in the case of Korea, there is usually at least one no-load open-end alternative and/or an exchange-traded fund to invest in. If not, even paying a 4 percent to 5 percent sales load to invest in an open-end fund would be preferable to a 30 percent CEF premium.

Open-Ending/Liquidating Opportunity

Almost all articles and columns written about closed-end funds talk about the possibility of funds "open-ending"—converting to an open-end fund—or liqui-dating. If a CEF selling at a 20 percent discount open-ends or liquidates, share-holders receive an almost overnight 20 percent profit. But it doesn't happen often; only approximately 2 percent of CEFs convert each year. Management usually has to endorse the conversion and few are enthusiastic about slaugh-tering a cash cow that systematically churns out fees whether shareholders, an almost captive audience, are happy or not.

Efforts in recent years to convert CEFs to open-end funds—some of which have included lawsuits—have failed more often than not because it usually takes 50 percent to 70 percent shareholder approval *in addition to manage-ment's willingness to convert.* In addition, if there is a legal battle, sharehold-ers get stuck with most of the legal bills—which reduces returns—and that's particularly painful if the open-ending initiative fails. However, institutional in-vestors have been increasing the pressure on fund's directors for conversions.

Getting Going with Closed-End Funds

The first place to start looking more closely at closed-end funds is the Monday *Wall Street Journal.* There you'll find headings showing their categories, where they are traded, their symbol, the market price and NAV, the discount or premium, and the 52-week market price returns plus dividends. The next stop should be exploring the Closed-End Association Web site, at CEFA.com. This site provides information on virtually every closed-end fund. There you'll find an education center, annual reports that can be downloaded, frequently asked questions, articles, recent reports, and news. If you enter a fund's symbol, you'll get recent and historical returns, a link to the fund's Web site where available, and a quote with the discount or premium du jour. In addition, the site provides Weisenberger reports on over 500 funds, showing 10-year NAV and market returns, top 10 sectors and holdings, and a 52-week chart of NAV and market value trends.

Morningstar's Principia Pro for Closed-End Funds provides many of the same statistics as their open-end service, and in addition, it provides excellent graphs showing monthly discounts or premiums going back 12 years (Figures 11.3 and 11.4); nowhere else can you get the premium/discount history as clearly shown. However, it doesn't provide such open-end services as a page devoted to larger funds with commentary and, particularly, category ratings (how funds perform versus similar funds).

Closed-end fund investing is not for everybody, least of all those who don't enjoy the investment process and/or are uncomfortable going against the crowd. But for some, it's a fascinating game where above-average returns are possible if you have the patience to wait for those few times (maybe three or four during a 10-year period) when the odds are heavily in your favor. But now it's time to move on to some alternative choices beyond the standard mutual fund categories. In Chapter 12, we discuss managed asset accounts, if you qualify, and what this approach to investing can do for you.

CHAPTER 12

Beyond Mutual Funds—Individually Managed Accounts

God shows his
contempt for wealth
by selecting the
nouveau riche to
give it to.

—Anonymous

Mutual funds are attractive because they offer diversification and relatively simple investing. They provide access to just about any conceivable investment niche and many, particularly index funds, are very cost-efficient. With their low minimums, mutual funds are available to just about anybody, even those with very modest means. However, mutual funds also have some disadvantages, and as your assets increase, they lose some of their luster—particularly if you have taxable accounts.

While mutual funds can be an excellent investment vehicle for the masses, there is one need that they don't satisfy: personal, professional attention that tailors your investment portfolio to your specific needs. For that, unless you do it all yourself, an individually managed asset account (IMA) is a good alternative. IMAs are not a brand-new idea; they've been around for decades, but until recently, they were only for the wealthiest investors. Now, however, if you have $100,000 or more to invest, you can get almost as much attention as the very rich have long enjoyed.

IMAs have grown rapidly in the past decade because they offer a higher level of personal attention than mutual funds provide. When you have an IMA account, you know the specific stocks and bonds in your account, and you will continually be updated on your portfolio via transaction confirmations and your monthly statement. This is very different from mutual funds, where the fund owns securities, and you own shares in the fund. With an IMA, you own 300 shares of Intel or Cisco Systems rather than so many shares of Fidelity or Vanguard fund. You also have a personal representative or contact, who keeps in touch with you regarding your account and advises you as your situation or your needs change.

Heard on the Street

"Once people reach a certain level of wealth, say, $100,000—liquid—or more, individually managed accounts (IMAs) is the next opportunity," says Robert Jorgensen. Chief Executive Officer of RunMoney.com, an online provider of IMAs. "What I'm excited about is what the mutual fund industry is not doing: Pushing back and insisting that the only vehicle out there is the community swimming pool—which I call mutual funds. High net worth investors want to invest in their *own* swimming pool.

"They don't want to be where the water goes up and down based on the number of people that are in there. A lot of investors jump in when the market is going up, [forcing the funds to buy] stocks at high levels. When the market goes down, they jump back out and here is the high net worth investor trying to manage his or her tax situation and the flow of the water is affecting the buy and sell decisions of his mutual fund manager."

Creating Services to Attract Your Assets

Brokers, fee advisers, and online services' IMAs offer customized, professionally managed portfolios of individual securities. Also called "wrap accounts," the fees for this type of investment service were very high in the past—and some still are. The Money Management Institute, the industry's trade association, wants to call them "individually managed accounts," to avoid the negative connotations associated with the old, expensive versions. The popularity of these IMAs is increasing: They boasted of assets of over $240 billion in 1999, up over 160 percent from $92.7 billion only 5 years previously. In 1999 alone, IMA account assets increased 28 percent, while the maturing mutual fund industry's net cash flow (new money invested versus money withdrawn), dropped by 39 percent.

The phenomenon is tracked by firms such as Cerulli Associates, a Boston-financial-services consulting firm that publishes the *Wrap and Managed*

Accounts Industry Survey every quarter. Cerulli projects that assets in IMAs will grow to $579.9 billion by 2004, and senior analyst Ryan Tagal told the *Wall Street Journal* (June 23, 2000), "The fund companies are all worried that their highest net-worth clients are going to be migrating to (these) separate-account products."

Brokers, too, have been under pressure from online competitors and fee advisers. As a result, they have made fee-based wrap programs a preoccupation for the foreseeable future; they recognize that investors are looking for more control, and are trying to offset the shrinkage of their tradional commission-based revenues. And although brokerage house profit margins on IMAs are smaller than for commission-based business, brokers recognize that IMAs garner annual fees that are paid whether transactions occur or not. IMAs offer brokers a relatively stable revenue base.

As a result, the whole field of investment advice is changing. As Cerulli's Tagal says, "There is no such thing as a broker anymore; they are financial advisers or financial consultants. A broker is kind of a bad word these days. . . . [But] most people [still] want financial planning and advice—kind of like being able to go to your doctor and ask candidly, 'What's my condition?' That's what brokers and financial consultants have had to evolve to." Brokers who offer IMAs can call themselves "advisers" and give the personal advice that their customers are demanding.

The largest IMA provider is Salomon Smith Barney's Consulting Group Program, with about a one-third market share of IMAs, followed by Merrill Lynch. Wall Street firms give IMA programs different names; for example, Morgan Stanley Dean Witter's various programs are lumped under "Investment Consulting Services." Less elegantly, Prudential calls its IMAs "Wrap Fee Programs." But, no matter what they're called, statistics, the extraordinary growth of assets, and anecdotal evidence all show the same thing: Many investors believe that fee-based services are a major improvement over the way they used to invest.

Some of this investor enthusiasm is probably due to the extra personal attention that IMA clients receive. They feel that since their average IMA investment is considerably larger than the average mutual fund account, they've earned the extras—the personal broker advice and attention, monthly statements, and so forth—that wrap programs offer. While many of them may have started out investing in mutual funds, as their investments have grown, they have reached the point that they feel it is time to move up to IMAs.

Reasonable Expectations

Unless you are truly wealthy, don't expect that becoming an IMA investor will automatically get you an invitation for a round of golf when your account manager comes to town. Still, you'll probably feel more of an affiliation than you do with the manager of your mutual funds. In the investment battle, both are hired guns, but in an IMA program, he's *your* hired gun. Clients feel more of a sense of participation, since they get personal attention with their broker, and notification whenever transactions are made in their accounts. There is no question that direct individual stock ownership livens up the investment process. Of course, if the securities markets aren't as profitable in the next 15 years as they were during the past 15, IMA clients may start to yearn for *less* participation, but for the time being, they like the feeling of being personally involved in with investments.

FUNDamental Facts

Professional Help When You Need It

It may turn out that wrap programs have a hidden benefit—they may cushion investor panic attacks during a plummeting market. As an IMA investor you can sell stocks any time, if you have the feeling that both your manager and broker/adviser are keeping their cool, reason might be more likely to prevail. If your advisers are doing their jobs, they might keep you from selling near a major bottom—a chronic problem for mutual fund investors, many who operate without professional guidance. But as there haven't been any real bear markets since IMA programs have become so popular, only time will tell.

Investment adviser W. James "Bear" Bower of Pebble Beach, California, talks about one of the key disadvantages of mutual funds: "embedded" capital gains. These are investment gains on securities that have been in the portfolio for a long time. When the fund sells, all fund shareholders—including recent investors—must pay the tax on these gains. As Bower points out sarcastically, "You have the joy of paying taxes on somebody else's profits."

Not so with IMAs. When you open an IMA, you start off with a clean slate, with no embedded gains. This is a distinct tax advantage. Another tax advantage is that your IMA can be coordinated with other investments. You can take gains or losses in your account and offset the impact of other investments you may have. For example, let's say you've sold real estate for a big gain. You can help offset its tax impact by taking losses in your IMA.

In the November 1999 issue of *Investment News,* Leonard A. Reinhart of Lockwood Financial Services, a large provider of wrap programs, said, "The biggest single advantage of separate accounts [IMAs] is tax efficiency. In most mutual funds, the portfolio managers have a problem. They have both taxable and tax-deferred assets in their fund. Who do they run it for? To date, they have been running it for their total return money." If you have a separate account in an IMA, you can control your tax situation.

Although it's beginning to improve, it has been hard for the average investor to get data about the impact of mutual fund taxes on their fund portfolios. Almost all rating services and personal finance magazines calculate pretax performance. As shown in Table 12.1, however, the November 1999 issue of *Investment News* provided a comparison showing the advantage of a typical separate account (IMA) over mutual funds, including their comparative tax efficiency ratings.

Nothing Is Perfect

While IMA "tax advantages" are undeniable, other advantages may be less certain. The idea that, as a group, IMA managers are somehow going to provide higher returns than mutual fund managers has not been shown, if for no other reason than that, in many cases, they are one and the same. Since the sudden spectacular growth of IMAs has occurred only recently, there is not enough history to draw any conclusions.

TABLE 12.1 Separate Accounts versus Mutual Funds—Separate Accounts the Clear Winner

ASSUMPTIONS	SEPARATE ACCOUNT (%)[a]	AVERAGE MUTUAL FUND (%)[b]
Unrealized capital gain *(no embedded capital gains in separate account)*	0	20
Average portfolio turnover *(buys and sells in portfolio)*	20–40	88
Capital gains realization rate *(in separate accounts, the individual decides when to take gain)*	5–25	50
Tax efficiency (5-year)[c] excluding fees	85–95	74

[a] Lockwood Financial Services
[b] Morningstar, Inc: December 1999—All Domestic Funds.
[c] Less tax liability in separate accounts versus funds due to personal control of account.
Note: Italics added.

> **FUNDAMENTAL FACTS**
>
> Mutual fund performance statistics are subject to independent audit and are reported to the SEC. Managers of wrap accounts are subject to SEC regulation also and report their returns regularly. Most wrap providers claim they do more due diligence and verification of money managers than is necessary with mutual funds. According to the Association for Investment Management and Research (AIMR), to which most wrap managers belong (and are deemed to be "AIMR compliant"), performance statistics are reported in a prescribed and uniform manner and are independently verified "to ensure fair representation and full disclosure of investment performance."
>
> Conclusion: IMAs report their results regularly and voluntarily, and although they are not as carefully regulated (by the SEC) as the mutual fund industry, they are presumed to conform to accepted practices.

Nuts and Bolts

Wrap programs come in many packages. Cerulli divides them into five segments, as described in the following subsections.

Mutual Fund Wrap Account

A professional adviser selects a portfolio of mutual funds consistent with your circumstances and risk tolerance. He or she may be a fee adviser or a broker at a national or regional brokerage firm. The adviser monitors the funds, makes changes and reports to you personally on the progress of your accounts—or lack thereof as discussed in Chapter 3.

Mutual fund wrap accounts have grown in popularity, particularly at full-service brokerage firms, where the fee is sizable. Fees may total 1 percent to 1.5 percent, layered on top of typical fund expenses. Together, these costs take a substantial bite out of annual returns:

Typical Mutual Fund Wrap Account—Estimated Annual Costs (%)	
Fund's average annual expense ratio (custodial services management, and administration)	1.4
Fund's average transaction expenses (cost of buys and sells in portfolio)	0.6–0.8
Mutual fund wrap fee (annual charge for managing account)	1.0–1.5
Total estimated annual costs	3.0–3.7

The estimate of average transaction expenses is probably conservative. On the other hand, there are fee advisers who charge less than 1 percent or invest heavily in index funds, that can reduce the total annual costs by as much as 50 percent. Mutual fund wrap accounts differ from normal mutual funds in one other way. Mutual fund wrap accounts are usually *advisory*, not discretionary. The broker does not buy and sell without consulting the client. In addition, a semiannual evaluation and portfolio rebalancing are usually included.

Fee-Based Brokerage Account

Investors who are used to dealing with commissioned brokers are migrating to these IMA-type accounts. Total assets invested in these accounts at the end of the first quarter of 2000 were over $150 billion, up more than $40 billion year over year. Typically, investors pay an annual fee of 1 percent or more and are permitted a specified number of transactions per year at a set rate or for free. Brokers provide advice, but it is not as systematized as that provided to wrap account customers. These are not pure IMA accounts, since they are merely a variation on the old commissioned-broker theme. The difference: It's fee-based and the number of transactions are limited.

"Rep" Portfolio Wrap Account

Customers receive personal services, including long-term planning, tax and asset allocation guidance, and regular reporting. Transactions are made at the discretion of the adviser without client involvement in the transactions, but these transactions are limited to trades involving a "select" group of securities from the brokers' approved lists.

"Senior Rep" Portfolio Wrap Account

These accounts are the province of broker representatives who have extensive experience in the business and who have been screened to meet certain standards. The services provided are comparable to those offered in standard rep portfolio wraps except that the senior reps have more flexibility to choose investments—they are not restricted to a "select" list.

Consultant Wrap Account (IMAs)

A broker or fee adviser who has knowledge of your circumstances introduces you to an investment pro: a money manager who your adviser believes will be a good match to manage your money. The manager, usually from a well-known money management firm, invests your account in individual stocks, bonds, convertible securities, and so on, making choices in accordance with your stated goals. He or she also takes into account your tax situation and any other preferences; for example, your stated desire to invest only in "socially conscious" securities.

Both the broker and the manager have defined roles. The broker's responsibilities include:

- Due diligence in checking the manager's qualifications, reputation, and competence.
- Marketing the program to prospective clients.
- Recruiting investors.
- Establishing client's goals and objectives and passing them along to the money manager.
- Introducing client to the money manager.
- Handling the paperwork related to the client's managed assets.
- Executing transactions—handling the buys and sells of securities in the portfolio as directed by the money manager.
- Sending bills, statements, and confirmations of all buy and sell transactions to the client.
- Monitoring the account's performance.
- Collecting the client's wrap fees at the brokerage firm and forwarding the appropriate portion of those fees to the money manager.

The money manager's responsibilities include:

- Providing regular performance statistics to the broker.
- Helping to sell the client on the program.
- Directing the broker which securities to buy and sell.
- Monitoring client's investment returns over time.
- Reporting performance to client.
- Communicating with client periodically.

The broker or adviser assigned to you represents you not only by monitoring but also by making sure that your money manager's investment strategy remains consistent with your goals and objectives. In addition, the broker handles routine administrative details, such as tracking your account balance or other account information and sending out dividend and interest checks.

The appeal of this kind of structure is that with a relatively modest account, you get access to the talents of money managers who normally would be dealing with more sizable accounts. This is possible because tasks are allocated: the broker or adviser does all the work of selling and opening accounts and relieves the manager of what is usually a fairly long and sometimes tedious process: signing up clients. Technology enables brokers to handle scores or even hundreds of clients with an ease unthinkable just a decade ago, when it would have been too labor intensive to be practical. Technology also enables managers' investment decisions to be implemented rapidly, in many accounts at once.

Wraps with RIAs (Registered Independent Advisers)

Even though independent advisers don't have the economies of scale of wire-houses, they are able to offer the same services using discount brokers. In some cases, overall costs, including the wrap fee, custodial, administrative and transaction charges, and the manager's fees, will be lower than the wire-house programs.

The Pros and Cons of Wrap Programs

Wrap programs are gaining in popularity, but it's important to weigh the advantages and disadvantages carefully before taking the plunge. Here's a partial list of wrap-program pros and cons:

Advantages

- *Avoidance of open-end funds' structural disadvantages:*
  1. *Avoidance of tax liability* The recognition of mutual fund capital gains is beyond your control. Fund management, and even fellow shareholders, can trigger capital gains taxes at inopportune times.
  2. *Fellow shareholders* Sellers or buyers of shares in volume during turbulent markets can affect your returns by bloating or depleting your fund's assets, usually at the wrong time.
- *Individual ownership of securities* The account manager can be sensitive to your tax situation; capital gains can be taken when it is to your best advantage. If you own 100 shares of Microsoft with a large capital gain, you can sell stocks with losses in your wrap account and sell your Microsoft for a gain, thus balancing the loss with the gain and reducing or eliminating your tax liability. Although it may be more psychological than actual, many investors prefer direct, rather than indirect, ownership.
- *Access to managers who manage large accounts ($1 million or more)* The "wholesale distribution" provided by brokers' wrap accounts provides access for smaller investors who wouldn't otherwise qualify.
- *Flexibility* If you fire your wrap manager, you don't have to sell the securities in your account. Because you directly own your stocks, you can keep them in your account or transfer them to another broker. If you fire a mutual fund manager, on the other hand, you sell the fund as well.

- *Manager's personal attention if needed* This is simply not available with a mutual fund.

- *Portfolio concentration* A typical managed account will contain 25 to 40 stocks, less than half of what you find in a typical mutual fund. There is the potential (it's by no means guaranteed) for better performance with a more focused portfolio.

- *Cost savings* In some cases, costs and fees are lower than they would be in a no-load open-end mutual fund.

Disadvantages

- *Costs* Although some wrap programs' annual costs are competitive, some are considerably higher than you'd pay in a mutual fund: 3 percent or more per annum. If you can't negotiate a lower fee, this is a distinct disadvantage.

- *Higher costs for the same manager* Some managers participating in wrap programs also manage no-load funds, where the management costs are lower.

- *More investment risk* While less diversification compared to an average fund allows higher returns, it also increases risk. If your account manager has a bad streak, the relative concentration will amplify losses.

- *Regulation* IMA programs submit to SEC oversight voluntarily. Compared with mandatorily regulated mutual funds, the possibility of shenanigans is higher.

- *Performance disclosure* Although there are performance reporting standards for private money managers, nothing compares with the audited performance statistics that mutual funds submit to the SEC and the extraordinarily detailed statistics compiled by Morningstar and other tracking services.

Determining Costs

The retail price you pay for the all-in-one wrap program varies by how much it is marked up by your brokerage firm. Full-service firms mark these fees up the most and, as you might expect, discount brokers and online providers, the least. That's why you want to take a close look at the internal costs (management fee, administrative costs, and your personal broker's advisory fee) of individually managed accounts before investing in them. These costs break down roughly as shown in Table 12.2.

It's ironic that posted (standard) fee schedules at full-service brokerage firms apportion more of your fees to the broker than to their managers—the people making the investment decisions.

TABLE 12.2 Typical Individually Managed Equity Account Fees for a $100,000 to $250,000 Account

	FULL-SERVICE BROKERS (%)	DISCOUNT BROKERS (%)
Money manager	0.50–1.00	0.50–1.00
Brokerage functions	1.20–2.00	0.10–0.35
Advisory function	included	0.25–1.00
Total	1.75–3.00	0.85–2.35

Negotiating Lower Fees

It's an open secret that clients can negotiate lower-than-posted wrap fees. Competition is bringing posted fees down and should continue to do so, so don't hesitate to try. Like buying a car, odds are, you *can* pay less than the posted sticker price.

A wirehouse branch manager and veteran of 30 years in the brokerage business explains,

> The posted rates on wrap accounts are now around 2 percent per year on accounts of $500,000 and above; but that's not what the firm *really* charges. Our brokers have the okay to discount up to 40 percent. If the customer has more money to invest later, or has been an especially good client, he'll probably get the maximum discount. But it doesn't stop there. It's even possible to get as much as a 50 percent discount, with management approval, for a few select clients.

This is not just one opinion; it's the industry norm. Most large brokerage firms have a discount—a "whisper" number that allows brokers to charge less than the posted price. But a lot of investors don't like to haggle. In an otherwise supposedly dignified business, bargaining may seem distasteful, but it's necessary.

With less than $500,000, you have less clout, and even at $100,000 you can probably get some reduction in fees. As they say in the car business, the "deal has to work" for you as well as the broker, and they want your business. Some old-line investment management firms look down their patrician noses at relatively new wrap programs. Their disdain has to do, in part, with wrap accounts' comparative microsize, which the old-liners view as not worth bothering with. The reason most often given, however is "outrageous" wrap fees. Brokerage firm managements, who should know better, know the fee math: A systematized annual 3 percent whack out of their clients' hides is 30 percent of stocks' historical returns.

> ### FUNDamental Fact
>
> Although they claim they are improving them, wirehouse in-house mutual funds have a long and singular record of mediocre to dreadful average relative performance (Chapters 5 and 7). The industry has a long way to go before it can demonstrate that it is as skillful managing money as it is moving and gathering it. Since their IMA programs are supposed to provide objective and unbiased advice, one would guess that they wouldn't include their own in-house managements on their carefully selected list of IMA managers. Guess again. Most offer in-house managed IMAs, and if history is any guide, most probably offer extra incentives to the sales force for steering clients in their direction. If you are evaluating wirehouse IMAs and the broker you're working with recommends an in-house manager, look for another broker.

Lower Cost Wraps

It doesn't matter what brokers expect—what matters is what you want to pay, and what services you can expect. And there is an alternative. In some cases, the same money managers whose services are offered by full-service brokers are also available at much lower cost. Charles Schwab, for instance, offers lower pricing for asset-based accounts. Schwab's Managed Asset Account Connection "offers investment advisers easy access to 50 of the country's leading institutional separate-account managers representing 100 investment styles." Although Schwab's program is the largest, competitors offer similar programs and their list is growing. There are two ways to gain access to these lower cost services:

1. If you are already working with a fee adviser (independent registered investment adviser), he or she sets up the account for you at Schwab for the selected manager. You have to work with an independent adviser to open a separate account with Schwab.

2. If you aren't working with an adviser, Schwab will provide a list of pre-screened advisers who will help with manager selection, setting up the account, and so forth.

You can't open up a separate account, also known as a wrap account, without a financial intermediary, typically, a fee adviser. Even so, using lower cost providers will reduce your fees.

Online IMA Programs

Predictably, wrap programs are also available in cyberspace. Two Web sites (runmoney.com and wrapmanager.com) are offering them already, and more are being rolled out to solicit client accounts. Although Cerruli reports that most investors particularly those with a couple hundred thousand dollars or more, feel they need some kind of advice, there are some who feel they don't. You may be one of them. If so, you can save even more on fees online. Currently, RunMoney.com charges all-inclusive 1.50 percent per year and Wrapmanager .com has a fee of 1.25 percent.

While these two Web sites will hook you up with a manager, the *Wall Street Journal* says more are coming onstream in the next year. Annual fees are in the 1.25 percent to 1.50 percent range now, but there is talk that they will be coming down to 1 percent, or possibly less. Minimums of $100,000 are also probably going to be reduced by some, possibly to as little as $25,000 per account.

One immediate concern might be, "With many e-commerce sites going under, how safe is my account?" The apparent good news is that investors' portfolios are held by independent custodians who administer your account. In one case, the custodian is a clearing subsidiary of a major wirehouse and in another, a national bank subsidiary. If online wrap programs have SIPC (Securities Investor Protection Corporation) insurance, in that respect, there is no more risk than with online or full service brokers.

Heard on the Street

Observers are predicting that the IMA movement is going to accelerate even more. Fund sponsors, such as Invesco and Alliance, already offer them, and Dreyfus and MFS Financial have announced new programs. There are rumors that others are going to be announced by Putnam, Janus, Fidelity, and others.

You aren't completely on your own if you use one of the online providers. When you contact them, they have licensed representatives who will lead you through filling out a profiling questionnaire either online or over the phone. Based on the information you provide, they will recommend independent money managers who appear to be a good fit for your investment needs. On each Web site, there is somewhat limited information about each manager— numbers of years in business, assets managed, performance for various periods, management style, and so on.

Staying in Touch

If you sign up, you are billed—or the all-inclusive fee will be deducted from your account, quarterly, or in advance. After that, you receive monthly statements, trade confirmations, quarterly performance reporting from the provider, and reports from the manager. You'll be able to visit your account online any time you wish. Although they're still in the formative stage, online providers are contemplating services that aren't even offered by full-service providers, such as instant notification by e-mail of transactions, the manager's reasons for making each trade(s), chat rooms with your manager, and so on.

As with discount brokers, there is access to some of the same managers available through wirehouses. What you *don't* get is personal TLC. Whether you are dealing with a wirehouse, a discount broker, or an online wrap manager, they're all working with the same basic profile, derived from your initial interview or questionnaire. This is likely to result in all of them giving you similar recommendations.

Unpopular funds and socially responsible funds are examined in Chapter 13. By unpopular, we don't mean unattractive—quite the contrary. They are interesting investment opportunities precisely because they're currently out of favor with investors. As for socially conscious funds, they are designed for people who don't want to support companies that abuse the environment, sell tobacco, have a history of improper treatment of their employees, and the like. There are several funds that refuse to include such companies in their portfolios. And far from suffering because of these exclusions, many of them have delivered superior investment results.

CHAPTER 13

Off the Beaten Path: Unpopular Funds and Socially Responsible Funds

It is better to be looked over than overlooked.

—Mae West

With all the options available, picking just a few out of the thousands of available funds can seem to be a daunting task. The majority of investors usually opt for the current leaders in the performance derby, but Morningstar's Russ Kinnel thinks this is a bad idea: "Anyone who buys a fund off a winners list probably deserves to be down 20 percent. You're inevitably picking a fund that focuses on stocks that are overheated" (May 6, 2000). There are, however, alternatives to following the pack: There are perfectly valid out-of-the-mainstream fund choices in which you can do better. These are the "wallflower" funds, which appeal to the contrarians among us; and "socially responsible" funds, which are popular among investors with a strong social conscience.

Wallflowers are currently unpopular mutual funds that merit attention because they are out of favor. Morningstar has studied unpopular funds for over a decade and has shown that buying wallflower funds has been a good idea. Socially responsible funds are tailored for investors who want their investments to complement their social or political principles. For the socially conscious investor, these funds preclude companies that deal with overseas sweatshops, sell tobacco or liquor, engage in practices that disturb the environment, and so forth.

Contrarian versus Momentum Investing

In recent years, two dominant and extreme investing strategies seem to have emerged. The most popular is "momentum" investing (where investors buy stocks or funds, regardless of price or valuations—simply because they are rising). This technique often works because of the laws of physics: A body in motion tends to remain in motion. The exciting, almost one-way markets of the late 1990s were ideal for momentum investors, allowing many to seem more skillful than they really were. Both talented and mediocre momentum fund managers garnered high returns as high stock prices climbed ever higher.

When it works, momentum investing provides almost instant gratification, as when Amazon.com tripled in price in a single year. But in a sideways, choppy, or down market, momentum investing provides dismal returns, because stock prices don't move up enough to allow investors to get in and out profitably, and frequent transaction costs take an additional toll.

Contrarians: Hoping for Reversion to the Mean

In Chapter 2, we saw how chasing performance reduces returns to below average, even below the returns of the very funds they invested in. The reason is that investors tend to be optimistic and buy when prices—and valuations—are high, and sell when they are low. In effect, these people are *fund*-momentum investors and most are not very good at it. Usually their portfolios would provide higher returns if left alone.

The opposite of momentum investors are what are called "contrarians." These patient folks go bottom-fishing for stocks and funds that have low prices and valuations, buying them when nobody else seems to want them. This is the classic "buy low, sell high" strategy, and when the market is choppy or sluggish, it can be a good way to go. However, this approach has its own problems: It worked miserably during the last half of the 1990s, during which cheap stocks stayed cheap, and in many cases, got cheaper; so did cheap funds.

Value-fund managers, who buy companies trading at a discount to their perceived value, watched as investors pulled hundreds of billions of dollars out of their funds during the 1990s, as people jumped onto the momentum-investing bandwagon, and some of these managers found themselves without jobs. But for decades, until it fell into disrepute in the 1990s, value investing was considered not only respectable, but shrewd. The most revered figures in the fund management business were almost all value managers.

Value investors try to capture the extremes of favor and disfavor and count on the "reversion to the mean" principle to secure their profits. It is a valid investment strategy that works, and even though it has been out of favor recently, in the long term it has worked well. It means, however, that an investor, or fund manager, must go against the crowd, which is sometimes hard to do psychologically.

Death of the "Dogs"

The most famous contrarian strategy in recent times was the hallowed "Dogs of the Dow." In this strategy, you buy the 10 highest-yielding stocks in the Dow 30 every year, looking for a rebound in their prices. It provided superior returns for decades—a book was even written about it. This strategy became hugely popular in the early and mid-1990s, and Wall Street distributors pandered to demand by dispersing pure and variations of "Dogs" unit trusts worth billions of dollars.

That's when the strategy stopped working. Dog lovers all bought the same stocks nobody else wanted, and the result was the stocks didn't drop enough in price to be real bargains. But just because the Dogs died and some fund managers are looking for work, it doesn't mean that value investing is dead. One constant on Wall Street is change, and it's just a matter of time before value investing returns to favor.

It's the Category, Stupid . . .

Although it seems hard to imagine now, investors weren't always obsessed with technology. In 3 out of 5 years—1989, 1990, and 1993—the technology sector was at the bottom of the category pile. Yet by the end of the decade, Fidelity Select Technology had posted a 10-year streak of average annual returns of 28.9 percent—thus beating the S&P 500 Index average annual return by over 10 percent annually. Late in the decade investors had become so enthusiastic they swapped out of index funds, which they had only discovered a couple of years previously, for technology funds.

If you can invest in an unloved category before it becomes popular, the profit potential is large. If you are in a rising-category fund—even with a dim-bulb manager—you are far better off than in a declining-category fund run by a genius. But how do you measure category popularity and profit from it? Morningstar provides a useful tool: They measure what investors are doing with their money (how much money is flowing into and out of different fund categories). They also recommend a strategy to profit from their findings, if you have the patience and discipline to be a contrarian investor.

Morningstar Wallflower Funds

Every January, *Morningstar FundInvestor* ($99 per year) reports on the three least popular fund categories of the previous year. A category's popularity, in this usage, is not defined by returns; instead it is determined by its money inflows and outflows, relative to all others. Even if a category has had net additions of cash during the previous year, if it is one of the three with the least cash added, it is deemed to be one of the unloved.

When trouble hits a category, many investors sell their stocks or fund shares to free up money to put in a more popular category. This selling drives down stock and fund prices. After prices fall, the media trumpets the mournful news, causing more selling. At year-end, the bad news is recycled again and the category's woes show up on the "Year's Worst" lists, causing even more selling. By this point, Morningstar ratings of funds in the troubled category have dropped to one or two stars (more selling), so there are very few interested buyers. The bad news is now stale and most investors are preoccupied with popular sectors where all the stars are. For the contrarian investor, history has shown that this is the time to consider these laggards—when they are "sold out."

Ideal Time to Buy

The strategy advocated by Morningstar is to buy one fund in each of the three unloved categories and hold on for 3 years. The strategy has one thing going for it: It is based on the orthodox, traditional, time-tested rationale of "buy low, sell high"—the way you're supposed to invest. Before popularity caused its demise, this is how buyers of "The Dogs of the Dow" prospered.

Backtesting this strategy to 1987, Morningstar's Peter Di Teresa, reported, "Unpopular categories beat the average equity fund over the next three years more than three fourths of the time. The odds versus popular categories have been even better. Unpopular categories have topped the popular ones over the next three years more than 80% of the time." As Olivia Barbee, *Morningstar FundInvestor's* managing editor, commented in 1999, "This is the closest thing investing gets to a sure thing."

Another reason to consider wallflower categories: Their breadth: Past unloved categories, include real estate, Europe, healthcare, Latin America, and convertibles. Consider the unpopular categories in 1998 and 1999:

1998	1999
Latin America	Latin America
Pacific/Asia ex-Japan	Precious metals
Natural resources	Convertibles

The breadth of the categories covers whole regions of the world, industries, and investment sectors, with funds diversifying their risk. Although it is a 3-year strategy, a look at the 1-year returns of 1998's recommended categories during its first year shows that it can get off to a terrific start:

1998 Category Returns (%) in 1999

Latin America	60.85
Pacific/Asia ex-Japan	72.28
Natural resources	30.26
Standard & Poor's 500 Index	21.04

You can't count on those kinds of spectacular returns in the future—the stars just happened to come together that year, boosting returns above the historical norm.

Heard on the Street

WHERE FUND MARKETERS SEE PROFITS, INVESTORS MAY FIND TROUBLE

"Looking for a reliable contrarian market indicator? Check out which sector the fund industry is loading up with new offerings. Consider the case of Internet funds. When 1999 dawned, there were only five, and all of them racked up stunning gains last year. By the end of May 2000, there were more than 30 Internet funds operating or in registration. Unfortunately, many came along just before the tech sector's huge sell-off. Having missed the triple-digit gains of 1999 (and 1998, for that matter), many of these funds are underwater since their inceptions. . . .

"The pattern continues. With a number of biotech funds posting gains in excess of 70% in 1999 and off to a good start again in 2000, a raft of biotech funds have been launched or are in registration.

"No one can predict with certainty when a sector's stocks have topped out, but if the fund industry's history is any guide, it is tough to be sanguine about these new biotech fund's prospects."

Morningstar FundInvestor, July 2000 (used by permission).

In 1999, Olivia Barbee reported less salubrious returns from the unloved category, "Three years ago . . . we suggested that investors buy 1995's unpopular bunch—precious-metals, communications, and Europe funds. The latter two picks are sitting on three-year returns in excess of 20%, but the precious-metals rebound is still aborning. In fact, investors who stuck with 1995's growth funds . . . reaped returns that were 12 percentage points better than those of the unpopular crowd. So the (Morningstar) study isn't infallible, but it has worked more often than not."

Strategy Specifics

Morningstar's strategy for investing in wallflower funds is based on the following rules:

- *Buy one fund from each category* They caution that buying in just one of the categories can be "risky."
- *Buy before summer vacation* Be sure to purchase by midyear (because you want to catch it before everybody else joins the club).
- *Limit your bets* Resist the urge to put more than 5 percent—or at most 10 percent—of your portfolio.

In its annual report on unloved funds, Morningstar also provides three recommended funds within each category (see Table 13.1). They include brief descriptions, usually with an assessment of relative risk. Morningstar's comments, coupled with the information on their Web site (morningstar.com), should put you on the right track if you want to use the strategy.

TABLE 13.1 One-Year Performance of Morningstar's 1998's Recommended Unloved Funds versus Their Category (%)

LATIN AMERICA	
Category	+60.85
T. Rowe Price Latin America	+59.38
Scudder Latin America	+47.16
Fidelity Latin America	+54.90
PACIFIC/ASIA EX-JAPAN	
Category	+72.28
Mathews Asia Gr. & Inc	+48.88
Mathews Pacific Tiger	+82.89
Newport Tiger	+73.14
NATURAL RESOURCES	
Category	+30.26
T. Rowe Price New Era	+21.11
Vanguard Energy	+20.98
Fidelity Select Energy	+34.25

Wallflower Wisdom

Before you adopt the wallflower strategy, there are other considerations to keep in mind. First, going against the crowd is not easy. You won't get much encouragement from the financial press. A few may point out relatively unpopular sectors, but most are preoccupied with chronicling the sectors' woes, which is discouraging.

And remember, any strategy should be spiced with judgement. For example, we recommend that investors avoid the precious metals category, even though Morningstar has repeatedly listed it as an unloved fund category, even though it usually doesn't make sense to second-guess a sound strategy. The precious metals category keeps popping up on unpopular lists—1992, 1995, and again in 1999—but the category has never paid off. In theory it should have, because gold demand has been running ahead of production for years. But governments worldwide keep selling their gold reserves and disrupting the normal forces of supply and demand. If and when they get out of the picture, supply and demand normalcy will return. Until then, the precious metals category seems destined to disappointment.

Another possible negative: If you need immediate gratification, this strategy is not for you—it requires patience. Locking into an unpopular category for an anticipated 3 years requires above-average resolve, considering that the average fund shareholder stays with his or her funds for only 1 to 2 years. However, if you have a contrary streak in you, the strategy is a good one. You can't fault a buy low, sell high strategy—particularly if it is applied consistently. Nor can you quarrel with the economics of investing in categories with low valuations relative to other categories.

Do-Good Investors

Some folks confine their investing to mutual funds that feature socially responsible companies. This concept is not new, and it is gaining in popularity. The idea is to avoid buying stocks in corporations that do "bad" things. Mutual fund managers who engage in socially responsible investing develop portfolios to reflect that commitment.

Socially Responsible Investing

Socially responsible investing (SRI) has become an important force—too big to ignore. SRI funds now represent 13 percent of the money invested in mutual funds in this country. Importantly, it has also delivered good relative returns in recent years. Today, it doesn't "cost" anything to be a good (i.e., socially conscious) investor. The general idea is simple: If you are interested in investing your money in the market but don't want to support corporate bullies or environmental polluters, or companies that use overseas sweatshops or sell tobacco, there's a mutual fund for you. The list of social concerns that SRI caters to is long. There are funds that refuse to include companies that make or sell liquor, run gambling enterprises, or engage in animal testing. And others have a human-rights focus, refusing to invest in companies that ignore or mistreat women and minorities.

The common theme of SRI investing is to find those companies that have committed themselves to community involvement, the environment, and other major social concerns. Socially responsible investing advocates use a screening technique to identify companies' behavior. They look at what companies *do*, such as complying with workers' health and safety standards, and at what companies *don't do,* such as polluting or making tobacco products.

Socially Responsible Mutual Funds

Morningstar listed a total of 54 SRI funds in the first quarter of 2000. To accommodate growing demand, three major fund families are currently adding more to their offerings. In August 1999, Dreyfus launched Dreyfus Premier Third Century Fund, and both Vanguard and TIAA-CREF announced SRI fund launches in the first half of 2000.

According to the Social Investment Forum in Washington, D.C., a national nonprofit membership organization devoted to the promotion of social and environmentally responsible investing, "more than $2 trillion is invested in a socially responsible manner." As noted earlier, SRI accounts for 13 percent of the $16.3 trillion under professional management in the United States, as reported by the *1999 Nelson's Directory of Investment Managers*—up from $250 billion 10 years before. The Forum's president, Steve Schueth, said in a news release on November 4, 1999:

> The clear message is that socially responsible investing is now firmly on a steady path of growth thanks to the nearly universal acceptance of social investment as a viable and value-added approach to asset management. Clearly, a growing number of American individuals and institutions are insisting that their money be invested in a fashion that is aligned with their values.

Domini—The First SRI Investor on the Block

The pioneer of SRI funds was Domini Social Equity Fund. Recently, it had a Morningstar four-star rating, and portfolio companies are screened to meet the needs of most socially responsible investors. The fund does not invest in "companies that manufacture tobacco, alcohol, nuclear power, [or] supply services to gambling operations . . ." according to their Web site (domini.com). Domini also believes that "good" investors have not sacrificed returns by owning this fund. Since inception (1991), the fund has outpaced the returns of the Standard & Poor's 500 Index, as Table 13.2 shows.

Domini management looks for companies that have strong worker involvement and corporate participation through employee stock ownership, as well as companies with fair labor practices and top retirement benefits. They also seek companies with high-quality products that are among the leaders in their industry groups.

Other mutual funds have followed Domini's lead, and SRI-correct fund investors have enjoyed bountiful returns. These funds choose to invest heavily in companies that, in addition to fitting the SRI mold, share other attractive qualities: They feature large-cap companies with a heavy tilt toward growth. Fund portfolios typically include blue chips like Microsoft, Wal-Mart, Coca-Cola, Hewlett Packard, Cisco Systems, AT&T, Intel Corp., and Home Depot.

SRI Comes in Many Flavors

SRI doesn't deal with only near-universal concerns like the environment; there are some narrowly focused funds. Morningstar's Emily Hall pointed out in an article June 6, 2000, that Meyers Pride Value Fund "screens out firms that are inhospitable to their gay and lesbian employees, while the Christian-oriented Timothy Fund avoids companies that provide domestic-partner benefits." Most SRI investing is less narrow in focus, however, and covers broader categories of the social investing universe. So, if this type of investing appeals to you, you should decide what particular concerns are most important to you.

SRI Fund Activism

Some SRI funds carry their interest beyond investing—they also get involved in shareholder activism to challenge some of the activities of companies in their portfolios. In the article mentioned earlier, Emily Hall said, "Some of the funds that engage in shareholder activism also donate a small percentage of their

TABLE 13.2 Domini Social Equity Fund—June 1, 1991 to March 31, 2000

	TOTAL RETURN (%)	ANNUALIZED RETURN (%)	AMOUNT ON $10,000 MARCH 31, 2000 ($)
Domini Social Equity Fund	383.96	19.54	48,396
Large Blend Category	292.95	16.76	39,295
Standard & Poor's 500 Index	369.29	19.13	46,929

assets to those in need. For example, Calvert Social Investment Equity invests 1 percent of its assets in community-based organizations such as low-income housing funds and community development funds." Hall went on to report that socially responsible investing has come of age. She pointed out that in the past 3 years, 21 percent of SRI funds in the Morningstar database had the highest— five-star—rating; and that in recent years, SRI investors escaped the horrible market performance of tobacco and nuclear stocks.

SRI in Cyberspace

GreenMoney (greenmoney.com), an online Web site, reports regularly on SRI investing. In July 2000, in "Investing with Your Values," they called 1999 "The Year of SRI." The online company cited increased media coverage by the *Wall Street Journal, Barron's,* the *Christian Science Monitor,* and *USA Today,* and noted that SRI investing can be quite profitable. The first book on SRI invest- ing, *SRI, Investing with Your Values: Making Money and Making a Difference,* published by Bloomberg, makes the case for SRI this way:

> One of the best ways to invest ethically is through several of the "screened" (for socially responsible practices) mutual funds. In 1999 eleven of the socially and environmentally responsible mutual funds returned 30% and more.

Here is GreenMoney's list of the top funds, screened for their compliance with socially responsible principles, along with their 1999 returns:

1. IPS Millennium 118.8%.
2. Green Century 76.4%.
3. Citizens Global Equity 74.1%.*
4. Citizens Emerging Growth 68.1%.**
5. Bridgeway Social Responsibility 49.4%.
6. Parnassus Fund 47.7%.
7. MMA Praxis International 42.4%.
8. American Trust Allegiance 38.7%.
9. Noah Fund 30.6%.
10. Dreyfus Third Century 30.2%.
11. Calvert World Values 30.1%.

---

*Included in *Forbes* (February 7, 2000) annual Fund Survey Best Buys.
**Awarded a first-time five-star ranking. Other Citizens' funds with five-star rankings: Citizens Index and Global Equity.

GreenMoney also pointed out that CBS Marketwatch included Citizens *Index Fund* on their "best of best, top performers"—one of only 15 out of 10,000 funds, based on 3-year returns as of May 20, 1999.

Split SRI Screens

If you're determined to be an SRI mutual fund investor, you have to add another layer of decision making to the investment process. One problem that you'll have to address is determining which SRI version is best tailored to your beliefs and objectives. As pointed out by the *Wall Street Journal*'s Karen Damato (May 18, 2000), in comparing funds, "The variations in stocks passing muster highlight the tricky task of deciding which stocks are indeed socially correct."

She pointed out three SRI funds: Citizens Index, Domini Social Equity, and Vanguard Calvert Social Index Fund. All three own the stock of Wal-Mart Stores. But Wal-Mart is a no-no with some other SRI funds because it's perceived as a retailer that "doesn't demonstrate the best treatment of employees . . . and its arrival in a rural community can be a nightmare for small local stores."

Wal-Mart is not the only company that gets mixed reviews in the SRI community. Coca-Cola, MCI WorldCom, Oracle, Pfizer, and Texas Instruments are all embraced by some SRI funds, but screened out by others. So, if the idea of socially conscious investing appeals to you, you'll want to check out the University page on the Morningstar Web site to get started. Just remember: From a financial standpoint, it would be unwise to abandon a well-thought-out investment plan and replace it with funds based solely on SRI criteria. A more sensible approach would be to start with a solid asset allocation plan and risk control, and then try to find a worthy SRI fund—in financial terms—that dovetails with your overall investment plan.

PART 4

Managing for Maximum Profits

CHAPTER 14

Fund Families Stalwarts— Stewardship instead of Salesmanship

It is a great nuisance that knowledge can only be acquired by hard work.

—Somerset Maugham

In many ways, fund families resemble companies in any business. In a typical growth cycle, the newcomers, like Avis, "try harder." Upstarts, with fires in their corporate bellies, try to win new customers, market share, recognition, and a place in the ranks. We've all read the stories about newcomers putting in crazy hours, sleeping on the office couch, living on cold pizza, and so on. You might call it being "hungry."

Established companies, on the other hand, have different priorities; old-timers are more concerned with protecting already-won turf. Instead of working long hours and going over spreadsheets and marketing plans on weekends, they put in normal workdays, go for lunch at the club, and spend their Saturdays on the golf course. This is usually called "comfortable."

Both portraits are formulaic: One is a profile of companies that are trying to make it, the other describes those who already have. Your personal finances aren't that much different. Early in life, you're hungry to "make it"; later in life, when you're comfortable, your priority shifts—you want to "keep it." Choosing fund sponsors whose corporate objectives parallel your own is a sensible strategy.

Marrying into the Right Family

Evaluating fund families is important, because top management sets the tone for the whole organization. The corporate soul affects how individual fund managers perform. If management's top priority is aligned with yours (top investment performance), individual managers will be working in a benign and supportive structure. Really talented people will be attracted to the firm and tend to stay. If top management's preoccupation is not with the investment process, but empire building and distribution instead, it is probably going to lead to mediocre investment returns.

If you're not interested in a heavy investment of your own time and effort—beyond initial choice and performance monitoring—you might want to invest with just one fund company. That way, you've only got one source to check when evaluating your investment performance. Obviously, if you decide to stick with just one company, the decision is even more important. With one-stop selection, the families that offer the widest selection of individual funds may be the best choice. However, if you don't mind dealing with different providers, or prefer to invest through fund supermarkets like TD Waterhouse, you can focus on particular strengths within several families.

Most personal finance magazines such as *Kiplinger's*, *Mutual Funds,* and *Forbes* rate fund families every year, and because they each use different rating criteria, the rankings of "best" and "worst," and everything in between can vary widely. One flaw in most rankings is that they usually require a minimum number of funds in a family and a relatively long-term assessment period. Thus, they tend to favor families that have been around for a long time, and, most of them ignore some good opportunities provided by newer entrants and/or families with only a few funds. So while it's important to check the print sources and established rankings, you need to cast your research net a little wider.

Recent Success Stories

Let's say you're in the "hungry" investing stage. If so, you're probably searching for growth funds. If that's the case, emerging fund companies are one of the best places to look. In recent years, one such hungry family was Marsico Capital Management. After a successful career as a category-trouncing portfolio manager of Janus Twenty and Janus Growth and Income Fund at Janus Capital, Tom Marsico went off on his own to set up Marsico Capital Management. His new company was well financed and staffed with serious investment talent, some of whom came with him from Janus. Marsico was deeply committed to establishing a successful company with his name on the door. During a period when most large-cap funds were struggling just to keep up with the S&P 500 Index, Marsico's large-cap funds returned 48.27 percent and 53.27 percent, beating the index's 35.97 percent return their first two years.

Another example was Massachusetts Financial Services (MFS), managers of America's oldest mutual fund, founded in 1924. For decades, MFS was known mostly for its bond funds—growth investors viewed them with massive indifference. In the early 1990s, however, two senior officers—John Ballin and Jeff Shames—determined to grow the company rather than continue its conventional, uninspired drift, and they shook up the sleepy MFS culture. Ballin and Shames were driven by a simple principle: "Money follows performance, everything else is trivial," They hired new people and concentrated on honing their stock-picking skills. Time proved them right. According to *Money* magazine, they ultimately improved their performance so much that in 1999 the once sleepy firm brought in almost as much money as giant Fidelity, seven times their size.

Selection Criteria

The more than 600 fund families on the market today collectively offer thousands of funds. This embarrassment of riches can make for an investor's nightmare, if your goal is to find the "perfect" family. Keep in mind that no magic combination of ingredients guarantees a fund family's success. Certain criteria, however, make success more likely. A desirable fund family has most of the following characteristics:

- *Experience.* A former portfolio manager who starts, or is running, a fund company of his or her own is ideal, because money management should be at the company's core, and marketing, distribution, and other considerations should be lesser priorities. Therefore, investment people, not distributors or marketers, should be at the top. That's the situation that existed at the start of the MFS and Marsico success stories, and it's a big part of why they did so well. A focus on money management pays off for shareholders, and not so incidentally, for management. And, if the fund managers have above-average track records, it's an added plus.

- *Resources.* If you invest in actively managed funds, you are obviously expecting them to outperform comparable index funds. That means getting your money's worth in terms of plenty of research and portfolio management, which is what you're paying the extra fees for, not start-up sponsors operating on a shoestring. You will miss the occasional star manager who rises out of nowhere, but usually a larger research effort is best.

- *Age.* Actual age of a fund family is not the issue here. An "old" revitalized management, an established investment management firm offering funds for the first time, or a new, well-financed, and fully staffed management can be equally desirable.

- *Style focus.* While the largest families are forced to try to be all things to all investors, medium-sized or small families often can be focused on their own proven expertise, such as small-cap or international stocks. Sometimes these are a better bet than the giants because they focus on areas where the managers have a record of past success.

- *Organization type.* As mentioned, sponsors whose primary business is investment management are much more desirable than are banks, insurance companies, or brokerage firm that establish fund families simply because they have existing or convenient "distribution channels."

- *Fund assets.* As covered in many other chapters, funds with small assets are desirable—avoid asset bloat.

Powerful Managers New to the Fund Business

Dresdner RCM Global Funds

Dresdner RCM Global Funds, owned by Dresdner Bank Group in Germany, seem to blow the efficient market theory to smithereens. Their performance has been so good, it's almost surreal. The awkward name stems from Dresdner Bank's 1995 takeover of San Francisco-based growth-investing boutique, Rosenberg Capital Management. Worldwide, with a pedigree that spans decades, the bank's investment division provides impressive capabilities with a network of 890 employees. Although their name may not be familiar, if you work for a large company, some of the roughly $90 billion they manage may be some of your retirement money. The firm counts many of the nation's largest private and public pension funds as clients (Dresdner has 6 million private and corporate clients in 70 countries).

The firm is not trying to be "we the people," with a broad selection of funds that can appeal to everyone. Instead, their funds focus on sectors where they have firepower. So far, most of the investors—owning $4 billion worth of Dresdner funds—bought in because they did a little homework, not merely because somebody sold it to them. While we know, without a scintilla of doubt, that past performance is no guarantee of future performance, both the frequency and degree of outperformance in this case are reasons to believe superior results have to be attributed to more than randomness as Table 14.1 shows.

While there are twenty footnotes to Dresdner's RCM's posted performance, none materially change the impact of their performance. The relative

TABLE 14.1 Dresdner RCM Funds—Cumulative Total Returns since Inception a/o 6/30/00 versus Various Indexes (indicated in italics)

	INCEPTION	CUMULATIVE RETURN SINCE INCEPTION (%)
Large Cap Growth Fund Class I	12/31/96	185.75
Standard & Poor's 500 Index		106.68
Tax Managed Growth Fund Class I	12/31/98	58.24
Standard & Poor's 500 Index		20.53
Biotechnology Fund, Class N	12/30/97	332.33
AMEX Biotechnology Index		298.23
Global Small Cap Fund Class I	12/31/96	252.81
Salomon Br. Extended Mkt. Index		34.91
MSCI World Cap Index		24.95
Global Technology Fund Class I	12/27/95	766.70
Lipper Science & Technology Index		330.68
Global Health Care	12/31/96	224.42
Russell Midcap-Health Care Index		56.39
International Growth Equity Fund Class I	12/28/94	163.21
MSCI EAFE Index		74.85
Emerging Markets Fund	12/30/97	69.21
MSCI Emerging Markets Free Index		14.62
Europe Fund Class N	4/5/90	144.06
MSCI Europe Index		280.13

Source: Dresdner RCM Global Funds Web site.

performance of Dresdner RCMs two large-cap funds might even shake the confidence of the staunchest efficient market advocate.

Until they began to offer mutual funds, the steep $10 million minimum required to open an account rendered Dresdner all but invisible to the average investor, which was fine with their top brass. Their mutual funds were started, in part, to give Dresdner RCM's own employees access to the same kinds of returns being produced for institutional clients. When their funds began to show up on the "best lists," in the financial press, alert investors began to come to them although Dresdner made minimal efforts to recruit customers.

WHAT A DIFFERENCE $9,999,000 MAKES

At that point the institutionally oriented management had to concede that there was no turning back and made their funds more widely available. Instead of $10 million to get in the door, IRA investors now need to pony up only $1,000—and what a difference $9,999,000 makes!

GRASSROOTS RESEARCH

One reason Dresdner is smoking the competition is their GrassrootsSM Research division. Developed over the past 15 years, Grassroots employs 290 independent researchers worldwide, managed by a 10-person staff in San Francisco. Based on 40,000 global industry contacts, reporters and field people generate 50 to 60 company and industry-specific studies per month. These studies provide fresh ideas, perspectives, and trends—all of which are reported to Dresdner's analysts and portfolio managers. Dresdner sees this Grassroots research as exemplifying its "commitment to going beyond traditional fundamental research."

Grassroots combines traditional centralized analysis with findings from the field about whether products or services really are in demand. Impetus for the program came from a bad experience Dresdner had in the 1980s (before the reporters were in place), when they owned Atari stock and didn't know that their video games weren't selling. Today, hopefully, feedback from reporters would alert analysts that games were sitting on store shelves.

TIAA-CREF

If you are looking for excitement, don't look to TIAA-CREF—it just isn't in that business. Instead, it offers a rock-solid organization with a deep corporate culture providing conservative and orthodox management, and *very* low, almost Vanguardesque, fees.

Although Teachers Insurance and Annuity Association-College Retirement Equities Fund (TIAA-CREF) is the largest private pension manager in the world, unless you are an educator or work for a nonprofit organization, you've probably never heard of them. Founded in 1918 by Andrew Carnegie, the $300 billion manager has turned 33,000 of its participants into millionaires. If it were ranked by size as a mutual fund company, it would be fourth largest in the United States. Its variable annuity, launched in 1952, was the first in the United States and the world. Until 1997, TIAA-CREF was a nonprofit, tax-exempt organization. While the company is no longer tax-exempt, it is still a nonprofit organization.

SUCCESSFUL FUND DEBUTS

Because TIAA-CREF has been well known and highly regarded in the investment community, its first fund launches caused considerable comment in the trade press. The commentary was largely about its low fees, and how, for the first time, there was a "real competitor" for Vanguard. While Vanguard, on average, charges 0.28 percent annual fees for the funds it manages, TIAA-CREF fees range from 0.29 percent to 0.49 percent. Both are about one full percentage point lower than the industry.

The organization is committed to holding expenses to their present levels until at least 2003, but their prospectus shows that they may charge higher fees at that time. The *Wall Street Journal*'s Jonathan Clements feels this won't happen: "I don't think TIAA-CREF's shareholders will end up [paying higher fees]. In its pension business, the firm has proven it can manage funds cheaply. Moreover, like Vanguard, TIAA-CREF is run solely for the benefit of its fund shareholders, with the long-term aim of providing fund-management services at cost."

Since inception, TIAA-CREF's publicly offered funds have garnered $2.8 billion in assets with only modest promotion; most of the incoming cash was the result their reputation and favorable press. Five of its funds have been in existence long enough to be tracked by Morningstar, and they have beaten the average fund in their respective categories by respectable margins—particularly notable considering their wide diversification. As of March 31, 2000, TIAA-CREF's Managed Allocation Fund's return (+53.97%) has been more than doubled the category average (+25.93%) since its 1997 inception.

UNIQUE FEATURES

TIAA-CREF blends indexing and active management in two of their funds. The division is not fixed—weightings are shifted as management perceives changes in the investment landscape. Their Growth & Income Fund's target index is the Standard & Poor's 500 Index and Growth Equity Funds tracks the broader Russell 3000 Index. These are the only two funds offered by a major fund company that incorporate "the best of both worlds"; they call it their "dual investment strategy." Another unique feature of TIAA-CREF funds is the low price of admission: A $250 minimum investment in any one of their funds makes it a great starter kit for children or anyone.

TELL IT TO THE JUDGE

If your are a fiduciary—a trustee or guardian—reluctant or uncomfortable making investment decisions, appropriate TIAA-CREF funds should be considered. If ever having to "tell it to the judge," in the future is even remotely possible, compared to most fund families, having chosen TIAA-CREF funds should be defensible:

- Reputation—excellent, widely known.
- Fees—some of the lowest in the industry.

- Investment approach—orthodox.
- Returns—competitive or above-average, compared with peers.
- Financial condition—very strong.
- Experience—verifiable, continuous experience for over 80 years.
- Wide diversification—broader than with most funds.

In investing, you can never completely "put it away and forget it," but with TIAA-CREF, it comes close. They have experience, depth, success, and a deep corporate culture favoring investors.

TCW Group

Established in 1971, the TCW Group (formerly known as Trust Company of the West) is a widely respected institutional money manager of both equities and bonds totaling over $75 billion. Their long list of clients ranges from Adolph Coors to the Maryland State Retirement System to Xerox Corporation. You could have invested in a TCW mutual fund as far back as 1993, if you had at least $250,000 *per fund.* As of March 1999, you can own shares in one of their funds with as little as $2,000.

Employee-owned, the Los Angeles-based TCW Group has a huge research staff compared with their assets. The 650-person company includes over 150 investment professionals including 55 portfolio managers/analysts, 70-plus research personnel, and 15 traders. TCW is an institutional money manager, with an excellent reputation among institutioal investors. Doug Foreman, chief investment officer of the organization, explains why his firm is beginning to offer mutual funds. His views are important, because they show how a fund sponsor's goals can parallel yours:

> As the industry and mutual fund assets grow, there are diseconomies of scale—any manager [who] tells you that as their asset base grows, that their excess returns aren't going to come down somewhat, is full of bull. There's no question that as you get bigger it gets tougher.
>
> So there is always room for a new kid on the block—the kid with good performance and a good investment culture. Savvy investors—and there are more and more of them out there—are looking for that kind of kid. You're going to have two types of mutual fund companies out there at the end of the day: Category one—big behemoths that are brand name, safe choice, mediocre performance, distribution-driven companies—you know the names already—we are never going to win at that game. That game is over and there is absolutely no point in our entering that market.

CATEGORY TWO—MORE POTENTIAL

Foreman puts his firm in a second category. He explains that many people are getting more and more sophisticated; they aren't seeking a financial planner, but are looking for good investment results. And they're willing to take a chance with a more performance-oriented fund family like his that has experience and a track record with large private accounts, but hasn't been in the mutual fund business before. Foreman thinks his firm offers an alternative to the well-known brand names in the fund business. And he has a point. With an experienced firm like his, managing a new, smaller fund provides a great opportunity for excellent returns, giving fund buyers a leg up on the large fund families.

TCW provides reasonably wide latitude to its managers. As the company tells it, "TCW's portfolio managers are free to differ as to investment philosophy, and they do so to a major extent. . . . There is room among our offerings for a wide variety of investment approaches *as long as each is well thought out and competently applied*" (emphasis added). And their results have shown the freedom they give their managers pays off.

Heard on the Street

"DEAR CLIENTS AND FRIENDS"

"While superior performance is only one measure of success, after all is said and done, it is perhaps the ultimate one. It is also something you simply cannot achieve over time without the other qualities we value so highly: teamwork, discipline, and consistency, to name a few. And that is why we take such pride in the fact that over the past 5 years, 88% of TCW's products and 99% of the assets we manage involving publicly-traded domestic and international securities beat their benchmarks. This is truly a remarkable record, and one we will strive to sustain in the future."

Excerpt from *Year-End Letter to Clients and Friends*, February 12, 2000—Robert A. Day, Chairman and Chief Executive Officer.

DISTINGUISHING CHARACTERISTICS

How does one management garner more than its share of winning funds, particularly across styles and sectors? Foreman explains the TCW culture:

First, foremost and last, Robert A. Day (TCW president and CEO) is an investor—he's a stock junky. It's very much an investment culture—it starts at the top and works its way down. His approach is, you hire good experienced pros in the different disciplines and areas and you supervise to make sure they're doing the things they need to do to stay out of trouble. Beyond that, you let those people basically manage their businesses in line with what they've communicated to people is the best way to manage assets in that particular discipline.

A DESIRABLE "PROBLEM"

Despite their superior performance records, TCW's funds haven't attracted much public notice—and that's *exactly* what you want. Fund assets are below $3 billion, less than 4 percent of the $75 million total under management. Even Galileo Select Equities, their flagship fund, run by highly regarded Glen Bickerstaff, is only $500 million—that's equal to Janus funds' *weekly intake* during their heyday. Bickerstaff's fund has room to grow and remain nimble in the large-cap sector for the foreseeable future.

From the investor's standpoint, modest fund sizes and orderly asset growth are attractive features of this company's funds. TCW is placing ads in a few trade magazines, but most investors come to TCW's no-load funds through fee-based investment advisers. TCW should prove to be an excellent fund manager over the long term, due to its unique and solid management approach.

Driehaus Capital Management

ACTIVE MANAGERS OF ACTIVE STOCKS

In a world where most fund families seem to have a numbing sameness about them, Driehaus Capital Management stands in stark contrast. If thumbing your nose at the establishment and achieving turbocharged returns have appeal, Driehaus may be your cup of tea. Why? Consider conventional wisdom and the way mutual funds are *supposed* to invest:

- *Portfolio turnover is* supposed *to be restrained.* The lower the turnover, the better. Driehaus funds' turnover rates (the amount of buying and selling in the fund portfolio) are routinely twice to three times the industry average.

- *Annual expenses are* supposed *to be as low as possible.* Driehaus funds' annual expenses are typically at least 1½ times the industry average.

- *"Momentum investing" is* supposed *to lead to bad ends.* It should routinely blow up its participants at the end of every market cycle. Founder Richard Driehaus, called the "Father of Momentum Investing," by *Worth* magazine, is alive and very well after many cycles during his 30-plus years career.

- *Technical analysis (using charts) is* supposed *to be akin to astrology.* Driehaus disagrees, "By placing heavy emphasis on the recognition of both favorable corporate developments and technical indicators such as increasing volume, we seek to make early identification of companies on the threshold of rapid stock price appreciation."

According to conventional wisdom, Driehaus's rule-flaunting should make his funds an investor's no-no. But he has reaped extraordinary returns for his investors: During the past 10 years, his domestic small-company and mid-size company growth portfolios garnered annualized returns of 32.9 percent and 34.7 percent, about double their respective categories' returns. In 1999, he and his firm took full advantage of an investment environment that favored their investment style: Unleveraged returns were a whopping 197 percent and 222 percent.

RICHARD DRIEHAUS'S "INVESTMENT PARADIGMS WORTH AVOIDING"

How does Driehaus do it? Take a look at his rationales for ignoring the dictates of conventional wisdom:

- *Perhaps the best-known investment paradigm is "buy low, sell high."* "I believe that more money can be made buying high and selling at even higher prices. . . . What is the risk? Obviously, . . . that I'm buying near the top. But, I would much rather be invested in a stock that is increasing in price and take the risk that it may begin to decline than invest in a stock that is already in a decline and try to guess when it will turn around."

- *Just buy stocks of good companies and hold onto them;* that way you don't have to pay close daily attention. "I would say: 'Buy good stocks of good companies and hold on to them until there are unfavorable changes.'"

- *Don't try to hit home runs; you make money hitting a lot of singles.* "I couldn't disagree more. I believe you can make the most only hitting home runs."

- *A high turnover strategy is risky.* "I think just the opposite. High turnover reduces risk when it is the result of taking a series of small losses in order to avoid larger losses."

The (momentum) stereotype . . . may describe some people, but it never sounds to me like what we do.

Driehaus officers don't believe that their investment methodology is extreme. William Anderson senior vice president and chief investment officer, International, believes that the term "momentum managers" is being misapplied to the firm. Anderson, a certified financial analyst with a BA in economics from Stanford and an MBA from the University of Chicago, said, "I've never liked that term very much. To me it applies to people who chase whatever is going up.

"We have half a dozen analysts here that work for me who travel overseas once a quarter, and as a group, we visit quite a few hundred companies all over the world every year. While we do buy companies that are growing and, typically, ones whose stocks are performing well, there is an incredible amount of fundamental research that is the basis of it all.

"In addition, it's a very disciplined process. We focus on a specific type of company—trying to find companies that are in the fastest part of their growth cycle. And we do a lot to try and control risk. We sell companies whose stocks are underperforming, and where the fundamental performances are subpar, and we're always looking for new ideas. One of the ways you control risk is finding new ideas and selling the relatively weakest stocks in our portfolio.

"The (momentum) stereotype—it may describe some people—but it never sounds to me like what we do. I guess we've gotten away from disagreeing with the title because people are going to use it anyway."

I would replace "bold" with "long-term" investors

What was Anderson's reaction to Morningstar's opinion that Driehaus funds were "suitable for only the boldest investors?"

"I think what their analyst is referring to, is that on a year-to-year basis, we have above average volatility, and that's always been the case.

"We're in companies that are changing very rapidly and inherent in that is the volatility in their outlook. What we feel we are suitable for is for people who want to take a long-term view and who are looking for superior returns over a three- to five-year cycle. We're especially well suited for people who don't have to pay taxes—although we do well even after adjusting for taxes. But we have generated more short-term gains historically. So I would replace "bold" with "long term," 10 to 20 years down the road.

"If you look at money that has been with the firm for 10 years, it's been pretty remarkable. We just got the numbers for the 10 years ending June 30th (2000), the EAFE Index was up 7.95 percent (average annual rate) and the average fund in the Lipper universe was up 9.9 percent and the top-performing fund was up 14.7 percent—our international composite was up 20.7 percent. You couldn't have been in our product the whole 10 years because it was a limited partnership for about half that time. Relative performance was the same on the domestic side. The point is, if people give us enough time, we can give them good performance. Driehaus Capital Management is a unique organization, and although their investment philosophy is unconventional by almost any measure, their results have been outstanding.

SHARED CHARACTERISTICS

There are sharp contrasts among the four profiled fund families, but they share common—and very attractive—characteristics:

- Powerful, experienced fund sponsors, just entering the fund business.
- Identifiable, superior relative performance.

- Investment-driven, rather than distribution driven, corporate cultures.
- Small funds benefiting from large infrastructure support.
- Excellent execution of differing methodologies.
- Years remaining before the size problem looms.

From *your* perspective, many of fund families have little to offer because, as TCW's Doug Foreman puts it, "Too much of their energy is invested in 'distribution'; performance—unless it's horrid—is almost incidental. Their distribution is smooth and practiced, designed to keep you in *their* 'comfort zone.'" Venturing outside and investing with the "new kids on the block" can significantly increase your returns.

CHAPTER 15

Recommended Funds

Even if you are on
the right track, you
will get run over if
you just sit there.

—Will Rogers

Most investors pick mutual funds before deciding where—or if—they fit their overall plan. By now, however, you know that fund selection should be one of your very last steps—after you've put together an asset allocation plan, and researched the fund categories that most accurately address your own short- and long-term goals. Only after you've done all that are you ready to look at specific funds, which explains the placement of our fund recommendations in the final chapter.

One caveat: While the mutual fund industry preaches long-term investing, it's difficult to stick to the long-term view in managed funds because some of the more important criteria for fund selection—management expertise and fund-family quality—are themselves not long-term factors. The average fund manager's tenure is 4 years, and fund families are continually merging or selling out. John Bogle says one-half of all funds disappear every decade. So with managed funds, you really can't "put 'em away and forget 'em." That doesn't mean that you can't start with a portfolio of terrific funds, however; you have to monitor them to make sure they continue to outperform. If they don't, you're better off invested in index funds.

With that preliminary warning, we can look at some of the great funds that are available. We present them according to the asset allocation categories presented in Chapter 4 so that you can more easily select according to your specific investment plan.

An All-Indexed Portfolio—Autopilot Investing

Index Funds

While a combination of the best of both the index and managed fund worlds is the optimal way to build a portfolio, some investors want all-indexed portfolios—an autopilot approach—so they don't have to be involved in the investing process. Others want to benefit from the long-term returns provided by securities, but find selecting the right fund a daunting task, so they end up preferring indexed funds more or less by default.

For such investors, we've pulled together a strong index-oriented portfolio. A few notes before we begin: The "all-indexed" portfolio has one nonindex fund because no convertible index fund exists. We've selected a managed no-load convertible fund from a powerful sponsor, one that has achieved above-average returns for over a decade. And, since Vanguard appears frequently throughout this chapter, here's some standard information relevant to *all* Vanguard funds:

- Investment minimum—$3,000; $1,000 for IRAs.
- Telephone 800-662-7447.
- Web site: vanguard.com

VANGUARD TOTAL STOCK MARKET INDEX FUND

Featuring large-, mid-, small-, and micro-cap U.S. stocks, this index fund "seeks to replicate the aggregate price and yield of the Wilshire 5000 Index," which tracks virtually all U.S. stocks. Large-cap stocks—representing approximately 70 percent of the total portfolio—dominate the fund. Medium-, small-, and micro-cap stocks make up the remainder, reflecting their respective weightings in the U.S. stock market. Since the fund includes companies of all sizes, you won't have to shift back and forth in the future. As of June 30, 2000, the fund's average annual return since its May 1992 inception has been 18.20 percent, compared to 16.60 percent for the average fund in its category (Morningstar large blend). The fund's annual expenses of 0.20 percent are very reasonable.

INTERNATIONAL STOCKS—VANGUARD TOTAL INTERNATIONAL STOCK INDEX FUND

This fund "invests substantially all assets in a combination of the European, Pacific, and Emerging Market Portfolios." These are Vanguard's three regional foreign index funds. The fund began in May 1996, and since then, the average annual return has been 9.09 percent. The average fund in this category returned 13.75 percent. Annual expenses total 0.32 percent.

REAL ESTATE INVESTMENT TRUSTS—VANGUARD REIT FUND

The fund "invests at least 98 percent of assets in stocks of real-estate investment trusts that are included in the Morgan Stanley REIT Index." One third of this fund's assets are in industrial or office properties, with another approximately 20 percent each in apartments and retail properties. Since its June 1996 launch, its average annual returns have lagged behind the Morningstar Specialty Real Estate category by just a sliver: 8.53 percent versus 8.81 percent. Annual expenses are 0.33 percent.

CONVERTIBLE SECURITIES—FIDELITY CONVERTIBLE SECURITIES FUND

Despite having had seven different portfolio managers since its 1987 inception, this fund has consistently outperformed its peers: $10,000 invested in February 1987 has returned $79,082 (16.66% average annual return), compared with $44,074 (11.69% average annual return) for the average convertible fund tracked by Morningstar. It's reasonable to expect future above-average, or at least respectable, performance because of Fidelity's impressive resources and experience. Annual expenses of 0.82 percent are very reasonable compared with the 1.50 percent for the average managed fund in the category. Minimum investment is $2,500 with $500 for IRAs (800-544–8888; fidelity.com).

BONDS—VANGUARD TOTAL BOND MARKET INDEX

This index "seeks to replicate the total return of the Lehman Brothers Aggregate Bond Index"; that is, all investment grade (average credit quality is AA) bonds that trade in the United States. The portfolio of government, agency, and corporate bonds has an average effective maturity of 9.1 years. This fund has done very well compared with its benchmark: Since its December 1986 inception, the average annual return of 7.52 percent has beaten the 7.02 percent return of the Morningstar Intermediate-Term Bond category. Annual expenses are 0.20 percent.

Because indexed REIT and international funds have historically achieved subpar returns, compared with managed funds, our (almost) all-indexed portfolio might seem overzealous. However, index funds in those less efficient markets may achieve better future returns since all markets seem to be getting more efficient. If so, a totally indexed portfolio might show improving relative performance in the future. However, if you are inclined to a more "hands-on" investment style, managed funds—or a mix of managed and index funds—should improve your returns.

Taking Control of Your Fund Portfolio— Recommended Funds

The following funds—both managed and index—are recommended if you want to be more involved. Here, the U.S. stocks allocations separate out three categories (large-, mid-, and small-cap) rather than lumping them together in a single fund as in the all-indexed portfolio. This allows you to customize the weightings between the small-, mid-, and large-cap sectors to suit your specific goals. In the following listings, index funds are identified by **(I)**, managed funds by **(M)**. And, of course, you can also use the previously recommended index funds if they fit your needs.

Large-Cap U.S. Stocks

TIAA-CREF GROWTH & INCOME FUND (M & I)

This fund is *the only major fund that combines active management and indexing,* and it spares you from having to choose between index and managed funds. Its "enhanced" approach to indexing tracks the Russell 3000 Growth Index, but when the fund's management finds plentiful opportunities in individual stocks, the portfolio is shifted toward active stock selection. Similarly, when attractive candidates seem to be scarce, indexing is given a greater weighting. Expenses are very reasonable, running at 0.43 percent annually, compared with 1.20 percent for the average large blend (mixture of value and growth stocks) fund.

The blend approach followed in this fund provides some protection from the effects of popularity shifts between value- and growth-stocks, and should ensure more consistent returns than either style would alone. As of June 2000, the fund's return since its September 1997 debut has been 73.38 percent, compared with 55.63 percent for the average fund in the large blend category (800-223-1200; tiaa-cref.org).

TCW GALILEO SELECT EQUITIES (M)

Managed by one of the *very* few large-cap managers to consistently beat the S&P 500 Index, 1999 was the tenth straight year that Glen Bickerstaff's returns (at TCW and his former employer) bested the large-cap S&P index. As of June 30, 2000, his winning streak remained intact; his fund was up 16.65 percent, while the S&P 500 Index was down 0.43 percent. Bickerstaff achieves his superior performance by skillful stock selection and by limiting the number of stocks in the fund. In mid-2000, the portfolio held only 30 stocks (versus approximately 100 in the average fund), and his 10 largest holdings represented just over half of his fund's assets. While this strategy has paid off so far, if Bickerstaff makes some bad picks, their impact on returns will be large. Of the three large-cap funds recommended, this fund has the highest risk profile because of the limited number of holdings (800-386-3829; tcwgroup.com).

VANGUARD INDEX 500 FUND (I)

This $100 billion (assets) granddaddy of S&P 500 Index funds has lagged behind its target index by an average of only 0.13 percent in the past 10 years, and by only 0.05 percent in the past 5 years. Manager Gus Sauter has so refined the science of indexing that in both 1998 and 1999 the fund actually *beat* its index by razor-thin percentages through the use of futures contracts. Annual expenses are 0.18 percent.

Mid-Cap U.S. Stocks

TCW GALILEO SMALL-CAP GROWTH FUND (M)

Although it calls itself a small-cap fund, at mid-year 2000, the fund held more large- than small-cap stocks. Large-cap stocks composed one third of the portfolio and the small-caps stake was actually less than 20 percent. Managed by a three-man team that includes Doug Foreman (Chapter 14), the fund has compiled a 411.73 percent return since its March 1994 launch, considerably better than the 279.18 percent achieved by the average mid-cap growth fund by mid-2000. Because the fund has a strong bias toward growth stocks with high valuations, it will probably remain volatile and suffer disproportionately during market downturns. Over the long term, however, excellent returns should more than compensate for shorter-term negatives. Management indicates that if performance begins to suffer from asset bloat, they will close the fund to new investors. Annual expenses are 1.13 percent; minimum investment (N class shares) $2,000 (800-386-3829; tcwgroup.com).

S&P MID-CAP 400 INDEX FUND (I)

This exchange-traded fund tracks the most widely watched mid-cap benchmark. Annual expenses are 0.25 percent. Traded on AMEX, symbol MDY.

SELECTED NEW MID-CAP FUNDS (M)

At inception, invest in new blend and growth mid-caps, using the new-fund selection criteria and timing strategy described in Chapter 8.

Small-Cap U.S. Stocks

SCHWAB MARKETMANAGER SMALL CAP FUND (M)

This fund-of-funds' attraction is that it should be able to provide relatively consistent returns in the small-cap sector, which is subject to feast-or-famine cycles. While its strategy precludes extraordinary returns in any one year, it should be able to delay the "size problem" longer than most successful small-cap funds because it spreads its assets among many funds (typically 10 to 13). Further, the blend investment style will help insulate investors from being marooned at the wrong end of the style sector. Since its October 1997 inception, total returns were 36.43 percent, compared with 19.08 percent for the Morningstar small blend category as of June 30, 2000. Assets are a modest $166 million, leaving fund management with plenty of maneuvering room for its fund collection within the small-cap fund universe (800-435-4000; schwab.com).

SELECTED NEW SMALL-CAP FUNDS (M)

At inception, invest in new small-cap blend and growth funds using the new-fund selection and timing criteria described in Chapter 8.

International Stocks

DRESDNER RCM GLOBAL SMALL CAP FUND AND DRESDNER RCM INTERNATIONAL GROWTH EQUITY FUND (M)

Although you can invest in either of these funds, buying both is recommended because that will provide style diversification, with exposure to both small- and large-cap international growth stocks. Since its 1995 inception, as of June 30, 2000 International Growth Fund's 5.5-year 183.21 percent returns beat the 102.79 percent achieved by the Morningstar Foreign Stock category. Global Small Cap Fund's 3.5-year comparative returns is even more impressive: 252.80 percent versus 70.51 percent for the World Stock (includes U.S. stocks) category. Minimum investment is $5,000 *per fund* (800-726-7240; dresdnerrcm.com).

DRIEHAUS INTERNATIONAL DISCOVERY FUND (M)

When conditions are favorable, as they were in 1999, this small, young fund provided torrid returns, up 213.65 percent its first year. Investors in this high turnover fund should be prepared for continued volatility, however. Another consideration: The fund's tax inefficiency makes it more appropriate for tax-deferred accounts. With assets of only $60 million, management can remain flexible and there is plenty of room for growth. Minimum investment is $10,000 (800-560-6111; driehaus.com).

Real Estate Investment Trusts

FORWARD FUNDS UNIPLAN (M)

This REIT, managed by UNIPLAN's Rick Imperiale (Chapter 9) has a distinctive structure that lessens the chance of underperformance: It targets the NAREIT Equity Index, employing a property-type profile that mirrors the index. Management divides the country into eight geographic regions. Within each of these regions, it compiles statistics on factors that influence supply and demand in the real estate market. The goal is to identify the property types in each region with the most favorable characteristics.

Individual REITs are selected according to their credit quality, capital structure, cash flow, funds from operations, management, and valuation. Imperiale's record for managing private accounts dates back to 1989, and he has achieved average returns beating the NAREIT index by over 5 percent annually. Since its May 1999 inception, the fund has returned 12.29 percent, versus 10.22 percent for the NAREIT Equity Index as of July 31, 2000. Approximate current yield is 4.4 percent. Minimum investment is $2,500 (800-999-6809; forwardfunds.com).

CGM REALTY

Portfolio manager Ken Heebner concentrates his bets; just five holdings made up 35 percent of his relatively small (20 stocks) portfolio at mid-year 2000. This less diversified portfolio leads to more volatility and poor relative performance over short-term periods when one or more of his larger positions are suffering. Long-term, however, Heebner's stock-picking abilities have provided superior returns. CGM Realty is in the top performance quartile of Morningstar's 3- and 5-year periods and in 6 years, total return has been 101.06 percent versus 65.96 percent for his average peer. The REIT sector made an apparent bottom in late 1999, and by June 2000, CGM was outperforming with a 15.55 percent return versus 12.83 percent for the average REIT fund. Approximate yield is 6.3 percent; minimum investment is $2,500 (800-345-4048; cgmfunds.com).

Convertible Securities

TCW CONVERTIBLE SECURITIES FUND (M)

This is the only recommended closed-end fund. Although TCW also manages an open-end convertible fund, the $250,000 minimum for the open-end fund rules it out for most investors. The closed-end fund began operations in 1987. Immediately after its IPO, it slipped to a predictable "morning-after" discount that exceeded 15 percent for 2 months. This discount gradually receded, however, helped by a 21 cents per share quarterly dividend initiated in 1988. By 1990, it began trading at a premium that averaged 4 percent for the next decade. Listed NYSE, symbol CVT.

The fund has a sizable stake in technology convertibles, so in 1999, as technology stocks and bonds weakened, the market price slipped again to a sizable discount, approximately 15 percent, where it remains. For the 10-year period ending July 31, 2000, average annual NAV returns were 16.79 percent, more than three percentage points higher than the average (open-end) convertible bond fund.

TCW convertible bond fund trades on the New York Stock Exchange—symbol CVT—and yields approximately 7.35 percent. Since the fund traded at a premium for almost a decade—in 9 years out of its 13-year life—it may do so again, which could provide a meaningful boost to future returns. Annual expenses are 0.68 percent versus 1.50 percent for the average convertible bond fund. The fund's NAV is reported weekly on a toll-free number: 877-829-6587.

CALAMOS CONVERTIBLE FUND (M)

Morningstar's William Harding (*Morningstar Mutual Funds*, September 29, 2000), sums up this fund's merits: "Management's attention to valuation and a well-diversified portfolio has led to below-average risk scores here. Moreover, the fund's returns land in the top quartile of its peers over the trailing five- and ten-year periods. This attractive risk/return profile and management's expertise in the convertible area make this a worthy option."

This is the most conservative of Calamos' funds. John Calamos' goal of achieving 75 percent to 80 percent of stocks' returns have been met. For the decade ending December 31, 1999, Calamos Convertible Fund achieved an average returned 15.57 percent return, which was 79.8 percent of the S&P 500's 18.20 percent return. Further, a $10,000 investment at the beginning of the period returned $42,495 compared to $36,350 achieved by the average convertible fund tracked by Morningstar.

Annual expenses are a bit higher than the average convertible fund, but they are more than offset by the fact that management is providing added value. Sporting an alphabet soup load structure, the best option is to invest in load-waived Class A shares that are available through financial intermediaries—broker wrap programs and investment advisors who use fund supermarkets. Minimum investment varies depending on where the fund is purchased (800-823-7386; calamos.com).

Bonds

Three Vanguard bond funds are recommended because their extremely low costs—averaging 75 percent less than the average bond fund—provide an almost unbeatable edge in the very efficient bond markets. The first one has already been discussed, in this chapter's Index Funds section: the Vanguard Total Bond Market Index.

VANGUARD LONG TERM CORPORATE (M)

This fund is invested in high-quality bonds. It is a bit more volatile than comparable funds because its maturities are longer, but the higher volatility provides an added benefit: higher yield—6.26 percent in 1999, compared with 6.01 percent for its Morningstar category. Over the longer term, the edge provided by lower expenses adds up. For the July 1, 1985, to June 30, 2000, period, this fund's cumulative total return was 272.76 percent, compared with 233.36 percent for the average fund in its category—an additional return of $3,940 on $10,000 invested. The fund should continue to outdistance its peers. Annual expenses are 0.30 percent.

VANGUARD GNMA (M)

As with other Vanguard funds, lower expenses provide an advantage over this fund's competitors. Income return in 1999 was 6.59 percent, versus 5.45 percent for the Morningstar Intermediate-term Government Bond Fund category. From July 1, 1985, to June 30, 2000, the total return was 242.16 percent compared with 190.77 for its average peer. Annual expenses are 0.30 percent.

PIMCO HIGH YIELD FUND

This fund has provided higher returns than most of its competitors. Pimco management, led by Bill Gross, has emerged as a bond-fund powerhouse. Morningstar gives it the highest rating in its category, and in the 7 years since inception, it has returned 102.00 percent compared with 76.31 percent for the average junk-bond fund. Annual expenses of the D class shares—the no-load class available to retail investors—are 0.90, compared with a category average of 1.29 percent. Morningstar's Sara Bush's assessment: "It's rare to find a fund that offers superior returns with less risk than its average peer. This fund . . . stands as one of the high-yield group's strongest choices." Make sure you specify D-class shares to avoid the class A, B, and C load minimum investment $1,000 (888-877-4626; pimcofunds.com).

Appendix A
Chapter Summaries

Chapter 1 seems like a long time ago; a lot of material has been covered since, and you can't expect to retain it all. As kids, when we left the schoolyard at dusk, we had a few special marbles we made sure went home in our pockets: "Keepers." Summaries from each chapter follow along with bulleted keepers— the most important points to take with you.

Chapter 1   Take Control of Your Mutual Funds

No one cares more about your money than you do, so before you even think about relying on experts, you should know that there are many ways to develop your own investment plan, more than ever before. By learning a few easy-to-follow principles like minimizing costs and the sensible asset allocation—plus diversification and a long-term perspective—you'll be prepared to make most of your own decisions. Even if you're a passive investor and rely on others to manage your portfolio, you still have to decide what types of funds to buy and which ones fit your objectives. Regardless of your approach, you have to keep score. The leading mutual fund mutual fund service, Morningstar, and other financial sources, will help you along the way. The question is, do you have the time and interest to take control?

If you're not inclined to deal with your investments, you can buy index funds and put them on "autopilot." It's a time-tested one-decision approach that will allow you to sit back and reap the benefits of a diversified low-cost portfolio that will serve you well over the years. Instead of worrying about what funds to buy, you'll be "buying the market." Index funds have proven records: The record shows that most professionally managed mutual funds have underperformed them.

Chapter 1 Keepers

- Take control. There are many ways to invest successfully; decide what's best for you and stick to it.
- Mutual funds are an almost ideal investment vehicle if you learn and follow a few simple rules—the do's and don'ts of fund investing.
- Controlling costs and your own emotions is achievable; forecasting the future is not—so don't try. Have confidence in the investments you've selected and those who are helping you and let time and the "magic" of compounding take care of the rest.

Chapter 2   Why You Can't Afford to Be an Average Mutual Fund Investor

All-too-often, investors—not just mutual fund investors—are their own worst enemies. It's human nature to bet on winners; the problem is, by the time we spot "winners," their race is almost over and another is about to begin.

Most investors pay little, or no, attention to costs; they have their gas pedals floored and their eyes glued to the rearview mirror. Mutual fund companies and distributors promote "winners" simply because they are the funds investors are most inclined to buy. "Best performer" fund buyers routinely defy two laws and get burned because prices tend to regress from both high stock valuations and price extremes.

When investors try to improve returns by trading more often, as they have in recent years, their increased activity reduces them instead. As a final insult, investors in taxable accounts are losing an average 2.5 percent in returns to taxes every year. The result is a toxic recipe that explains how the average investor accomplishes the seemingly impossible feat of achieving lower returns than the very funds he or she invests in. When you do the opposite of the average investor, in addition to increasing your returns, you will benefit in other ways: Investing will take much less of your time and it will reduce psychological wear and tear.

Chapter 2 Keepers

- Invest in funds that fit your personal asset allocation plan; don't follow the crowd.
- If you can't resist timing, buy unloved sector funds (Chapter 13) and sell funds that have become disproportionately large allocations; regression to the mean can then work for, rather than against, you.

- Control costs—don't overspend for expert advice and services. Most experts overcharge and underdeliver.

Chapter 3 Financial Sources

Americans spend staggering sums on financial services; Warren Buffett estimates a whopping $130 billion a year: "Perhaps $100 billion of that relates to the FORTUNE 500 . . . investors [who] are dissipating almost a third of everything that the FORTUNE 500 is earning for them—$334 billion in 1998—by handing it over to various types of chair-changing and chair-advisory 'helpers.'"

You have to rely on Buffett's "helpers" to some degree, even if you are a rugged individualist. If you require a lot of help, it gets expensive, because hand-holding doesn't come cheap on Wall Street.

Complicating matters is the reinvention of what help is. After titanic resistance, Merrill Lynch, among others, has announced a corporate restructuring that includes changing the name of its brokerage business from "national sales," to "advisory," consistent with how it now views itself: "One of the world's leading financial management and advisory companies."

A spokesperson told *Investment Advisor* magazine that top brass was "positioning Merrill in a way where we can help or advise our clients in their financial life holistically. . . . We don't want to just sell stocks and bonds." Pass the granola.

How do you make sure you are the diner—not the dinner?

Follow these principles:

Chapter 3 Keepers

- You simply can't afford helpers who—if you aren't careful—will siphon off as much as 20 percent or even 30 percent of expected annual returns.
- Take advantage of the huge increase in services and information that technology is providing at *much lower* cost.
- Hire good "help" only when you have to. *Unassisted,* you ought to be able to invest at least half of your portfolio in well-run index funds.

Chapter 4 Asset Allocation

More than anything else, your investment success will be determined by your portfolio's foundation: asset allocation—and your own self-discipline. Asset allocation is how you divide up your money into the different investment categories such as stocks, bonds, and convertible bonds, and then their subcategories—large-cap, mid-cap, and small-cap stocks, and so forth.

If you want to be a successful investor, you have to have a plan geared to your circumstances and risk tolerance; and you have to adjust as the years go by as follows:

Chapter 4 Keepers

- When you're young, take more risk—invest for growth.
- As you grow older, shift gradually from growth to less risky investments.
- Keep in mind: *Your returns will be more a function of asset allocation than any other factor.*

Chapter 5   Index Funds

If you don't want to worry about your investments, or even think about them, buy index funds and leave them alone. They are one-decision, maintenance-free investments in portfolios of stocks and/or bonds that replicate widely followed market indexes, such as the Standard & Poor's 500 Index or the total U.S. stock market. Only when there are changes in the index it tracks, does the index fund's portfolio change. Managed funds differ—they are actively managed—with decisions being made on what securities to buy and sell. Managed funds try to beat the market; index funds want *to be* the market.

Index funds are low-cost investments, charging a small fraction of managed funds' fees—allowing most of your money to work for you instead of being siphoned off by managements who usually trail the indexes.

Exchange-traded index funds (ETFs) were added to the mix in the mid-1990s, creating a new—and more liquid market—where investors can trade all day—an innovation that may be almost too convenient.

Index funds work best in efficient markets where there is a large and active marketplace for stocks and bonds.

Chapter 5 Keepers

- Well-run index funds have proven performance due to low-costs. The average actively managed fund has been unable to outperform the market consistently.
- Large-cap stock and investment-grade bond index funds, invested in securities that trade in efficient markets, have worked best.
- Index funds provide opportunity for investors who want minimal involvement in the investing process.

Chapter 6   Picking Winning Managed Funds

Who should manage your money? If you're going to rely on experts, which ones do you choose? Does past performance assure future success?

These questions can be difficult to answer, but aggregating opinions of leading industry sources show that consistent themes run through their comments: management character and integrity, clearly defined long-term investment objectives and policies, discipline, low portfolio turnover, and tax efficiency. Additional desirable qualities: length of track record, performance consistency, and management tenure. And not to be forgotten, low costs—emphasized by Vanguard's John Bogle.

Corporate culture, hard to quantify from long distances, means simply how managements treat their shareholders. *Money's* Jason Zweig, points to Longleaf Partners' funds management stated objective, "Fund investing should be a partnership between the portfolio manager and the investing public . . . we will remain significant investors with you in Longleaf."

It might sound a little corny, but can you point to many fund managements that are as candid and open? Precious few, but like the U.S. Marines, you "only need a few good men."

Chapter 6 Keepers

- Corporate culture, though sometimes hard to quantify, is important when you choose who will manage your money; you want stewardship—not salesmanship.

- Managers with lower turnover, tax efficiency, and low costs tend to do better over long periods.

- Managements with a long and consistent record of superior returns are preferred.

Chapter 7   Bonds and Bond Funds

When you buy bonds, you are buying the IOUs of corporations and governments (local, state, and federal). Compared with stocks and used properly, they provide relatively safe havens, as well as current income, predictability and stability. The trade-off is that bond returns may not keep up with purchasing power, and if interest rates soar, bond prices will fall. Bonds pose market risk (falling prices) and investment risk (default). If you are a conservative investor, you should stick to high-quality bonds and relatively short maturities. You'll sacrifice some returns, but you'll have a safer investment. Bonds are rated as far as safety by major rating services.

With bond *funds,* you buy a diversified portfolio of bonds that deliver income either monthly or quarterly. While they add a measure of stability and predictability to your portfolio, they are not as predictable as individual bonds because of their perpetual nature. The most common classifications are managed and index open-end funds, unit investment trusts, and managed closed-end funds.

Like individual bonds, there are lower and higher risk bond funds, depending on the average quality and maturity of their portfolios. The average quality of a bond fund's portfolio is disclosed in the prospectus and by fund rating services such as Morningstar. Bond funds usually offer more safety than individual bonds, especially for smaller investors because of their instant diversification. Government bond funds are safest but have the lowest returns.

Chapter 7 Keepers

- Bonds add safety, predictability, and income to a fund portfolio, but historically have provided lower returns than common stocks.

- Bond funds are convenient and diversify your fixed income allocation. However, they are less predictable than individual bonds because they are perpetual with an elastic shareholder base.

- Index bond funds offer stability, diversification, and the lowest cost.

Chapter 8   New-Fund Investing

Numerous studies have shown that new funds outperform their older peers: A disproportionate number of new funds show up on the list of top performers year after year. You can boost the odds of above-average performance by investing in *diversified* new funds at inception.

There is no time in the life of a fund where investors and fund management's self-interests are more closely linked. Both have invested at the outset and performance is the number one priority.

Information on new funds is more difficult to get; there are no write-ups, star ratings, or proven track records. They are not in the spotlight, but that's a benefit. They usually start out with a very small asset base—a decided advantage—and until they garner star ratings, it is easier for them to remain nimble.

You can't buy new funds indiscriminately. Studies have found that in addition to newness and a small asset base, top-performing funds tended to be managed by independent managers—as opposed to brokers, banks, and insurance companies and that new small-cap growth funds performed best on a risk-adjusted basis.

New funds from strong sponsors, piloted by experienced portfolio managers with identifiable superior track records are particularly desirable.

Be careful in fund selection because Wall Street typically launches many new funds at the height of their sector popularity. Avoid those like the proverbial plague.

There is no single reason for new fund outperformance; more probably, it is a combination of favorable factors and the lack of structural handicaps such as asset bloat and management inattention that afflict older funds.

While a disciplined, new-fund investment strategy boosts returns, it is also tax *in*efficient and is best used in tax-deferred accounts.

Chapter 8 Keepers

- New funds can boost your returns in the small- and mid-cap stock sectors.

- Stick with diversified new funds from strong sponsors, managed by a portfolio manager with an identifiable superior track record.

- A new-fund investing strategy includes selling those that fail to perform after 6 months and those that do well after 18 to 24 months, and replacing them with new funds that have desirable characteristics at their launch.

Chapter 9   Real Estate Investment Trusts (REITs)

REITs are publicly owned corporations that invest directly in real estate and come in several flavors—equity REITs, mortgage REITs, or both (hybrids). They are not taxed at the federal level as long as they pay 95 percent of their earnings to shareholders in the form of dividends.

Generous dividends and soaring real estate prices in the 1970s caused a great deal of interest in the early days of REITs. Floods of them came on the market at the peaks of real estate cycles giving them a boom-and-bust reputation, and the public's appetite for REITs has largely disappeared. Although large institutions typically have 10 percent to 15 percent of their portfolios in commercial real estate, they invest directly, so when the public isn't interested, "nobody" is, and that creates a REIT investment opportunity. Many investors wrongly equate REITs with the dreadful real estate limited partnerships that imploded after the 1986 Tax Reform Act.

The overall perception of REITs is beginning to change and given equity REITs' record of good returns, investor psychology appears to be improving. During the first half of 2000, the REIT stocks were the second best performing industry category in the United States.

There are good reasons to consider REIT funds. They offer professional management, property-type and regional diversification, bondlike income, and appreciation. In addition, they are traded daily on exchanges and the Nasdaq, and are liquid (not usually a feature of real estate investing).

Another advantage of REITs is their inflation-hedge characteristics—most commercial real estate leases are indexed to the CPI or other inflation indicators. Further, since most studies show a low correlation between REIT and both stock and bond prices, they can reduce volatility in an investment portfolio. An added plus: On average, insiders own approximately 12.5 percent of their own properties.

Real estate will always be cyclical, but stricter lending practices may make it less so; industry observers seem to agree that future peaks and valleys should be more moderate.

Chapter 9 Keepers

- REITs have a relatively low correlation to stock and bond price changes; they will reduce your portfolio's volatility.

- Compared with stock yields of 1 percent to 1.5 percent, REIT fund yields of 4 percent to 8 percent are common, providing bondlike income with the prospect of moderate growth.

- REITs are an inflation hedge—real estate prices and rents tend to rise with inflation and it appears that boom-and-bust cycles may be moderating.

Chapter 10   Convertibles

A convertible bond is a debt instrument and has many of the fixed income characteristics of a straight bond, with a difference: Investors have the right to convert their bond into a fixed number of shares of common stock of the issuer whenever they wish.

Convertible bond investors aim to capture most of the returns of common stocks, without taking as much risk. Convertibles' math is complicated and most of the time, it is played by the pros. Because of complexity, most investors ignore individual issues—as they do convertible bond funds that routinely show up in Morningstar's "unloved" fund rankings.

Information on convertibles is scanty—there are few Web sites devoted to converts—and daily news is usually buried toward the end of the *Wall Street Journal*'s "Credit Markets" column.

While it's possible you could be a convertible bond investor, their complexity and obscurity make it unlikely. It's a game best left to the pros—enter convertible bond *funds*—who take care of all those numbers.

The safety net provided by convertibles was demonstrated by the Japanese and Asian stock market meltdowns. In both cases, convertible bond prices declined much less and investors who held on, "got even" much sooner.

Chapter 10 Keepers

- Convertible bonds are a way to capture most returns provided by stocks with less risk and more income.
- Convertible bond funds provide the opportunity to invest in higher risk sectors you might otherwise avoid altogether.
- Convertible bonds' complexities make funds the most realistic way to invest.

Chapter 11 Closed-End Funds

A closed-end fund (CEF) is created by a one-time initial public offering (IPO), after which, the fund is "closed"; it will not issue new or redeem shares. CEF shares trade as stocks on the major exchanges and the price is determined by supply and demand.

Occasionally CEFs sell above their NAVs, but discounts are more common; in May 2000, 94 percent were selling at discounts. Why? Part of the reason is public psychology and the other is mechanical: Investors know that they may never be able to realize the underlying value (NAV). When overall market psychology is negative, or a particular sector is unpopular, discounts tend to widen.

The discount problem also persists because CEFs have a checkered past, with a history of IPOs near market and sector highs, and dilutive rights offerings. Also, they don't get as much publicity as open-end funds that are continually marketing new shares.

Occasionally, there is good news for CEF shareholders—when managements decide, or are pressured, to convert to open-end fund status. If a CEF selling at a 20 percent discount "open-ends," there is an immediate 20 percent profit.

CEFs can provide the opportunity for fund investors to participate in small niches such as small single country funds and venture capital private placements.

Bond fund investors can profit from opportunistic trading if they catch bond CEFs at discounts before they narrow, but since most fixed income investors seek predictability and safety, trading bond CEFs has limited appeal. Additionally, most bond CEFs are leveraged, adding to their unpredictability.

Chapter 11 Keepers

- Stock and bond CEFs differ from open-end funds in that they trade according to supply and demand and usually at a discount to NAV.

- Opportunistic fund investors can profit by buying CEFs at unusually wide discounts, expecting that they will narrow.

- CEFs can provide the opportunity to invest in very small market niches such as small single country funds and venture capital private placements.

Chapter 12   Beyond Mutual Funds

Mutual funds work well for people because they offer instant diversification and make investing relatively simple. With their low minimums, they are available to just about anybody with money to invest. But there is another way if your assets have grown enough to qualify for individually managed accounts (IMAs).

Brokers, fee advisers, and online services are now offering professionally managed portfolios of individual securities. Called "wrap" or "individually managed" or "consultant wrap" accounts, they have grown rapidly in recent years—reaching assets of $240 billion in 1999.

To meet demand, some mutual fund sponsors companies have launched wrap programs; many more are on the way.

There is a clear tax advantage. Unlike with funds, new investors are not stuck with embedded gains (those that have been there for years) that can emerge at any time.

There is also a psychological appeal: Many people like to own their own shares of Cisco Systems, Merck, and Intel, rather than shares of a Janus or Fidelity fund that in turn, owns the individual securities. There is more of a feeling of personal involvement. During rising markets, it's simply more fun.

Depending on where you sign up, wrap fees can be high, but you can negotiate so that in many instances, total wrap costs are less than mutual fund costs. If you qualify, reasonably priced wraps are a compelling alternative to mutual funds.

Chapter 12 Keepers

- Wrap accounts manage individual securities in accounts meeting minimums, usually $100,000 or more.

- IMAs are more tax efficient than mutual funds.

- With the growth of IMAs, wrap fees are coming down due to increased competition; in some cases, total costs are less than those of mutual funds.

Chapter 13   Off the Beaten Path

With all the confusing options available, most investors buy brand names or funds with above-average recent performance. While both approaches are comfortable ways to invest, they usually result in mediocre or—in some cases—horrid returns.

If you have a contrary streak, another way of picking funds is investing in the *least* popular wallflower sector funds that "nobody else" loves. Least popular is defined not by how they've performed, but by how much money has been invested in them relative to the total fund sector universe.

Morningstar reports the unloved sectors every January, and based on historical results, advocates buying one fund in each of the three unloved categories and holding for three years.

Morningstar backtested the strategy to 1987 and found that "unpopular categories beat the average equity fund over the next three years more than three fourths of the time." It doesn't always work, but the overall results have been too rewarding to ignore.

Another out-of-the-mainstream (but becoming less so) method of investing is Socially Responsible Investing (SRI). It used to be that SRI investors shunned companies that did "bad" things like selling liquor, operating gambling enterprises, engaging in animal testing, or manufacturing armaments.

More recently, SRI criteria has been broadened to include what companies do, such as supporting women and minority rights, day care, and so on.

There is no shortage; there are SRI funds with more than $2 trillion in assets.

Although "Big tobacco's" travails probably distort the recent past's returns, SRI investing doesn't necessarily mean you have to sacrifice returns. *Green-Money* reported, ". . . in 1999, eleven of the socially responsible mutual funds returned 30% and more."

Chapter 13 Keepers

- Unloved fund sector returns have been higher than either average or the most popular fund sectors, but to benefit, you have to go against the crowd and have patience.
- SRI funds have delivered excellent results in recent years to investors who don't want to support companies that, in their view, do not practice socially responsible policies.

- Off-the-beaten-path investing has provided above-average returns to contrarian and socially conscious investors.

Chapter 14 Fund Family Stalwarts

With over 600 fund families offering thousands of funds, selecting outstanding fund families makes sense. We identified four that share certain desirable characteristics.

Again, as in past chapters, "corporate culture" is a key element. While the four families spotlighted are very different in some ways, they also share highly desirable characteristics:

- All have "earned their stripes" in the big leagues—competing in the institutional arena and achieving superior returns for many years—even decades.
- All have substantial resources—research infrastructures, support personnel, and financial muscle—to continue their success and growth.
- None, considering their investment styles and objectives, are too large to accomplish their objectives.
- All are relatively new to the fund business.
- All have returns-driven—rather than distribution-driven—corporate cultures.
- Institutionally managed assets dwarf fund assets.
- Compared with competitors, fund assets are small—allowing plenty of time before asset bloat becomes a problem.

Chapter 14 Keepers
- Dresdner RCM Global Investors
- TIAA-CREF Mutual Funds
- TCW Funds Management
- Driehaus Capital Management

Chapter 15 Recommended Funds

The funds recommended here—both indexed and managed—fit into the asset allocation categories recommended in Chapter 4: All categories are covered: Large-, mid-, and small-cap U.S. stocks, international stocks, REITs, convertibles, and bonds.

Chapter 15 Keepers

- If you want to buy funds and leave them on autopilot, choose the all-indexed portfolio.
- If you want to take control, you can select fully managed funds or mix index funds with their managed brethren.
- If safety is uppermost in your plans, and you want or need income, the bond section provides several low-cost alternatives.

The Future

The next steps are yours: You can be as involved or uninvolved as you want to be and still be a successful investor. Whatever paths you take, since the future is uncertain, plan for the unknowable, avoid the crowd, and have some fun along the way.

Happy trails.

Appendix B
Compound Interest Table

Using the example from Chapter 1, if you invest $1,000 in a mutual fund at age 30, and your average annual return is 6 percent per year, you will have approximately six and one half times your money or $6,510 when you're 65, 35 years later. If your return is 10 pecent, it is even more dramatic. Your gain at 65 would be over 28 times, or $28,100.

YEAR	3.0%	3.5%	4.0%	4.5%	5.0%	5.5%	6.0%	6.5%	7.0%
1	1.03	1.04	1.04	1.05	1.05	1.06	1.06	1.07	1.07
2	1.06	1.07	1.08	1.09	1.10	1.11	1.12	1.13	1.14
3	1.09	1.11	1.12	1.14	1.16	1.17	1.19	1.21	1.23
4	1.13	1.15	1.17	1.19	1.22	1.24	1.26	1.29	1.31
5	1.16	1.19	1.22	1.25	1.28	1.31	1.34	1.37	1.40
6	1.19	1.23	1.27	1.30	1.34	1.38	1.42	1.46	1.50
7	1.23	1.27	1.32	1.36	1.41	1.45	1.50	1.55	1.61
8	1.27	1.32	1.37	1.42	1.48	1.53	1.59	1.65	1.72
9	1.30	1.36	1.42	1.49	1.55	1.62	1.69	1.76	1.84
10	1.34	1.41	1.48	1.55	1.63	1.71	1.79	1.88	1.97
11	1.38	1.46	1.54	1.62	1.71	1.80	1.90	2.00	2.10
12	1.43	1.51	1.60	1.70	1.80	1.90	2.01	2.13	2.25
13	1.47	1.56	1.67	1.77	1.89	2.01	2.13	2.27	2.41
14	1.51	1.62	1.73	1.85	1.98	2.12	2.26	2.41	2.58
15	1.56	1.68	1.80	1.94	2.08	2.23	2.40	2.57	2.76
16	1.60	1.73	1.87	2.02	2.18	2.36	2.54	2.74	2.95
17	1.65	1.79	1.95	2.11	2.29	2.48	2.69	2.92	3.16
18	1.70	1.86	2.03	2.21	2.41	2.62	2.85	3.11	3.38
19	1.75	1.92	2.11	2.31	2.53	2.77	3.03	3.31	3.62
20	1.81	1.99	2.19	2.41	2.65	2.92	3.21	3.52	3.87
21	1.86	2.06	2.28	2.52	2.79	3.08	3.40	3.75	4.14
22	1.92	2.13	2.37	2.63	2.93	3.25	3.60	4.00	4.43
23	1.97	2.21	2.46	2.75	3.07	3.43	3.82	4.26	4.74
24	2.03	2.28	2.56	2.88	3.23	3.61	4.05	4.53	5.07
25	2.09	2.36	2.67	3.01	3.39	3.81	4.29	4.83	5.43
26	2.16	2.45	2.77	3.14	3.56	4.02	4.55	5.14	5.81
27	2.22	2.53	2.88	3.28	3.73	4.24	4.82	5.48	6.21
28	2.29	2.62	3.00	3.43	3.92	4.48	5.11	5.83	6.65
29	2.36	2.71	3.12	3.58	4.12	4.72	5.42	6.21	7.11
30	2.43	2.81	3.24	3.75	4.32	4.98	5.74	6.61	7.61
31	2.50	2.91	3.37	3.91	4.54	5.26	6.09	7.04	8.15
32	2.58	3.01	3.51	4.09	4.76	5.55	6.45	7.50	8.72
33	2.65	3.11	3.65	4.27	5.00	5.85	6.84	7.99	9.33
34	2.73	3.22	3.79	4.47	5.25	6.17	7.25	8.51	9.98
35	2.81	3.33	3.95	4.67	5.52	6.51	7.69	9.06	10.68

7.5%	8.0%	8.5%	9.0%	9.5%	10.0%	10.5%	11.0%	11.5%	12.0%
1.08	1.08	1.09	1.09	1.10	1.10	1.11	1.11	1.12	1.12
1.16	1.17	1.18	1.19	1.20	1.21	1.22	1.23	1.24	1.25
1.24	1.26	1.28	1.30	1.31	1.33	1.35	1.37	1.39	1.40
1.34	1.36	1.39	1.41	1.44	1.46	1.49	1.52	1.55	1.57
1.44	1.47	1.50	1.54	1.57	1.61	1.65	1.69	1.72	1.76
1.54	1.59	1.63	1.68	1.72	1.77	1.82	1.87	1.92	1.97
1.66	1.71	1.77	1.83	1.89	1.95	2.01	2.08	2.14	2.21
1.78	1.85	1.92	1.99	2.07	2.14	2.22	2.30	2.39	2.48
1.92	2.00	2.08	2.17	2.26	2.36	2.46	2.56	2.66	2.77
2.06	2.16	2.26	2.37	2.48	2.59	2.71	2.84	2.97	3.11
2.22	2.33	2.45	2.58	2.71	2.85	3.00	3.15	3.31	3.48
2.38	2.52	2.66	2.81	2.97	3.14	3.31	3.50	3.69	3.90
2.56	2.72	2.89	3.07	3.25	3.45	3.66	3.88	4.12	4.36
2.75	2.94	3.13	3.34	3.56	3.80	4.05	4.31	4.59	4.89
2.96	3.17	3.40	3.64	3.90	4.18	4.47	4.78	5.12	5.47
3.18	3.43	3.69	3.97	4.27	4.59	4.94	5.31	5.71	6.13
3.42	3.70	4.00	4.33	4.68	5.05	5.46	5.90	6.36	6.87
3.68	4.00	4.34	4.72	5.12	5.56	6.03	6.54	7.09	7.69
3.95	4.32	4.71	5.14	5.61	6.12	6.67	7.26	7.91	8.61
4.25	4.66	5.11	5.60	6.14	6.73	7.37	8.06	8.82	9.65
4.57	5.03	5.55	6.11	6.73	7.40	8.14	8.95	9.83	10.80
4.91	5.44	6.02	6.66	7.36	8.14	8.99	9.93	10.97	12.10
5.28	5.87	6.53	7.26	8.06	8.95	9.94	11.03	12.23	13.55
5.67	6.34	7.08	7.91	8.83	9.85	10.98	12.24	13.63	15.18
6.10	6.85	7.69	8.62	9.67	10.83	12.14	13.59	15.20	17.00
6.56	7.40	8.34	9.40	10.59	11.92	13.41	15.08	16.95	19.04
7.05	7.99	9.05	10.25	11.59	13.11	14.82	16.74	18.90	21.32
7.58	8.63	9.82	11.17	12.69	14.42	16.37	18.58	21.07	23.88
8.14	9.32	10.65	12.17	13.90	15.86	18.09	20.62	23.49	26.75
8.75	10.06	11.56	13.27	15.22	17.45	19.99	22.89	26.20	29.96
9.41	10.87	12.54	14.46	16.67	19.19	22.09	25.41	29.21	33.56
10.12	11.74	13.61	15.76	18.25	21.11	24.41	28.21	32.57	37.58
10.88	12.68	14.76	17.18	19.98	23.23	26.97	31.31	36.31	42.09
11.69	13.69	16.02	18.73	21.88	25.55	29.81	34.75	40.49	47.14
12.57	14.79	17.38	20.41	23.96	28.10	32.94	38.57	45.15	52.80

Appendix C

The Lessons from Japan

Lessons
from Japan

THE CONVERTIBLE MARKET—FULL CYCLE IN EQUITY MARKETS

By Nick P. Calamos

t may not be popular to discuss stock market cycles today because for so long many market experts have been calling for a bear market in U.S. stocks while the market has continued upward. But, it may be a good time to at least consider that some downside protection is warranted. It is always difficult to leave a good thing behind and the stock market has obviously been very good. We do not advocate market timing, but intelligent risk reduction should be part of every investment program. We feel that the convertible market today offers a good opportunity to lower equity risk while still offering participation in some of the upside potential in the equity market.

CALAMOS ASSET MANAGEMENT, INC.®

CALAMOS® ASSET MANAGEMENT, INC.
is a leader in convertible securities with over two decades of experience in investment and risk management.

Specializing in convertible securities investment since 1983, Nick P. Calamos, Managing Director and Senior Portfolio Manager, oversees the research and portfolio management for the firm. A Chartered Financial Analyst (CFA) and a member of the Investment Analysts Society of Chicago, he was instrumental in developing the CALAMOS Convertible Research System (CCRS), a sophisticated, proprietary research system that monitors and scans the entire convertible market for the best available investment opportunities. Mr. Calamos has been quoted as an authority on convertible securities by leading financial publications and has been a frequent speaker at various conferences and seminars throughout the country. He holds a B.S. degree in Economics from Southern Illinois University, and an M.S. degree in Finance from Northern Illinois University.

Headquartered in Naperville, Illinois, CALAMOS ASSET MANAGEMENT, INC. (CAM) presently manages approximately $5.5 billion as of March 31, 2000, for major institutions and individual investors, and oversees six mutual funds. CAM offers a Balanced Convertible Program, an Investment-Grade Convertible Program, as well as a program designed for Non-U.S. Investors.

CALAMOS ASSET MANAGEMENT, INC.®

Convertible bonds offer higher yields than equity along with fixed income features that can help preserve wealth in a declining equity market environment. In the past, convertibles have provided a high return alternative to the bond markets (see Table 1) while still providing significant equity participation in the bull phase of a market cycle. In fact, over the 22-year period covering 1973 through 1995 the convertible market provided 99% of the upside total return of the S&P 500 with one-third less risk. With a risk level equal to long-term government bonds, convertibles yielded significantly higher returns. Importantly, this period includes full market cycles in the U.S. bond and stock markets and points to the long term value of convertible investing.

Another excellent example of how the convertible asset class can work for investors throughout a market cycle and more directly during the bear phase can be seen in the Japanese experience. The Japanese convertible

*I*t is remarkable how closely the bull market in Japanese equities and convertibles resemble the U.S. market today. This **Special Report** focuses on how convertibles offer an opportunity to lower equity risk while retaining a good portion of the upside potential.

bond market is the largest convertible market in the world. During the great bull market in Japan from 1978 to 1989, the convertible market was hard pressed to keep up with the rocketing equity markets. By 1985, the Japanese convertible market captured approximately 85% of the upside of the Japanese equity market. Since convertible bonds have a built-in protection component derived from its fixed-income features, one would expect the convertible market to lag the bull phase of the equity market. The 85% upside capture was impressive but began to fade as the equity market entered an exponential climb (see Figure 1), and by 1988 the convertible bond market captured about 63% of the upside of the long bull market. Despite the convertible market performing much better than the bond market during the bull phase of the market, the upside lag in the convertible market relative to equities appeared to be large. But then the world changed. The Japanese miracle began to unravel and the equity markets entered the bear phase.

Table 1
IBBOTSON PERFORMANCE COMPARISON 1973-1995

ASSET CLASS	% ANN. RETURN	12/72= $1	% STD. DEVIATION
Convertible Bonds	11.7	$12.73	12.47
S&P 500	11.84	13.11	17.27
Long-term Corporate	9.66	8.34	12.44
Intermediate Corporate	9.91	8.79	8.93

Source: Yamaichi Research Institute

The Japanese convertible bond market is the largest convertible bond market in the world.

Figure 1
GROWTH OF $1 INVESTED IN VARIOUS JAPANESE ASSETS
From 1978 to 1988 (in Japanese Yen)

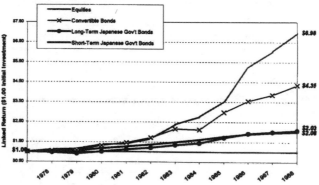

Source: Yamaichi Research Institute

Table 2
RETURNS ON VARIOUS JAPANESE ASSETS
1978-1996
(all returns in YEN)

ASSET CLASS	% CUM. RETURN	% ANN. RETURN	% STD. DEVIATION
Japanese Convertible Bonds	416.97	9.0	11.8
Japanese Equities	306.8	7.7	19.5
Long-term Japanese Gov t Bonds	276.4	7.2	6.7
Short-term Japanese Gov t Bonds	199.5	5.9	3.1

Source: *Yamaichi Research Institute*

bond market is now higher than its 1989 peak! (See Figure 2)

In fact by 1993, the convertible market surpassed its high of 1988. Over the complete market cycle, the convertible market was the best performing asset class with a +9.03% annual return compared to equities at +7.66% with convertibles experiencing nearly 40% less volatility than the equity market. The convertible market did a remarkable job of preserving wealth for investors in the bear phase of the cycle while still building wealth in the bull market period (See Table 2).

From 1989 until 1996, the Japanese equity market declined approximately 60% from its peak. In Japan, it may be time to step up equity exposure while in the U.S. the opposite may be true. Despite the 60% decline in equity values since 1989, the Japanese convertible

The lesson from the Japanese markets is not unlike the long-term lessons experienced in the U.S. markets. Over complete market cycles, the convertible bond is a remarkable investment vehicle. But, this sometimes gets lost in the bull market phase of a cycle.

Figure 2
GROWTH OF $1 INVESTED
IN JAPANESE STOCKS & CONVERTIBLES
From 1988 to 1996 (in Japanese Yen)

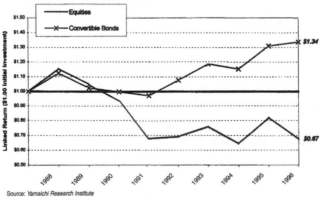

Source: *Yamaichi Research Institute*

Figure 3
**GROWTH OF $1 INVESTED IN VARIOUS JAPANESE ASSETS
JAPANESE EQUITIES AND CONVERTIBLE PERFORMANCE
From 1978 to 1996 (in Japanese Yen)**

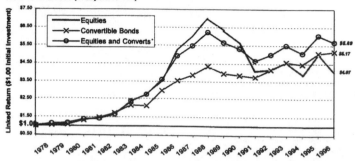

Source: *Yamaichi Research Institute*   *combines 20% convertibles and 80% Equities

During the first year of the Japanese equity market correction, the convertible market declined –9.0%, nearly as much as the equity markets –9.3%. The long-term Japanese government bond also declined –9.0% that year. During the next two years, the convertible market was off –2.5% and –2.7% while the equity market declined –10.9% and –27.4%. The convertible market provided excellent protection and in fact has appreciated in value over the bear phase of the market because of the security s bond attributes. Since the Japanese bond market continued to perform well, the fixed-income feature of the convertible increased in value. More importantly, many bonds were maturing at par value and moved to par despite the performance of the underlying equity.

Today, in the U.S., it is typical to see 5 to 7 year maturities on convertible new issues. These shorter term to maturity bonds should provide good protection of principal in declining equity markets. The typical convertible had 15 to 20 year terms to maturity in the last U.S. bear market.

If an investor began to blend convertibles into their portfolio during the last few years of the Japanese bull market in equities, they would have substantially enhanced returns and reduced risk. Obviously, selling all equities in 1989 and purchasing convertibles or government bonds would have provided excellent returns and required perfect market timing. But instead of attempting to pick the market top, as equity valuations became stretched and hit historic highs in 1986, 1987 and 1988, blending convertibles into the equity mix would have had a significantly positive impact on performance. As the investor avoids market timing and instead blends convertibles into the asset mix, he reduces equity exposure each leg up in the market and retains a significant portion of the upside potential of the equity market. Figure 3 demonstrates how an investor would have fared if 20% of the equity portfolio had been rolled into convertible bonds each of the last three years of the bull market. This would be a logical approach toward maintaining appropriate risk tolerance in an expensive market without making major market timing decisions.

Today, U.S. equity valuations are stretched by any historical valuation measure. In fact, it is remarkable how closely the bull market in Japanese equities and convertibles resemble our market in equities and convertibles today. This is illustrated in Figures 4 and 5.

Blending convertibles into the asset mix seems to make good sense today.

Figure 4
**GROWTH OF $1 INVESTED
IN U.S. CONVERTIBLE MARKET & S&P 500
From 1982 to 1996**

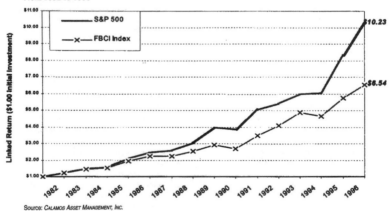

Source: *CALAMOS ASSET MANAGEMENT, INC.*

CALAMOS ASSET MANAGEMENT, INC.

Somewhere in the market cycle, risk reduction takes
precedence over return. It may be prudent to reduce
equity risk but still participate in a portion of the upside
should the bull market continue. Blending convertibles
into the asset mix seems to make good sense today.

Figure 5
**GROWTH OF $1 INVESTED
JAPANESE CONVERTIBLE MARKET & EQUITIES
From 1978 to 1988 (in Japanese Yen)**

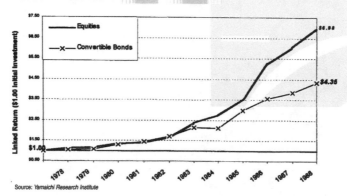

Source: *Yamaichi Research Institute*

Lessons from Japan:
The Convertible Market—
Full Cycle in Equity Markets
is one in a series of *Special Reports*
discussing the role of convertible investments.

© Copyright 2000
CALAMOS® ASSET MANAGEMENT, INC. (4/00-4M)

Past performance is no guarantee of
future results.

1111 East Warrenville Road · Naperville, Illinois 60563-1493 · 630.245.7200 · 800.323.9943 · http://www.calamos.com

CALAMOS ASSET MANAGEMENT, INC.

Index

G

H

About the Authors

Jerry Tweddell is a former stockbroker with more than 25 years of experience in both individual and institutional investing. He was a vice president in the San Francisco office of S.G. Cowen & Co. He is currently an independent investment advisor, offering investment management and consulting services to individual investors. He is the coauthor of *Winning With Index Mutual Funds—How to Beat Wall Street At Its Own Game* (1997, AMACOM Books). A graduate of St. Lawrence University, he lives in Sonora, California.

Jack Pierce retired from Donaldson, Lufkin & Jenrette, where he acted as their first West Coast Branch Manager, based in San Francisco. He spent over 30 years as a stockbroker and regional manager at major Wall Street firms, specializing in retail and institutional investing. He is the coauthor of *Winning With Index Mutual Funds—How to Beat Wall Street At Its Own Game* (1997, AMACOM Books), and has written numerous magazine articles on finance He graduated with a degree in Economics from the University of the Pacific. He lives in Greenbrae, California.